· ABOUT THE BOOK

In the late 1960's many segments of our society reflected concern with the sequential but interactive phenomena of the knowledge explosion and technological revolution, the thrust for innovation and change, and most recently the ability to cope with and adapt to rapidly accelerating rates of change. As individuals and in formal groups, we were developing a greater appreciation of the necessity of studying and knowing something about the future—we began to know that it would be a far different place from what we know as the present.

At the 1966 National Conference of Professors of Educational Administration, a committee was appointed to consider the future of educational administration. Its purpose was to project the nature of education in 1985, and thus encourage proactive behavior by educational administrators. This book is a modified and edited version of the final report to the 1970 conference. An extensive bibliography increases the book's value as a tool for working with the concepts of futurism.

The 1985 Committee of
The National Conference of
Professors of Educational Administration

EDUCATIONAL

FUTURISM

1985

*Challenges for Schools
and their Administrators*

McCutchan Publishing Corporation
2526 Grove Street
Berkeley, California 94704

Members of the 1985 Committee

of

The National Conference of
Professors of Educational Administration

WALTER G. HACK, Chairman
Professor of Education
The Ohio State University
Columbus, Ohio

CONRAD BRINER
Professor of Education
Claremont Graduate School and University Center
Claremont, California

STEPHEN J. KNEZEVICH
Professor of Educational Administration
University of Wisconsin
Madison, Wisconsin

RICHARD C. LONSDALE
Professor of Educational Administration
New York University
New York, New York

ROBERT E. OHM
Dean and Professor of Education
University of Oklahoma
Norman, Oklahoma

GERALD E. SROUFE
Executive Director
National Committee for the Support of the Public Schools
Washington, D. C.

Preface

In the late 1960s many segments of our society reflected concern with the sequential but interactive phenomena of the knowledge explosion and technological revolution, the thrust for innovation and change, and most recently the ability to cope with and adapt to rapidly accelerating rates of change. As individuals and in formal groups, we were developing a greater appreciation of the necessity of studying and knowing something about the future—we began to know that it would be a far different place from what we know as the present.

Individuals interested in public education held these same concerns. The 1950s and 1960s saw significant changes and were characterized by an accelerating rate of change toward the end of the last decade. Professors of educational administration, as one of many groups, recognized that the acceleration of change added to the urgency of action in the professional field of education, since there is less and less time to make decisions, mount programs, correct inadequate programs, or take counter actions when new variables are introduced. Thus, it was natural that a professional organization should structure a formal response to the concern for the nature of public education in the future.

At the 1966 National Conference of Professors of Educational Administration, it was proposed that a committee be appointed to consider the future of educational administration. Conferees who were appointed to the committee included Luvern Cunningham, University of Chicago; Keith Goldhammer, University of Oregon; Walter G. Hack, Ohio State University; and Stephen J. Knezevich, American Association of School Administrators. During the following year the committee worked to define its role and function. The members decided to concern themselves with the relatively short-range future, so they named the committee in terms of its work parameters—the 1985 Committee. The basic purpose of the committee was defined as describing educational administration in the future to stimulate proactive behavior in educational administrators. The approach was to prepare a set of working papers to spell out salient characteristics of educational administration in 1985. These papers were to be used by members of the National Conference of Professors of Educational Administration to consider the implications for programs designed to prepare educational administrators.

Shortly after the creation of the original committee, several changes in membership were made due to a shift in the professional responsibilities of Professors Cunningham and Goldhammer and to the recognition that additional competencies were needed in order to do the job. From 1967 on, the 1985 Committee was composed of Conrad Briner, Claremont Graduate School, Stephen J. Knezevich, University of Wisconsin; Richard C. Lonsdale, New York University; Robert E. Ohm, University of Oklahoma; Gerald Sroufe, National Committee for Support of the Public Schools; and Walter G. Hack, Ohio State University, Chairman.

The committee presented progress reports on its work during the 1967 and 1968 sessions of the conference, and lodged its final report in August 1970. At that time, the conference authorized the modification and editing of the final report for general publication.

The members of the committee on the publication team wish to express their appreciation to the National Conference of Professors of Educational Administration for its support during the development of the work. We also wish to recognize the confidence its membership expressed in encouraging its publication and distribution. Our greatest benefit, however, was the opportunity to interact in an activity of such importance to our professional peers.

Table of Contents

Walter G. Hack

1

On Confronting the Future

INTRODUCTION

When they consider the future of education, most professional educators assume that education in the future will not be what it is today and that they will not be content to let the future take care of itself. As professionals in education, we are aware of being buffeted by the tides of change. Change is often a result of unplanned events or unanticipated influences. Much of it comes from sources beyond the sphere of education and often beyond our understanding.

The professional educator, as he plans, develops, and works in an educational unit, finds himself in a reactive posture most of the time. He reacts to such phenomena as teacher militancy, federal funding, and national assessment—all in the educational context. He also reacts to mass concern for pollution and ecology, to overpopulation, and to cries for the reordering of national priorities. As a consequence, he stands in double jeopardy. He does not know what the future holds; moreover, he does not know how to influence it to make it more to his liking.

One response to this dual concern was that made by the National Conference of Professors of Educational Administration in the establishment of the 1985 Committee. The Committee's job was to project the nature of education in 1985 and thus encourage proactive behavior by educational administrators. Although "futurism" has been explored in many other contexts, in 1966, no comprehensive effort had yet been mounted in the field of public elementary and secondary education.

We encountered substantial problems as we started our work. In retrospect, however, working through these problems provided an exciting and productive experience and, in one sense, gave us the impetus to share with the reader a new and valuable perspective for educators and educational systems. In essence, as a group of colleagues with common concern for increased institutional effec-

1

tiveness in the future, we developed a way of looking at futurism, a way of working together, and a general approach usable by other groups interested in futuristic educational planning, such as groups of teachers, administrators, governing board members, or interested citizens.

The first problem was to define the scope of the work. It is difficult to establish clear and discrete parameters in the study of much of today's educational system. It proved to be a rigorous intellectual exercise to establish meaningful parameters in the context of 1985. We finally decided to concern ourselves with the counterpart of grades kindergarten through 12 in today's public school system.

A second problem was to decide what aspects or key component parts should be considered in developing a picture of education in 1985. Many of the contemporary or traditional concepts of education and educational systems were found wanting. Eventually, several related concerns emerged as aspects or components through which we could best describe public education in 1985. These units were identified as the future environment, educational program, governance structure, operational school unit, and administrator. "Future environment" evolved into "futurism"; the five units became the content components (Chapters 2 through 6) of this book.

The third problem was to establish a working definition of the future. In the early stages of our work, the term had a narrow, temporal connotation: it was something that was going to happen. We recognized the basic contradiction between the notion of anticipating or predicting the future and the idea that educators in general and educational administrators in particular should assume a proactive posture to influence the molding of the future. A conceptual hurdle was cleared when we recognized the concept of futurism as a way of thinking. Chapter 2 deals extensively with the concept, which is in every way the primary consideration in our effort. We rejected straight-line projections or other predictions of specific features or characteristics of the future. Instead we considered alternative futures and focused on policies and programs likely to be necessary in them.

A fourth problem was the recognition of the crucial role of values in futuristic considerations. As each of the five chapters on the major components of education in 1985 was drafted all of us found it necessary to handle questions of values as a part of issues related to alternative futures, criteria, priorities and the like.

A fifth problem was to decide what specific policies and procedures would be necessary to place an administrator in a proactive posture to positively influence the future. Our conclusion was to narrow our focus to a smaller sector concerned with graduate programs in educational administration (one that had sponsored the Committee's work). Since educational futurism has profound implications for university preparation programs for educational administration, the behavior of administrators trained in these institutions should be influenced by proactive and futurist-oriented programs and professors. Thus, as a kind of application of futurism to a given institution, we developed a number of "criteria for survival" to answer the question: What must a given institution do to make its program in educational administration survive and be relevant in 1985?

GUIDELINES FOR THE APPLICATION OF FUTURISM IN EDUCATION

On the basis of the experience of the authors and the contention that the approach described is applicable and appropriate to other groups of educators, several guidelines are presented below for the use of this approach.

(1) The study and application of futurism is quite idiosyncratic since the future will be determined by how individuals and groups see it and behave in it. Individuals and groups must start with themselves and their given organizations to ascertain and plan their own institution's future. Futuristic planning must be recognized as having a developmental character. The work is incremental; there are no fast or firm answers. Very little work can be simply delegated and then considered complete when the report is lodged. Instead, all opportunities for exchange of work, mutual critique, and interaction should be taken. Tentativeness, constant modification, and updating is the norm. One must be realistic with a group of teachers, for instance. The job is likely to continue for several years without a visable product. Individual opinion will be challenged. Futurist planning in the superintendent's cabinet will involve a commitment of time and a reasonable degree of staff stability.

(2) Given the above orientation to the work expectations, a team should be assembled. The members of the team should be diverse in orientation but have as a common concern the basic objective of planning futuristically for a given institution or organization. In recent years educational institutions have developed capabilities to provide such personnel. Individuals from citizens' committees, government-sponsored programs such as Model Cities programs, and

other organizations such as Urban Education Coalitions and NAACP could provide input along with professional staff in a city school system.

(3) Initially, team members should read widely in the literature on futurism. The bibliography on futurism in the appendix provides a good starting point. Bibliographies and footnotes in other chapters can also be used to orient team members in the general concept of futurism. The principal American journal devoted to futurism is *The Futurist* published bimonthly by the World Future Society. An increasing number of other journals carry occasional articles on futurism. General reading should eventually give way to specific reading as the parameters and components of the futurist study begin to emerge.

(4) The parameters of the futurism project should be defined but kept flexible. A useful idea is to define a counterpart institution that can be projected as existing into the future. If a school system is projected into the future to perform certain vital educational functions, one should not assume that it will necessarily serve children and youth 5 through 18, that it will have a curriculum based primarily on subjects derived from traditional disciplines, or that there will be buildings designated as attendance centers. Parameters probably should be broader than those denoting today's institutions, since roles and functions will change. Later in the development of the team's work, parameters might be tightened if this is the alternative future to be projected.

(5) As study of futurist literature progresses and parameters are considered, the major components to the study should be sorted out and identified. Thus, guidelines 3, 4, and 5 are not separate. Attention should flow back and forth among them. It is here that group interaction should provide clues and stimulation for further exploration. In all probability most studies of educational futurism could use a modification of the major components or content chapters identified in the present book as topics for exploration. These should be examined critically and not accepted without careful analysis, however.

The unique present role and function of each institution will dictate a unique description of alternate futures. Thus, the governance of public education described in Chapter 4 should not be accepted at face value if one's State Department of Education is conducting a futurist study of public education in the state.

(6) As the major components of the future of education in the study setting are tentatively determined, individuals or small groups

will probably be the most effective units to review authorative statements of significant research and to ascertain the alternative futures
in each of the given component areas. In reviewing the work that has
been done, a great deal of conflicting opinion and even fact will be
found. The authors' experience suggests that members of the study
team look for or develop complementary alternative futures in order
to increase the probability for a given future. The identification of
common patterns of influencing variables can be used to conclude
that a given future is possible as well. For example, if there is evidence of the probability of increased population density of a certain
order, then (along with other elements in the pattern of variables)
one could conclude certain demographic futures.

As indicated earlier, it is imperative that drafts of these tentative reports be shared with all members of the team to provide
insights into new patterns of alternative futures and influencing variables, as well as mutual stimulation to provide and to test the appro-
priateness of the topics. Naturally, it may be necessary to abandon or
redefine some topics and generate new and more appropriate topics.
Consequently this step might be recycled several times. After several
analyses and revisions, common threads should appear and a futures
"gestalt" should emerge.

The study team should report to a large constituency at this
point to obtain feedback from others who are part of or vitally
concerned with the organization. The team must always recognize its
own limitations in this "far out" activity. Progress reports may elicit
new ideas, insights, and problems. They might also develop some
group or community readiness for change which can enhance the
carrying out of long range plans.

(7) The next step is to develop policies and strategies enabling
us to get from here to there, making proactivity on the part of the
educator really meaningful. For instance, a team of school administrators in a city school system could develop policies and long range
plans for their school system. This could include plans not only for
school curriculum and buildings but also for new types of positions,
functions, services, and relationships. It could spell out administrator
and board responsibility for exerting influence on policy development at state and federal legislative levels as well as in noneducational agencies. Or, a group of teachers concerned with the future of
the teacher counterpart might seek means to change the specific role,
function, and status of the teacher. Teacher organization policy
might reflect a shift in priorities from specific welfare concerns to

acquiring voting membership on the legislative and governing bodies of school systems.

(8) The final step in this series of guidelines for applying futurism in education is to make it work. This involves the integration of policies and planning into the ongoing operation of the institution. Futurist planning capabilities can be integrated into organizations through the establishment of standing committees or agencies, as in teachers' or administrators' organizations. A city school system, a state education agency, or the U.S. Office of Education might establish, staff, and fund a continuing unit charged with a specific and discrete function of projecting future plans.

A word of caution is in order for all the proposed futurist planning bodies. Although the state of the art of futurism is perhaps analogous to or only slightly beyond that of alchemy, it is not a toy. If the awesome responsibility of futurism is perceived and assumed by dedicated and reasonable men, then we may restore the believability of juxtaposing the two words "bright" and "future."

Richard C. Lonsdale

2

Futurism: Its Development, Content, and Methodology [1]

THE DEVELOPMENT OF FUTURISM

The first report of the National Goals Research Staff, released by the White House in July 1970, "emphasized the importance of defining policy alternatives for the nation as it speeds toward the year 2000 in an era of inquiry, confrontation and technological achievement,"[2] but concluded that the White House cannot set goals for America. Rather, "the Government should instead provide the information the public needs to engage in debate about the sort of society it wants."[3] Appointed by President Nixon in 1969, the goals staff forecasted a slowing down of our national population growth to yield less than the widely predicted 50-percent increase in population between 1970 and 2000. It called for schools to give less emphasis to imparting information and to do more to help students sift data and to establish their own values. Although it presented few firm alternatives and seemed to avoid a number of important and politically sensitive issues, the report nevertheless showed a significant effort on the part of the national administration to get the people to "begin now to define what we wish to have as our national goals, and to develop in both our public and private institutions the specific policies and programs which will move us toward those goals."[4] As such, the report represented the recognition at the top governmental level of the existence and importance of the developing field of study called "futurism."

Although forecasts of the future and descriptions of ideal futures have been widely scattered through the world's literature over the past 2,500 years or so, it was only during the sixties that there began to emerge a more intense and organized concern for and study of the future. The emergence was certainly stimulated by the demands for change marking the decade and the sense of increased speed of change in world society. Perhaps as we approached and passed 1967, people became intrigued by the notion that we had entered the final third of the twentieth century. In his introduction to *The Year 2000* by Kahn and Wiener, Daniel Bell suggested that the current outpouring reflects the desire of society for economic growth, for upgrading the people's standard and conditions of living, and for controlling change for specified ends.[5] As a result, more and more people have begun to talk of the year 2000 and the twenty-first century, causing Bell to voice concern lest we develop an infatuation with "2000," producing a fadism that will wear out the subject, arousing unfulfillable expectations, and overemphasizing the technological gadgetry that will supposedly transform our lives.[6]

This concern for the future falls into three time ranges: the near range, or the next few years; the middle range, extending to about 1980-1985; and the far range, from 1985 to 2000 and beyond. Despite the turbulence of our times, which might warrant giving all our attention to the near range concerns, it has been in the middle- and far-range futures that there has come the notable upsurge of interest since about 1960. Although relatively few predictions extend to the twenty-first century, at least one book focuses on *The Next Hundred Years*[7] and another on *The Next 500 Years*.[8]

With the new interest in the future has come a new professional specialist, the "futurist." At his best, the futurist is a true interdisciplinarian. Perhaps he is even what Buckminster Fuller calls the "comprehensivist," a member of an intellectual elite who assembles the results provided by specialists working on complex problems and issues of specialization.[9] Just as attention to comprehensive study of parts of the world led in the middle of this century to "area" studies and the area specialist, before long there may develop a new pattern of specialization in a future time period, such as the decade of the 80's. If he were to plan his career with sufficient vision, a young man finishing his graduate study in the early seventies could become a "decadist": first a futurist specializing in the eighties, then an interdisciplinary analyst and critic of the eighties while living during that decade, and thereafter an historian of the eighties.

The most serious futurists have generally been affiliated with one of the research organizations or commissions committed to the study of the future, such as the Rand Corporation and the National Planning Association. The Hudson Institute, at Croton-on-Hudson, New York, is another private, nonprofit research organization studying public policy issues, especially those related to long-range planning and to United States national security and international order. Abroad are the *Futuribles* Project in Paris directed by Bertrand de Jouvenel, and the Committee on the Next Thirty Years in England, established by the English Social Science Research Council. Perhaps the most eminent collection of futurists in this country is the Commission on the Year 2000, appointed by the American Academy of Arts and Sciences and chaired by sociologist Daniel Bell of Harvard University. The progress report of that commission, published as the summer 1967 issue of *Daedalus,* and reprinted by Beacon Press in 1969, is one of the most sophisticated and reflective in all of the growing literature of futurism.

Symptomatic of the growth of the field was the formation of the World Future Society, an Association for the Study of Alternative Futures, in the summer of 1966. In February 1967 the group began publishing a bimonthly popular journal, *The Futurist: A Journal of Forecasts, Trends and Ideas About the Future.* The society held its first General Assembly in May 1971 in Washington. In 1968, the Institute for the Future was established at Middletown, Connecticut. Other future-oriented groups have also begun to spring up in connection with other universities.

In the field of education, "Designing Education for the Future" was a four-year project from 1965 to 1969, supported by eight of the Rocky Mountain states and funded by the United States Office of Education. It sponsored seven conferences and issued reports on each of them. A final report summarized and evaluated the project, which was directed by Edgar L. Morphet. Under a grant from the Office of Education, two Educational Policy Research Centers were established in 1967, one at Syracuse University and the other at the Stanford Research Institute. Their purpose is "to develop a capability for thinking about the future in such a way as to permit the assessment of educational policies within the context of conjectures about alternative long-range futures."[10]

A service of the Syracuse center has been the publication of *Essential Reading for the Future of Education: A Selected and Critically Annotated Bibliography.*[11] This bibliography is reprinted in the Appendix. The Syracuse center also began publishing bimonthly *Notes on the Future of Education* as of November-December 1969.

It hardly seems likely that futurism is a passing vogue. It seems more likely that the increased concern for the future and attempts to predict it are an expression of man's increasing urge to exert some amount of control over his future, more to "proact" to it and less simply to react. It was this motivation that caused the Planning Committee of the National Conference of Professors of Educational Administration, at the Indiana University conference in 1966, to appoint a "1985 Committee." Out of the work of this committee over the past three years has come the present book.

The rest of this chapter will define three concepts of importance to futurism, report some of the ways in which futurists have approached their analytical task, note some specific predictions of particular relevance to education, indicate the methodology futurists are using in predicting the future and conducting research, comment on the development of formal instruction in futurism in universities, and pose the challenge of the S-curve versus the J-curve as they symbolize the future.

CONCEPTS

In the developing field of futurism, three concepts have gained wide currency and special utility: *alternative future, scenario,* and *system break*. In general, the futurist concentrates not on predicting *the* future, but on developing *alternative* futures. These are different, often contrasting, sets of future conditions, some of them representing an extrapolation of related aspects of the present or highly likely near range environment. Others may be like leaps into the blue, with few apparent roots in the present. Alternative futures may be broad, even sweeping, descriptions. *Scenarios,* on the other hand, lay out more specific pieces of the future. They indicate a sequence of events leading up to the future situation, "focusing attention on causal processes and decision-points." as Kahn and Wiener put it.[12] Scenarios indicate the step-by-step developments from the present to an hypothetical future situation. They lay out alternatives available at each step for preventing, changing, or enhancing the process. There may be more than one scenario leading to an alternative future, so that the scenarios become the streams feeding into the lake of an alternative future. Scenarios and alternative futures together constitute raw material from which may be extracted specific issues for analysis and examination, alternative policies for systematic comparison, and various criteria for the guidance of decisions. Multiple scenarios suggest alternative routes to be shunned or followed. The steps in these scenarios are branching points in sequential decisionmaking.

Scenarios may be based on fairly straight-line, evolutionary, "surprise-free" projections of current trends or conditions. But the transformation of the present into the future has never been entirely free of surprises, nor is it likely to be in the years ahead. These surprises may derive from *system breaks,* as Boulding called them, representing a sudden change in an evolutionary system.[13] Wars, earthquakes, or assassinations are system breaks with negative values. Space flight, the invention of transistors, or a decline in population growth in the last third of the twentieth century have more positive values. Although they are almost impossible to predict and sometimes are difficult to recognize while they are occurring, system breaks can be inserted arbitrarily in scenarios to give planners or administrators practice in dealing with disruptive uncertainty, with discontinuities rather than continuities.

THE TAXONOMICAL PROBLEM

Futurists interested in developing any wide-ranging predictions or composites of predictions confront a taxonomical problem. What systematic classification shall be used to describe the future? For the futurist concerned with what one writer has called "predictography," the problem is the temporal reverse of the historian's problem in historiography. It is classification of the probable range of man's future progress. Various writers, individually and collectively, have used different, but not totally dissimilar, approaches.

Reporting for the Commission on the Year 2000, Bell analyzed four sources of change in society: the growth of technology, the increasing diffusion of goods and services, developments in the structure of society (*e.g.,* centralization nationally, and the lodging of sources of innovation in such intellectual institutions as universities and research institutes rather than in the older industrial corporations), and emerging new relationships between the United States and the rest of the world.[14]

The same group suggested two different classifications of future problem areas. One included the adequacy of the governmental structure, the changing nature of values and rights, the structure of intellectual institutions, the life cycle of the individual, and the international system. A second classification included technological changes, psychological and social problems, political problems, economic and demographic problems, and the international question.[15] A chapter by Kahn and Wiener, "The Next Thirty-Three Years: A Framework for Speculation," in the same report, separated the basic, long-term, multifold trends of Western society into the following classifications

(1) Increasingly sensate (empirical, worldly, secular, humanistic, pragmatic, utilitarian, contractual, epicurean or hedonistic, and the like) cultures;

(2) Bourgeois, bureaucratic, "meritocratic," democratic (and nationalistic?) elites;

(3) Accumulation of scientific and technological knowledge;
(4) Institutionalization of change, especially research, development, innovation, and diffusion;
(5) World-wide industrialization and modernization;
(6) Increasing affluence and (recently) leisure;
(7) Population growth;
(8) Urbanization and (soon) the growth of megalopolises;
(9) Decreasing importance of primary and (recently) secondary occupations;
(10) Literacy and education;
(11) Increasing capability for mass destruction;
(12) Increasing tempo of change; and
(13) Increasing universality of the multifold trend.[16]

The bulk of the commission's progress report in *Daedalus* consists of an analysis of the following problems:

Can Social Predictions Be Evaluated?

Forecasting and Technological Forecasting

Information, Rationality, and Free Choice in a Future Democratic Society

Planning and Predicting: or What to Do When You Don't Know the Names of the Variables

Modernizing Urban Development

The Relationship of Federal to Local Authorities

The Need for a New Political Theory

University Cities in the Year 2000

Educational and Scientific Institutions

Biological Man and the Year 2000

Deliberate Efforts to Control Human Behavior and Modify Personality

Religion, Mysticism, and the Institutional Church

Memorandum on Youth

The Life Cycle and Its Variations: the Division of Roles

The Problems of Privacy in the Year 2000

Some Psychological Perspectives on the Year 2000

Notes on Meritocracy

Communication

Thinking About the Future of International Society

Political Development and the Decline of the American System of World Order

The International System in the Next Half Century[17]

In commemoration of its 50th anniversary, the American Institute of Planners mounted a three-year national and regional consultation to look into "The Next Fifty Years, 1967-2017." National and regional conferences were held from 1966 to 1969, and three volumes of papers were published under the editorship of William R. Ewald, Jr.[18] These papers centered around the following themes: the limitations and potentialities of man, including the problems of the individual in a mass society; the development of cities and metropolitan areas; the role of the arts, the spirit, science, and technology in creating the future; urgent problems relating to minority groups, education, health, leisure, transportation, and housing; the process of planning and change; and the need for a national policy of development.

In analyzing prospective changes in society by 1980 the earlier mentioned eight-state project, "Designing Education for the Future," invited a series of papers that clustered around a somewhat similar set of topics. These included trends in population and natural resources; governmental relations at urban, metropolitan, and federal levels; the activities of nongovernmental, private association; economic development and industrial relations; communication and transportation; the future of medical science and of the humanities; and the processes of change and of planning and decisionmaking.[19]

A study of the above classifications of predictions of the future raises the question whether professors, practitioners, and other students of education will find it most valuable to study these broad subject categories or to develop a more relevant system of classification focused on the school, *i.e.,* a school-centered view of the future. As professional educators we have as much justification for holding education at the center of the social environment as other specialists have for spotlighting health or communication or agriculture. There is an advantage in thinking of the school, in systems fashion, as interacting with an inner ring of immediate subsystems of future knowledge and one or more outer rings of more remote subsystems. Thus, in the inner ring there might be predictions about such areas of knowledge as biomedical developments concerning man, the family, occupational patterns, learning processes, information systems, and organizational behavior. Outer rings might include such areas of knowledge as population growth, economic resources, transportation, and international relations. Let us contemplate some specific predictions first in the inner ring and then in the outer rings.

SOME PREDICTIONS OF PARTICULAR
RELEVANCE TO EDUCATION

Biomedical Developments Concerning Man

What the psychiatrists call the "social breakdown syndrome" may become the leading psychiatric illness in the future. It occurs when individuals and even family groups cave in before extreme environmental pressures, as when critical illness strikes a member of a family group.[20]

Miniature radio transmitters implanted in the human body, after the manner of devices presently used for stabilizing the heart beat may be used to monitor behavior controlled through a given learning program. Computer records could thus be made of routine behavior at predetermined intervals.[21]

The Family

Specialization of family functions may yield a new social pattern where a certain, smaller number of families may be allocated a child-rearing function, while other childless family units would have a socially approved opportunity to function as individuals, free from child-rearing restraints.[22]

Occupational Patterns

Much more typically than now, the lifetime career pattern may be marked by a sequence of careers, often markedly different in requisite knowledge and skills. Such a worker, changing occupations in midlife, will not be seen as a late-bloomer who failed to settle early enough on a career goal, but as a normal individual living a fuller life.

There may develop a federally regulated, "central human resources exchange," using computer-based information to allocate human resources among organizations. This would set priorities on the use of manpower, relieve dislocations caused by technological unemployment, and yet, ideally, preserve a freedom of choice for both individuals and organizations.[23]

Learning Processes

A breakthrough may be achieved in "interanimal memory transfer" as research reveals a biochemical component of learning permitting, as it were, learning by injection from one animal to another.[24] Where we now look to computer-aided instruction to routinize the learning of certain kinds of skills, we may in the future see possible a mass conditioning by hypodermic-transmitted instruction.

Information Systems

One of the most certain predictions is the increasingly pervasive influence of the computer. "Computer utilities" may become as commonplace as electric utilities are today. Libraries will become parts of informational service networks; Hospitals, likewise, will become parts of medical informational networks. Computer tapes will revolutionize a coordinated system of book manufacturing and information storage and retrieval.[25]

Organizational Behavior

The new capabilities of computer-based informational systems will routinize much day-to-day decisionmaking and thus stimulate the creative potential of administrators to engage in longer range planning. Just as a captain of a large airliner must begin a course change well before the plane changes direction or elevation, so the top leaders of organizations will learn to exercise longer range control in order to accomplish organizational change.

Bureaucracy may well die out, as Warren Bennis has predicted, and be gradually replaced by the increasing use of "adaptive, rapidly changing *temporary* systems." These would be task forces built around organizational problems to be solved, using an organic rather than a mechanical model, and with emerging rather than predetermined role expectations in an "organic-adaptive structure."[26]

Postindustrial Society

Perhaps in an outermost ring of earth-based systems surrounding our arbitrarily selected center of education would fall such a projection as that called "post-industrial society" by Bell and Kahn and Wiener. Though they see postindustrial society emerging more fully by 2000, it may have taken considerable shape by 1985 and is even now apparent in its early forms. Some of the features of this postindustrial society may be summarized from *The Year 2000*.

The very name "postindustrial" presupposes a progression or evolution of modern society along a continuum from preindustrial or small and partially industrialized to large and partially industrialized to mature industrial to mass consumption to early postindustrial to visibly postindustrial. It is hypothesized that by 2000 the postindustrial stage will have been reached by the United States, Japan,

Canada, Scandinavia, Switzerland, France, West Germany, and the Benelux countries. The United Kingdom, the Soviet Union, Italy, Austria, East Germany, Czechoslovakia, Israel, Australia, and New Zealand will by then have reached the early postindustrial stage. The other countries of the world will be spread out along the continuum, with large parts of Africa, the Arab world, Asia, and Latin America still at the preindustrial or small and partially industralized extreme end of the continuum.[27]

Because most problems of production will have been solved and the consumption of products made widespread throughout the societies at this stage, industrial institutions or organizations will have lost their primacy in society and key values will no longer derive from the business firm and from its entrepreneurs, managers, and policies. Instead, intellectual institutions will supplant the business firm as the major new institutions of society. These will include research corporations, universities, and various kinds of regional compacts for dealing with current problems. They will be the major innovative institutions, using the organization of theoretical knowledge as the basis for their innovations. Just as new kinds of nongovernmental, nonindustrial, nonuniversity institutions have emerged during the past 25 years or so since the end of World War II and have become new sources of changes (*e.g.*, Argonne, Brookhaven, Lincoln Lab attached to M.I.T., and Jet Propulsion Lab attached to Cal Tech), so new needs for planning, research, and services will spawn new social forms in the next three decades. These, however, can be expected to be mainly research and intellectual institutions.[28]

The primary occupations of agriculture, fishing, forestry, and mining and the secondary occupations responsible for processing the products of the primary occupations will decline in importance. Growing in importance will be the tertiary occupations, which serve the primary and secondary occupations and the quarternary occupations, which serve the tertiary occupations and each other. These two groups are what we now think of as the service occupations. The quarternary occupations will attract a major portion of the most productive and creative people.[29]

At the present time the standard work year is around 1920 work hours, based on a 40-hour week for approximately 50 weeks, less holidays. In the postindustrial society of 2000, the work year will be reduced to 1095 work hours (made up of a 7.5-hour working day, 4 working days per week, 39 working weeks per year with 10 legal holidays) and 13 weeks vacation per year, or 146 working days and 219 days off per year. Thus, a person could spend 40 percent of his days on a vocation, another 40 percent on an avocation, and have 20 percent for just relaxing. Some 50 percent might work a normal work year, another 20 percent might do additional moonlighting, 10 percent might be half-time hobbyists, and the remaining 20 percent be variously nonemployed or, in today's term, unemployed.[30]

For our purposes, one of the most significant characteristics of the postindustrial society—and one which even sheds light on events and trends of today's world—would be what Kahn and Wiener call the "alienation amidst affluence."

> Thus there may be a great increase in selfishness, a great decline of interest in government and society as a whole, and a rise in the more childish forms of individualism and in the more antisocial forms of concern for self and perhaps immediate family. Thus, paradoxically, the technological, highly productive society, by demanding less of the individual, may decrease his economic frustrations but increase his aggressions against the society. Certainly here would be fertile soil for what has come to be known as alienation. . . .
>
> Of course, it is important to note that the lower middle class, making, say, five to twenty thousand dollars a year, are by 2000 not going to be very different from the lower middle and middle middle classes today. The upper (and middle) middle class in the year 2000 make, say, twenty to one hundred thousand dollars a year and will not necessarily feel independently wealthy. Both groups by and large will probably continue (with some erosion) with current work-oriented, advancement-oriented, achievement-oriented values. The extreme alienation we are talking about is restricted to minorities, which will be important in part because they are likely to be concentrated in the big cities, in part because they appeal to many of the more intellectual members of that ordinarily alienated group—adolescents—and mostly because their members will be literate and articulate and have a large impact on intellectuals and therefore on the culture generally.[32]

A mark of the postindustrial society, therefore, will be a shift from stoic or bourgeois values to epicurean or materialistic values. By "stoic," in modern terms, we mean "the responsible, duty-minded, hard-working, public-spirited American who feels obligated to do a good job for his government, company, or other institution, and works well without necessarily getting much recognition, supervision, or special reward."[33] By "epicurean" we mean the gentleman and humanist emphasizing sensation, emotion, and pleasure; bent on acquiring socially approved skills and experiences; with a suspicion of power, an untamed individualism, a disdain for the culture of others, and leisure as a goal.[34] A kind of epicurean view already characterizes the European upper and middle classes today. The more demanding and difficult professions would have to recruit their new personnel from those with stoic life patterns and from the children of parents who already identify with these professions.[35]

What is projected for the postindustrial society, therefore, is a shift in influence from industrial to intellectual institutions, in occupations from production-oriented to service-oriented ones, in the work year from about 240 to 146 days, in a sense of commitment from involvement to alienation, and in values from the stoic to the epicurean.

Other Alternative Futures

The literature of futurism naturally contains other models of alternative futures. Few of these are discrete; they tend to overlap each other. Thus, there are some common elements between the postindustrial society model and the "temporary society" conceived by Bennis and Slater, who analyze its impact on family units, formal organizations, and the broader society. As primary consequences of the temporary systems characterizing the temporary society, they foresee that "the process of individuation—the separation of the individual from those permanent groups that provide him with ready-made values and traits and from which he derives his identity, will accelerate"[36] and will be accompanied by strong feelings of alienation, anomie, and meaninglessness. Secondary consequences of temporary systems will be an interchangeability achieved through uniformity, an other-directedness leading to more flexible moral patterns and weakened internal controls of a fixed kind, and an intensification of the marital relationship resulting from an increase in the emotional functions imposed on marriage.[37] One of the competencies to be developed in the temporary society will be "learning how to develop intense and deep human relationships quickly—and learning how to 'let go.' In other words, learning how to get love, to love, and to lose love. . . ."[38]

John McHale suggests that a "planetary society" might include a number of alternate models of cities, rather than any standard model. Thus, there might be such urban forms as the ceremonial city, the university city, the scientific city, the festival city, the recreation or "fun" city, the communications city, the convention city, the museum city, and even the experimental city.[39] Most of these types may already be seen emerging in existing cities.

In an intriguingly imaginative and wide-ranging discourse on "An Operating Manual for Spaceship Earth," Buckminster Fuller sketches what seems like a Utopian society of the twenty-first century:

But we can scientifically assume that by the twenty-first century, either humanity will not be living aboard spaceship Earth, or, if approximately our present numbers as yet remained aboard, that they then will have recognized and organized themselves to realize effectively the fact that humanity can afford to do anything it needs to do.

As a consequence Earth-planet based humanity will be physically and economically successful and individually free in the most important sense. While all enjoy total Earth, no human will be interfering with the other and none will be profiting at the expense of another. Humans will be free in the sense that 99.9 percent of their waking hours will be freely investible at their own discretion. They will be free in the sense that they will not struggle for survival on a "you" or "me" basis and will therefore be able to trust one another and be free to cooperate in spontaneous and logical ways.[40]

Classes of Alternative Futures

Futurists have proposed various ways of classifying possible alternative futures. Kahn and Wiener set forth a surprise-free "standard world" along with eight "canonical variations" on this standard world, as follows:

A.   More Integrated
  1.   Stability-oriented
  2.   Development-oriented
B.   More Inward-Looking
  3.   With an eroded Communist movement
  4.   With an eroded democratic morale and some Communist dynamism
  5.   With a dynamic Europe and/or Japan
C.   Greater Disarray
  6.   With an eroded Communist movement
  7.   With a dynamic Communist movement and some erosion of democratic morale
  8.   With a dynamic Europe and/or Japan [41]

The Director of the Educational Policy Research Center of the Stanford Research Institute, Willis W. Harman, described five alternative futures: anarchy; the garrison state, representing massive repression of militancy; disruptive violence, followed by social restructuring; gradual evolution; and suppression of violence, with a return to a previous power balance.[42]

From the same Educational Policy Research Center, Arnold Mitchell, building on the work of Robert E. Kantor, divided Americans into three kinds of people—each with markedly different sets of needs, values, and beliefs—operating on three different levels of human fulfillment. At the "man-against-society" level there is a perpetual, inevitable, unresolvable clash between the individual and society, where central needs of the people center around survival and security. People in this group, constituting perhaps 25 or 30 percent of Americans "are largely the disenfranchised, minorities, the poor, and the unsuccessful."[43] At the "homeostasis" or stability level, the goal is to reach equilibrium and consistency where life will be predictable and good. "Such people are likely to be materialistic, conforming, competitive, outer-directed, hard working, possession-conscious, stereotyped, achieving. Their beliefs are geared to the here and now, pragmatic, and strongly behavioristic."[44] This level may constitute 65 or 70 percent of the population, including the middle and upper classes. The final level is the "unfolders," including only two, three, or maybe five percent of the population. For them the goal of life is the full expression of the person himself. Man lives in harmony with his own nature and the natural environment. These are the self-actualizers. Using these three levels or models of social subgroups, one can build a variety of alternative futures that depend on the varying mix of the three levels one predicts. Mitchell identified a possible "cybernetic society, rich, well-regulated, impersonal"; a materialistic one, suffering as now the artifacts of industrialization; "a more humanistic future, less rich and powerful than the others, but more attuned to human wants";[45] or even a hippie society where everyone does "his thing" in the belief that this will bring about the common good. Dismissing each of these as unsatisfactory, Mitchell finally proposed a "synergistic society" in which perhaps 15 or 20 percent of the people might be raised to the unfolding level, where virtue would pay; where the prime societal value would be "the building of a working physical, social, economic, political, spiritual, and cultural ecology";[46] and where the dominating need would be to become fully human or self-actualizing.[47]

Resulting Issues

Just this selection of predictions raises critical issues symptomatic of policy and, indeed, moral dilemmas of the future. For example:

(1) How much of our resources should be allocated to the eradication of various specific illnesses?

(2) Should career changes be entirely the free choice of the individual, or should they be in part socially determined?

(3) Shall freedom of learning include the freedom not to learn? What authority and permission will be needed for the administration of drug stimulants to learning?

(4) What personal and social data shall be stored, and for what uses?

(5) How can we ameliorate the tensions that will build up as the disparity widens between the quality of life in the postindustrial nations and the preindustrial or the small and partially industrialized ones?

(6) What mix shall formal organizations strive for in selecting employees from among those at the man-against-society level, the homeostasis level, or the unfolding level? How compatible will these groups be—how possible of integration within an organization?

It is because of such issues as these that future administrators of formal organizations will be increasingly confronted with value decisions as their need to make technical decisions wanes.

THE PROCESS OF PREDICTION

A look at the process of prediction is useful to the professor of educational administration and the practicing administrator because of its significance for better understanding the process of long-range planning in education, which is gaining increasing recognition as an important competence of upper level local school administrators and of state and federal educational officials.

Because of the overdefiniteness of the term *forecasting,* some futurists have sought to use more conditional terms, such as *conjecture, anticipation,* or *prevision,* to describe the process of hypothesizing the future. *Forecasting,* however, continues to be used and is often equated with *predicting.* Roger Revelle identified three kinds of forecasting.[48] First, the projection of trends produces behavioristic models through the simple extrapolation of time series in what is also called deterministic forecasting. Some futurists believe that these extrapolations are too narrow, too econometric. A second kind of forecasting is the working out of consequences of models. A third kind is normative forecasting or the development of normative models describing the kind of future world you want. An example of normative forecasting was the essay written by the prominent Russian nuclear physicist, Andrei D. Sakharov, circulated from hand to hand without official sanction in Russia and published in the *New York Times* on July 22, 1968. Fred Ikle described two broad categories of predictions.[49] "Guiding predictions" aim "to describe the consequences of a course of action and of some of its alternatives so that we can shape the future more to our liking."[50] Another category of predictions includes guessing games, the futuristic novel written for entertainment, and predictions aiming at the spiritual edification of the predictor.

Three major steps are involved in the process of making guiding predictions.[51] The first step is to develop descriptions of the future. These may be based on logical truths; the inductive process; or tacit knowing, intuition, or common sense. The second step is to relate these predictions to actions by evaluating the consequences of alternative courses of action. The third is to predict the relevant values or meanings, that is, to evaluate the desirability of predicted aspects of alternative futures. A danger here is that of assuming that values remain constant, when in fact they may change radically over a period of time. There are two notable features of social predictions (predictions about phenomena that can be changed by human action). One is that they may be self-fulfilling or self-defeating; the very act of predicting may increase or decrease the probability of the event. The other is that the predictor may be aided by advance signals of future plans and events, such as those given by political leaders about what they intend to do.

The errors that mark many predictions, especially when seen in retrospect, come from several sources.[52] One is the failure to seek alternatives to the given prediction. A second is the avoidance of horrible courses of action for lack of nerve in contemplating them. Thus, predictors tend to estimate the probability of nuclear war as exceedingly low, because they know how unpleasant their lives would become if they acted as if they believed a higher estimate of probability. A third error is to base predictions on matters and problems of concern to us now, forgetting that these concerns can change.

One of the needs in forecasting is for more combination or integration forecasting, in contrast to extrapolation forecasting. This need is met in the construction of alternative futures that describe a hypothetical set of interrelated events or conditions in the future. Thus, "a good prediction does not just say A will happen, but that it is the most likely thing, and that the most likely alternatives, if A does not happen, are contingencies B and C."[53] After describing four alternative futures, Daniel Bell commented:

> It may well be that the actual future, the year 2000, will in no way look the way we are hypothetically assuming it will. But then we would have a means of ascertaining what intervened to cause a change. In effect, we are setting up a kind of controlled experiment, a "prospective experiment," and allowing our heirs to match our "as ifs" with the reality.[54]

In a brilliant essay, John Platt illustrated another approach to the challenge of predicting the future.[55] He developed a "crisis intensity chart" in which he ranked "a number of present or potential problems or crises, vertically, according to an estimate of their order of intensity or 'seriousness,' and horizontally, by a rough estimate of their time to reach climactic importance."[56] His eight levels of intensity were estimates of the size of population that might be hurt or affected by the crisis and, beginning with the most intensive, were "total annihilation; great destruction or change (physical, biological, or political); widespread almost unbearable tension; large-scale distress; tension producing responsive change; other problems—important but adequately researched; exaggerated dangers and hopes; and noncrisis problems being 'overstudied'."[57] His categories of "estimated time to crisis," if no major effort were made to bring about a solution, were 1 to 5 years, 5 to 20 years, and 20 to 50 years. He ranked "nuclear or RCBW (radiation chemical biological warfare) escalation" on the first level of intensity for the next 1 to 5 years and also 5 to 20 years, but indicated that by 20 to 50 years this must be solved or we all will be dead. In contrast, "man in space" and "most basic science" were ranked at the bottom in intensity for the next 1 to 5 years.[58] Platt's purpose in presenting his time-intensity analysis of problems was to show the desperate need justifying a mobilization of all scientists to help see us "through this dangerous transition period to the new world instead of to destruction."[59]

RESEARCH IN FUTURISM

Several research techniques have been developed, most of them using the process of predicting in one way or another, to carry on research in futurism. Thomas Green, of the Syracuse University Educational Policy Research Center, has described five of these.[60] The *Delphi technique* was developed by Olaf Helmer and his colleagues at the Rand Corporation. Their purpose was to measure group opinions concerning urgent defense problems. It is an oracular procedure for "assembling systematically a body of expert judgment through a process which appears to bring consensus."[61] A panel of experts is asked to render certain forecasts, doing so individually and without face-to-face confrontation. The results of this survey are returned to the same panel members, giving them the opportunity to revise their forecasts or to give their reasons for remaining outside the central tendencies. The results of this second survey, together with the reasons given, can be returned to the panel members again for a final chance to revise their opinions. The technique provides for a convergence of opinions and their defense, along with defended minority views.

At the Syracuse Center, W. Timothy Weaver has done an extensive analysis of the research using the Delphi technique. He concluded a summary of this analysis with the following assessment of the utility of the technique:

> To sum up quickly, although Delphi was originally intended as a forecasting tool, its more promising educational application seems to be in the following areas: (a) a method for studying the process of thinking about the future, (b) a pedagogical tool or teaching tool which forces people to think about the future in a more complex way than they ordinarily would, and (c) a planning tool which may aid in probing priorities held by members and constituencies of an organization.[62]

A *cross-impact matrix* is a refinement of the Delphi technique for the purpose of assessing the impact of events on each other. A Delphi-like procedure can be used to measure the mode of the relation among forecasted events, the strength of their relationship, and the time lag for the relationship to be felt. A computer analysis of the matrix can yield "a set of modified probabilities for a complex set of events occurring by a given target date."[63] The method can be used in the generation of scenarios.

Simulation/gaming techniques are being experimented with as a way "to assess the trade-offs between alternative paths to the future and alternative goals in relation to specific policy choices."[64] Researchers at the Syracuse Center are also experimenting with *forecasting value changes* with respect to such values as community, independence, privacy, and respect for authority. One purpose is to see how values shift in relative importance as elements in alternative futures. *Evaluating policies* is a research effort to assess such elements of a policy as its cost, efficiency, effectiveness, and capacity to leave subsequent options open.

As a result of a survey of futures research in the United States, McHale estimated that in 1970 there were about 600 full-time and about 500 part-time workers concentrating on futures research, of whom a disproportionate number came from the fields of the physical sciences and engineering.[65] The objectives represented by ten or more studies were technological forecasting (41), socio-economic forecasting (21), economic projections (21), market analysis (15), and corporate planning studies (10).[66] In order of their frequency of use in futures research projects, the nine most frequently used techniques of research, according to McHale's survey, were scenario building, Delphi techniques, simulation/gaming, trend extrapolation, dynamic modeling, cross-impact analysis, correlation plotting, expert position papers, and relevance trees.[67]

The process of predicting and related research processes in the area of futurism have not been refined to any great extent. But they are significant not only because they provide the methodology for building the content of futurism, but also because of their possible adaptation by the practicing administrator in carrying out his role as planner for the near-range future.

THE DEVELOPMENT OF FORMAL INSTRUCTION IN FUTURISM

The emergence of any new area of specialization usually spawns in short order a new association of those who become interested in the specialization and a corresponding set of new courses in the specialization in the colleges and universities of the nation. The first development has already been reported above as the formation in 1966 of the World Future Society. The second development has also begun to appear. Eldredge estimated on the basis of his survey of education in futurism in 1969-1970 that about 100 instructors were already offering about 90 courses in as many institutions during that period. Among those instructors, social scientists predominated—in contrast to McHale's finding that physical scientists and engineers predominated among workers in futures research. Eldredge concluded that formal education in futurism will continue to expand, showing up in many disciplines either as new courses or as altered subject matter in traditional courses.[68] Although he made no reference to futurism courses offered within the field of professional education, an earlier informal survey published by *The Futurist* did list several such courses. It also reported a Program for the Study of the Future, established at the University of Massachusetts.[69]

THE S-CURVE VERSUS THE J-CURVE

Any serious study of futurism can lead to a pervasive feeling of alarm or even deep pessimism about the future. The rational basis for this feeling is symbolized by the J-curve graph. The best known illustration of this exponential curve of growth seeming to reach to infinity is the one representing the increase in the world's population from about a billion in 1840 to about three billion in 1963 and to more than six billion in 2000, with the statistical prospect of doubling about every two generations thereafter. Various facets of today's ecological crisis can be similarly graphed, as can the explosion of knowledge. The very speed of change indicated by the steep ascent of the J-curve is the cause of the "future shock" analyzed by Alvin Toffler in his book of that title. Were the J-curve the inexorable wave of the future, doomsday would seem certain.

But there is growing evidence that the exponential increase in many changes is now beginning to taper off, bending the J-curve into an S-curve, which has always symbolized change from one state of relative stability to a different state of stability. Thus, population growth is showing signs of leveling off—several decades in the future, but, nevertheless, leveling off. Limits seem to have been reached in weapon destructibility—a fact that still leaves open the danger of nuclear holocaust. In less emotionally charged areas, the speed of communication may have reached its peak (unless a speed faster than light can be found), and a peak is in sight in the speed of computer operation.

Most significant, it is through human effort and decision that some of the pessimistic J-curves seem destined to be turned into more optimistic—at least more manageable—S-curves. There is some promise that the growing realization of the environmental crisis may lead to action having that effect on the gloomy ecological J-curves. And one new and growing organization in this country has adopted the slogan, "Stop at Two," to advocate the kind of family planning resulting in a limit of two children. That group, called Zero Population Growth has even adopted the graphic symbol of a J-curve transformed into an S-curve. It is this very symbol that best poses the challenge of futurism: for man to control the future for his own welfare rather than being overwhelmed by a future carrying him to his ultimate destruction. No process can be more crucial to this challenge than education.

FOOTNOTES

1. This is a revision and enlargement of a paper, "Predicting Future Environments," presented at the NCPEA at the State University of New York at Albany in August 1968. Some parts of this paper have been adapted or taken from the writer's "Education and Educators in a Changing Society, Part Two: Some Implications for Education and the Preparation of Educators," *Preparing Educators to Meet Emerging Needs* (Denver: Designing Education for the Future, 1969), 7:19-31.

2. James M. Naughton, "Panel Finds Need to Inspire Debate on Nation's Goals," *New York Times,* 19 July 1970, sec. 1, p. 1.

3. Ibid.

4. Ibid., p. 47.

5. Daniel Bell, "Introduction," in Herman Kahn and Anthony J. Wiener, *The Year 2000* (New York: Macmillan, 1967).

6. Daniel Bell, "The Year 2000—the Trajectory of an Idea," in "Toward the Year 2000: Work in Progress," *Daedalus* 96 (Summer 1967): 641.

7. Harrison Brown, James Bonner, and John Weir, *The Next Hundred Years: Man's Natural and Technological Resources* (New York: Viking, 1957).

8. Burnham P. Beckwith, *The Next 500 Years: Scientific Predictions of Major Social Trends* (New York: Exposition Press, 1967).

9. R. Buckminster Fuller, "The Prospects for Humanity," *Saturday Review* 47 (August 29, 1964): 43-44.

10. Thomas F. Green, "The Educational Policy Research Center at Syracuse: Problems and Prospects," *Journal of Research and Development in Education,* 2 (Summer 1969): 49.

11. Michael Marien, comp., *Essential Reading for the Future of Education: A Selected and Critically Annotated Bibliography* (Syracuse, New York: Educational Policy Research Center, Syracuse University Research Corporation, September 1970).

12. Herman Kahn and Anthony J. Wiener, *The Year 2000: A Framework for Speculation on the Next Thirty-Three Years* (New York: Macmillan, 1967), p. 6.

13. Kenneth E. Boulding, "Expecting the Unexpected: The Uncertain Future of Knowledge and Technology," in *Prospective Changes in Society by 1980,* Designing Education for the Future, no. 1., eds. Edgar L. Morphet and Charles O. Ryan (New York: Citation Press, 1967), p. 203.

14. Bell, "The Year 2000," pp. 642-644.

15. Ibid., p. 649, and Karl Deutsch, "Baselines for the Future," *Daedalus* 96:659-661.

16. Herman Kahn and Anthony J. Wiener, "The Next Thirty-Three Years: A Framework for Speculation," *Daedalus* 96 (Summer 1967): 706. Also Kahn and Wiener, *The Year 2000,* p. 7.

17. Daniel Bell, ed., "Toward the Year 2000: Work in Progress," *Daedalus* 96.

18. William R. Ewald, Jr., ed., *Environment for Man: the Next Fifty Years* (1967); idem, *Environment and Policy: The Next Fifty Years* (1968); idem, *Environment and Change: The Next Fifty Years* (1968)(Bloomington: Indiana University Press).

19. Edgar L. Morphet and Charles O. Ryan, eds., *Prospective Changes in Society* (New York: Citation Press, 1967).

20. Herman E. Hilleboe and Ray E. Trussell, "The Medical Sciences," in *Prospective Changes in Society,* p. 58.

21. Gardner C. Quarton, "Deliberated Efforts to Control Human Behavior and Modify Personality," *Daedalus* 96:846.

22. Margaret Mead, "The Life Cycle and Its Variations: The Division of Roles," *Daedalus* 96:872.

23. Edward A. Shaw, "Speculations About Man and His Work—A.D. 2000," *Personnel Journal* 46 (July-August 1967): 423.

24. David Perlman, "The Search for the Memory Molecule," *New York Times Magazine*, 7 July 1968, pp. 8-9.

25. William T. Knox, "The New Look in Information Systems," *Prospective Changes in Society*, chap. 13.

26. Warren G. Bennis, "Beyond Bureaucracy," in Warren G. Bennis and Philip E. Slater, *The Temporary Society* (New York: Harper & Row, 1968), chap. 3.

27. Kahn and Wiener, *The Year 2000*, Table 22, p. 60.

28. Daniel Bell, "Alternative Futures," *Daedalus* 96:667.

29. Kahn and Wiener, *The Year 2000*, pp. 62-63.

30. Ibid., pp. 195-96.

31. Ibid., p. 199.

32. Ibid., p. 208.

33. Ibid., p. 190.

34. Ibid., pp. 191-92.

35. Ibid., p. 207.

36. Philip E. Slater, "Some Social Consequences of Temporary Systems," *The Temporary Society*, p. 79.

37. Ibid., pp. 79-88.

38. Warren G. Bennis, "The Temporary Society," *The Temporary Society*, p. 127.

39. John McHale, *The Future of the Future* (New York: George Braziller, 1969), pp. 291-92.

40. R. Buckminster Fuller, "An Operating Manual for Spaceship Earth," in *Environment and Change: The Next Fifty Years*, ed. William R. Ewald, Jr. (Bloomington: Indiana University Press, 1968), pp. 377-8.

41. Kahn and Wiener, *The Year 2000*, Table 2, p. 9.

42. Willis W. Harman, "Contemporary Social Forces and Alternative Futures," *Journal of Research and Development in Education*, 2 (Summer 1969): 81-83.

43. Arnold Mitchell, "Alternative Future Societies," (speech given at San Francisco, December 11, 1969) (Menlo Park, California: Stanford Research Institute, n.d.), p. 5.

44. Ibid., p. 4.

45. Ibid., p. 9.

46. Ibid.

47. Ibid., pp. 1-15.

48. Roger Revelle, "The Need for Normative Statements," *Daedalus* 96:968.

49. Fred C. Ikle, "Can Social Predictions Be Evaluated?" *Daedalus* 96:733-9.

50. Ibid., pp. 733-734.

51. Ibid., pp. 739-750.

52. Ibid., pp. 750-753.

53. Karl Deutsch, "Alternative Futures," *Daedalus* 96:677.

54. Bell, "Alternative Futures," *Daedalus* 96:667.

55. John Platt, "What We Must Do," *Science* 166 (November 28, 1969): 1115-21.

56. Ibid., p. 1117.

57. Ibid., Table 2, p. 1119.

58. Ibid.

59. Ibid., p. 1115.

60. Green, "Educational Policy Research Center at Syracuse," pp. 49-66.

61. Ibid., p. 57.

62. W. Timothy Weaver, "The Delphi Forecasting Method," *Phi Delta Kappan* 52 (January 1971): 267-71.

63. Green, "Educational Policy Research Center at Syracuse," p. 59.

64. Ibid., p. 61.

65. "A Survey of Futures Research in The United States," *The Futurist* 4 (December 1970): 200-204.

66. Ibid., p. 201.

67. Ibid.

68. H. Wentworth Eldredge, "Education in Futurism in North America," *The Futurist* 4 (December 1970): 193-196.

69. "Professors Teach the Future," *The Futurist* 4 (June 1970): 97-100.

70. "To Them, Two Children are Fine, but Three Crowd the World," *New York Times*, 12 January 1971, p. 30.

Stephen J. Knezevich

3

Perspectives on the Educational Program in 1985

Since the dawn of history man has plotted and planned ways to gain a better glimpse of what is to be. Fascination with the future waxes and wanes in intensity and the styles of forecasting change, but the desire to know more about tomorrow never dies. Five thousand years ago man turned to oracles and astrologers. These mystics it was believed were born, not made, and had the rare ability of sensing what "signs" to seek and how to interpret them. They issued predictions in general, if not vague, terms and, as a consequence, one could read into them what he wished.

According to Bell, we are experiencing a resurgence of interest in the future.[1] "Signs" of the future, however, are not sought in the malodorous examination of the entrails of freshly killed chickens or in the generation of pseudoscientific charts of the movement of heavenly bodies. It is believed now that educational missions, programs, and strategies likely to prevail in the year 1985 can be derived from the organized and systematic studies of the future that trace their origins to the late 1960s. The new breed of futurists rejects the occult arts of the ancients in favor of more rational and scientific approaches.

Even more startling is the growing conviction that man can intervene to influence the course of events in education as he does in other endeavors. This stands in stark contrast to the cliché "what will be, will be." According to the argument of the ancients, the future is wrapped up in the stars; heavenly bodies are beyond the control of mere mortals on earth. Questioning the grip of the stars, the moon, or other heavenly bodies on man's fate, the present day futurist is more inclined to say "the future is what we make it" or "the future belongs to those who plan for it." This point of view implies the possibility of control or, at least, of anticipating events far enough in advance to maximize the positive and minimize the negative. Recognizing the fallibility of mortals, the multiplicity of variables involved in futures determination, and the limitations of available data the emphasis is placed on generating a set of alternative futures or choices. Given a set of reasonable alternatives, plans can be developed to anticipate, if not influence, each of the most likely educational futures.

The historic mission of the schools, stated in general terms, has been to prepare the "young" to meet the challenges of future worlds. For the most part the schools were to serve a narrow segment of the total population. What programs or strategies could best realize this future-oriented mission stimulated an endless debate that has been going on now for more than 3,000 years. The critics of educational institutions argue that the programs are cast in a narrow and conservative mold of preserving the past even though present civilization may be threatened. In short, "transmitting the cultural heritage" was overplayed and overemphasized the past.

Through the philosophical debates described by Plato, the writings of John Dewey, and the "Great Society" goals of a U.S. president runs the theme that educational programs can be a powerful force in the building of an ideal society. Over the years, practical considerations reduced the probability that schools would assume a dynamic role in the solution of social and economic ills of a nation, but this did not stifle the historic debates. It was easier to talk about building a new social order than it was to gain a consensus on what that meant and then allocate to schools the magnitude of resources to get the job done. It is predicted that educational missions and programs will be the subjects of even greater controversy in the years between 1970 and 1985 as the schools become more involved in the persistent social problems of the times. In short, Plato and Dewey are likely to look like winners in the great debate as education is designed more and more to be an instrument of social and economic policy for the nation. Furthermore, adults as well as children and youth will participate in the noble experiment.

This, then, is one alternative future for educational institutions in 1985, namely that they will be dedicated to a more active role in the improvement of man and his society. This would call for plans to design an immensely complex and expensive-to-support educational system. Moreover, an educational system designed purposely to do more than merely transmit the cultural heritage—that is, to contribute more directly, and with the short run in mind, to the resolution of controversies in civil rights, poverty, and other social tensions—is destined to become more controversial, if not explosive. Agreement on inadequacies does not automatically result in consensus on new educational directions to be pursued.

Another alternative future could also come to pass. It could be argued that the intense and prolonged social and political controversy in which educational institutions became embroiled during the 1960s and 1970s greatly weakened and splintered schools. A consequent loss of public support would mean that schools, as now defined, would cease to function and exist in 1985. The demise of schools could be projected on other grounds as well. New developments in technology by 1985, and certainly by 2000, could create new forms of communication and social interaction that would eliminate the need for the kind of educational institutions that now exist. Educational functions in 1985 or 2000, could be distributed among other continuing or newly created social institutions. This alternative future implies that the best use for professional planning during the 1970s would be to provide for the orderly demise of schools and the efficient transfer of responsibilities to other social agencies. Public education, after all, has been in existence for a relatively short period: only three centuries.

The probability of realizing an alternative future in which there are no formal educational institutions in operation or existence as early as 1985 is not considered to be very high by the author. Institutions are organized to maximize the probability of survival. Bureaucracies are created to resist forces that would destroy them as well as forces that would drastically modify purposes or change directions by some 180 degrees. The disappearance of schools by 1985 is even less likely than an alternative future in which the educational institution in 1985 pursues missions, programs, and strategies very much as it did in 1970. Schools in 1985 will be different, but formal educational institutions will be around in the year 2000 as well as 1985. How different they are likely to be is the subject of this chapter. The changing missions, programs, and strategies are among the key variables that will define educational institutions of the future.

This chapter seeks to identify the alternative futures most likely to be experienced by educational institutions. It starts with a review of social, political, and technological forces likely to have a major impact on education by 1985. These factors will stimulate the generation of new educational programs by 1985 and will make possible the implementation of a new store of strategies by members of the profession. Finally, there will be an examination of the new roles and relationships between actors inside and outside educational institutions, such as pupils and teachers, teachers and administrators, schools and their publics, and the like.

FORCES LIKELY TO CHANGE THE SHAPE OF EDUCATION BY 1985

Experimentation has not always been greeted with enthusiasm. Nor has the lot of the change agent always been a happy one. Equally suspect is the assumption that education is now and always has been insulated from the winds of change. Compounding historical errors leads some to the erroneous belief that educational institutions of today look and perform precisely as they did 100 or 200 years ago. A more complete review of educational history would reveal many reform efforts, some successful and others abortive. Modifications of missions, programs, and strategies have occurred in the past. Some may be impatient with the slow rate of change or its shallowness. Nonetheless, change is no stranger in schools.

A more accurate historical picture shows that innovative action during one period may stimulate a reaction or resistance to change during another period. Thus, during the 1930s the famous progressive education experiments of more than two decades before were harshly repudiated. The negative reaction to innovation under the guise of progressivism inhibited bold departures from traditional educational practices for at least a decade. Since 1945, however, the educational environment has been more conducive to change. The clamor for educational innovations showed no signs of abating as late as 1970. Future projections of educational missions, programs, and strategies described here are based on the assumption that the educational spirit of the 1970s and early 1980s will be at least as enthusiastic toward innovations as it was in the 1960s.

General Sources of Change

Bell believes it is easier to talk about the sources of change in society than it is to predict specific events at some future point in time. He cites four major sources of change in society:[2]

(1) Technology is on all lists. Technology multiplies the number of possibilities "for mastering nature and transforming resources, time and space"[3] and thereby is a prime stimulator of future change. No one questions that the computer will have a profound impact on society. Bell views technology not simply as machines but as a "systematic disciplined approach to objectives, using a calculus of precision and measurement and a concept of systems that are quite at variance with the traditional and customary

religious, aesthetic, and intuitive modes."[4] He emphasizes the intellectual rather than purely physical dimensions of technology.

(2) The second source of change is "the diffusion of existing goods and privileges in society, whether they be tangible goods or social claims on the community."[5] This diffusion alters the size and scale of servicing institutions as we come closer to the realization of the promise of equality. It can be related to what others have called the rising expectations for services obtained from social institutions.

(3) The third source of change is related to new structural developments particularly the trend toward greater centralization within the American political system. The economy is being transformed into what Bell calls the postindustrial society. Major occupational opportunities will shift from production-oriented to service-oriented occupations. Intellectual institutions such as universities and research organizations will be the primary sources of innovation rather than the industrial corporations.

(4) The fourth major source of change, and perhaps the most important, is the relationship between the United States and the rest of the world. What happens in the cold war, the middle East, or southeast Asia will have a decisive impact on the future course of events in the United States.

A fifth force of no less significance can be added to the four described by Bell. It is the interaction between population and environment, often vaguely referred to as "ecology." Major population shifts, changes in distribution, and variation in racial and socio-economic composition within rural and urban areas have always had a powerful impact on social institutions such as the schools. Unchecked population growth has been feared since at least the time of Malthus. The fear in the United States is less for the assumed starvation and more for the society's inability to provide the quality and quantity of social services needed. Of even greater concern is the propensity to increase water and air pollution as well as irritants to human senses such as excessive noise and offensive odors. The future size of families, concentrations of population in urban and suburban areas, and the ability of government to regulate use of natural resources will have a significant impact on the 1985 environment.

Most futurists agree with Bell that "bewitchment with technology" is dangerous and that what matters most in the future is not gadgets, but the development of "the kinds of social arrangements that can deal adequately with the problems" likely to be encountered. He adds that "the only prediction about the future that one can make with certainty is that public authorities will face more problems than they have in any previous time in history."[6]

The demand for greater accountability, basically a political term, is likely to intensify during the 1970s and deserves recognition as a sixth force for change. By 1985 administrators will have adjusted to the impact of this thrust and generated a series of procedures to satisfy public information and demands for accountability in the use of resources for educational purposes. This force doubtless will continue to generate a host of clichés. "Reaching the unreachables" may be the "in" slogan for education 1985 along with "relating what's relevant."

Specific Innovations and Changes

Performance (incentive-fee) contracting, a companion concept to accountability, was introduced to education in the late 1960s. To illustrate, considerable research and experimentation on this method of serving the educational market will be completed in the 1970s. The shift to a mixture of school employees and commercial contractors for instructional services performed previously by teachers employed by the school district is considered a dramatic one in 1971. Incentive-fee instructional performance contracts will be one of the many options available to administrators in 1985. Performance contracting will produce changes that move beyond instructional services and encompass any and all types of services required by the educational institutions. What can be done best through performance contracting and what is done best through direct employment in an educational institution will be defined. The mode of contracting will be seen as less relevant than the quality of services purchased under contract arrangements, that is, the capability of the contractors to deliver on promises. In this respect the organized teachers will represent one agency offering instructional services to school districts for a "fee" (or salary schedule).

Kahn and Wiener developed a table of what they called "One Hundred Technical Innovations Very Likely By The Last Third Of The Twentieth Century."[7] These could be viewed as illustrations and specific technological factors that will produce change. At least one third of the innovations included had implications for educational missions, programs, and strategies. These are shown below with the same numbers used in the list prepared by Kahn and Wiener:

1. Multiple application of lasers and masers for sensing, measuring, communication, cutting, heating, welding, power transmission, illumination, destructive, defensive and other purposes.

13. Major reduction in hereditary and congenital defects.

17. New techniques and institutions for adult education.

22. More sophisticated architectural engineering (*e.g.*, geodesic domes, "fancy" stressed shells, pressurized skins, and esoteric materials).

24. Three-dimensional photography, illustration, movies, and television.

29. Extensive and intensive centralization (or automatic interconnection) of current and past personal and business information in high speed data processors.

30. Other new and possibly pervasive techniques for surveillance monitoring, and control of individuals and organizations.

33. New and more reliable "educational" and propaganda techniques for affecting human behavior—public and private.

34. Practical use of direct electronic communication with and stimulation of the brain.

38. New techniques for very cheap, convenient, and reliable birth control.

43. New techniques and institutions for the education of children.

58. Chemical methods for improving memory and learning.

63. Mechanical and chemical methods for improving human analytical ability more or less directly.

70. Simple inexpensive home video recording and playing.

71. Inexpensive high-capacity, world-wide, regional, and local (home and business) communication (perhaps using satellites, lasers, and light pipes).

72. Practical home and business use of "wired" video communications for both telephone and TV (possibly including retrieval of taped material from libraries or other sources) and rapid transmission and reception of facsimiles (possibly including news, library material, commercial announcements, instantaneous mail delivery, other printouts, and so on.

75. Shared time (public and interconnected?) computers generally available to home and business on a metered basis.

81. Personal "pagers" (perhaps even two-way pocket phones) and other personal electronic equipment for communication, computing, and data processing program.

83. Inexpensive (less than $20) long-lasting, very small battery operated TV receivers.

84. Home computers to "run" household and communicate with outside world.

85. Maintenance-free, long-life electronic and other equipment.

86. Home education via video and computerized and programed learning.

88. Inexpensive (less than one cent a page), rapid high-quality black and white reproductions; followed by color and high detailed photography reproduction—perhaps for home as well as office use.

94. Inexpensive road-free (and facility-free) transportation.

97. New biological and chemical methods to identify, trace, incapacitate, or annoy people for police and military uses.

The focus of this writing is on the first half of the 30 years that remain of this century. A sizable number of the innovations on the list by Kahn and Wiener may well appear by 1985; others would be delayed until the end of the century.

Kahn and Wiener generated yet another list of "Ten Far-Out Possibilities."[8] The following have implications for education after the year 2000, but they are unlikely to have an impact as early as 1985.

1. Life expectancy extended to substantially more than 150 years (immortality?)
5. Interstellar travel
7. Practical and routine use of extrasensory phenomena
9. Lifetime immunization against practically all diseases

The organized and more rational studies of the future are concerned more with identifying alternatives than with producing a single prediction. The task that confronts long-range educational planners is to build on the more general data by extracting those considered to be most significant in developing a series of varied futures for education.

EDUCATIONAL MISSIONS IN 1985

During the 1960s schools were criticized with increasing frequency for limiting their missions so severely that they failed to contribute more to the solution of persistent social problems. During the past decade, education became a stage on which the ills that troubled groups of people were called to the attention of the public. Schools became a focal point of action in resolving socio-economic problems. This suggests the following as far as likely alternative futures for educational missions are concerned.

The continuing debate is more likely to alter priorities and introduce new missions than it is to sunder educational institutions. The traditional and conservative role of transmitting the cultural heritage will become only one of many roles. It will be granted a lesser priority for school resource allocation than those programs dedicated to the great social and political issues of the 1970s and 1980s. It appears reasonable to expect that the social ferment, knowledge explosions, and technological developments will continue unabated, with the rate of new developments being at least equal to that of the present. The big issues of the 1950s and 1960s, namely pupil and faculty integration, staff negotiations, and decentralization will be resolved by 1985 only to be replaced by a new set of social, economic, and political concerns. There will be no shortage of new scientific miracles in 1985 that some will feel should be adapted to revolutionize education. Nor will there be any fewer social crises of the type that easily provide more ammunition with which to criticize what and how things are done in schools.

Conceptualization of the educational institution as an agency contributing to the amelioration of a variety of societal problems will be in vogue well past 1985. Public education in 1985 will be viewed as an institution capable not only of contributing to the resolution of problems in the long run, but also of coping with short-run effects. Education will become more important than ever and a prime contributor to the building of the superculture of 1985. This task is likely to be performed more effectively and efficiently by a specialized educational institution than by a multipurpose social organization that would tend to rank other functions above education. The more complex world of 1985 will have an even greater need for a relevant and formal set of educational institutions.

All this is related to the concept that the deliberate intervention of human instruments, principally through governmental institutions, is a desirable and significant way to control change and to achieve specified ends. It is, therefore, highly probable that schools will become what John Dewey called "strategic outposts on the social frontier." The problems of indecisiveness about what to do in education will increase rather than decrease. Furthermore, educational institutions in 1985 will continue to face rising expectations, that is, higher standards of excellence will be demanded by those served.

Whether measured by the magnitude of the risk capital called research and development or by the increased expenditures encountered in preparing a new educational practice model, innovation demands additional resources above and beyond those required to maintain the status quo. If education is to be part of the innovative society and an institution with new missions during the 1970s and 1980s, it must be assumed that there will be significant increases in allocations of fiscal resources for schools. New ideas are hard to obtain and even harder to implement in a marginal or subsistence economy.

By 1985 a more definitive statement of educational missions translated into more specific and behavioral terms will be accomplished. The more comprehensive missions will produce what can be called a "programmatic curriculum." The present subject matter curriculum format, which emphasizes knowledge for the sake of knowledge, will finally be superseded by a format that clusters educational experiences around measurable objectives. A "programmatic curriculum," by definition calls for the organization of educational programs rather than the traditional courses of study and even such variations as the broad fields, fused, or correlated curriculum. A program, in turn, is derived from a mission statement; it is generated when all activities are related to a mission rather than a subject field.

Behavioral objectives, discussed with increasing frequency during the 1960s, will be the guidelines for educational operations in 1985. Pipe defined a behavioral objective, also known as a performance objective, as "a description of the desired outcome of a learning experience, stated in terms of the behavior to be exhibited by the student as evidence of competence."[9] He stipulated further that the behavioral objective has at least the following characteristics:

(1) It describes the observable action that is to be evidence of competence;

(2) When necessary, it describes the conditions under which the action is to be performed; and

(3) When necessary, it describes the criteria by which to judge acceptable performance.

Systems techniques like what is presently known as PPBS (Program Planning Budgeting System) will be implemented more completely by 1985. An essential part of this approach is the development of a programmatic format for education. Missions are translated into measurable objectives which in turn give rise to a clustering of activities and educational experiences around such measurable objectives.

EDUCATIONAL PROGRAMS

Range of Experiences

To satisfy a broader range of social and educational concerns within one social institution, public schools will be extended and expanded in all directions. Although the "school-age" group will continue to be served, far more than one fourth of the population will demand educational opportunities in 1985. By the middle of the next decade nursery education will be accepted as the starting point in formal preparation. This implies that the public school kindergartens, which had their beginnings 100 years before 1985 and were accorded only limited acceptance in nonurban areas as late as 1970, will finally gain universal acceptance. An educational program consisting of five years of specialized instruction for children from two to six will be part of almost all school systems by 1985. These so-called *preschool* (actually pre-grade-one) programs will place heavy emphasis on social, emotional, and physical health developments of the pupil as opposed to the traditional academic dimensions. Primary or infant school centers are likely to be separate from and more widely dispersed within urban concentrations in particular than present day elementary schools.

It will be inappropriate·to speak of a terminal point in education in 1985. Individuals will spend a lifetime in a variety of educational programs and "schools" gaining new ideas or further sharpening old skills. If education is narrowly defined as the time during which a person dedicates a majority of his efforts and time to attending a formal institution of learning, then the terminal point is reached when either no time during a year or less than a majority of time is spent in formal studies or skill development. Within this narrower conception of education, the termination of formal schooling (where a majority or more of time is devoted to the pursuit of studies) in 1985 will include completion of opportunities available through what is now called a two-year community college.

Universal community college educational opportunities will be established in all states by no later than 1985. A community college is defined here in its most comprehensive sense. It would include postsecondary programs of vocational-technical education, remedial education in the basic academic skills, adult education, avocational or special interest development, community services, counseling and guidance services, retraining for those whose occupational skills are made obsolete by new technologies, and part-time learning opportunities as well as the college transfer or parallel opportunities encompassing many of the elements in the first two years of a four-year or baccalaureate degree granting institution of higher learning. In short, the so-called *noncredit* and credit programs will both be available. By 1985 a new system of recognition will have been developed to signal completion of learning experiences that are not recognized in collegiate degree programs and for that reason have acquired the inaccurate designation of *noncredit* courses.

Community colleges in the United States will have repeated during the 1945-1985 period what the secondary schools experienced during 1890-1930. The dream of universal elementary education was conceived in the eighteenth century and realized, in large part, in the United States during the last half of the nineteenth century. Universal secondary education was only a dream in the first half of the nineteenth century. This ambition was not to be fulfilled until about the middle of the twentieth century. Likewise the seeds of the concept of a universal public community college education can be traced to the early part of the twentieth century. The fruition of this expanded educational concept will not be realized fully until about 1985. Enrollments in community colleges in 1985 will be of the magnitude of that noted in secondary schools in 1965.

Four-year and degree-oriented collegiate institutions of 1970 will double in number and in size by 1985. They will command a sizable portion of the total resources allocated by society for education. The emphasis in these institutions will be on learning opportunities for students at the junior, senior, graduate, and postgraduate levels. The research dimensions are likely to be expanded rather than diminished. As many futurists have suggested, the production of new knowledge will come from specialized research organizations and universities rather than from industry or the independent inventor. The development of "human capital" and new ideas will become more important in the last three decades of this century and will acquire greater significance than the accumulation of financial capital. The knowledge-producing function of universities will be part of the movement toward greater institutionalization of change in 1985.

The term *dropout* will be redefined in the light of a higher standard for measuring whether a person has terminated his formal education (in the narrower sense) prematurely. By 1985 completion of grade 14, or the second year of a community college, will be the new standard rather than the present grade 12. Progress in the reduction of secondary school dropouts, which in 1970 totaled 28 per cent of those who were in fifth grade eight years before, will reach a point by 1985 where less than ten per cent will terminate formal education prematurely based on our present standards, that is, before completion of grade 12.

The futurists point to the great strides in medical science continuing throughout this century. The average productive life span in 1985 will be extended far beyond present levels. By the same token the rapid pace of technology will mean that a sizable portion of the population will find their occupational skills rendered obsolete. The longer lifespan increases the probability that a person will pursue more than one career during a lifetime. Career shifts and career cycles will be of considerable concern to educational institutions. Massive retraining programs, at least twice during a lifespan for most adults, and continuing new career development programs will be accepted and significant functions of postsecondary institutions teamed with some industries in 1985.

Educational programs will be expanded on all fronts to provide for the diverse needs of the talented and those less well-endowed intellectually, physically, socially, or economically. Work-study experiences will be available for those 15 and older who can benefit from them. Cooperative work opportunities will bring industrial establishments and formal educational institutions into closer working relationships. Secondary schools as well as those concerned with initial or retraining phases of technical-vocational experiences will include job placement for their graduates. This function has been neglected and ignored as recently as 1971.

Pupils with all types of exceptional characteristics will be involved in educational and rehabilitation experiences by 1985. Neither physical, emotional, nor mental handicaps will deprive an individual of an opportunity to participate in some type of an institution of formal learning. This, of course, will necessitate development of a broad series of special learning experiences for those who cannot learn at the same rate or with the same type of materials as others in better circumstances or with more talent. Futurists predict that between 1970 and 2000, medical technology will greatly reduce the number of congenital and hereditary defects. One alternative future projection for exceptional education programs is that by 1985 their enrollments will begin to decline rather substantially. By the end of the century only nominal needs may remain.

Futurists again project increasing affluence and leisure in the last third of the century. A work week in the neighborhood of 35 hours seems highly probable by 1985. How to maximize enjoyment from increased time off will be of increasing concern during the 1970s. The long-stated educational objective of "worthy use of leisure time" will receive serious concern by 1985. Educational programs devoted to more productive and enjoyable leisure time for the entire labor force, as well as for those retired from the labor force, who can be expected to live longer and healthier lives, will gain high priority by 1985.

Curriculum or Program Revisions

Curriculum revisions have been a way of life ever since schools were organized as specialized educational institutions. At times additions and deletions were relatively minor, or there were long time spans between them. The increased rate of development of new courses of study and the continuing reorganization of the subject content in science, mathematics, and other fields at the elementary and secondary school level during the post-World War II period will be extended during the next two decades. Incorporating the new knowledge produced in all disciplines will be a continuing challenge to keep the curriculum relevant in 1985 as well as in 1970. Every phase of the school's curriculum will have undergone a significant revision at least twice by 1985. This will embrace the academic and vocational programs as well. As indicated earlier, a "programmatic curriculum" will be in vogue by 1985.

More than likely a continuing massive curriculum reform to ensure the relevance of its content, to produce new and meaningful programs, and to generate a unique instructional organization will demand a research and development investment of well over $10 billion. Local school districts and the states do not have the fiscal capacity to dedicate resources of such magnitude for nonoperating expenditures. Most of the funds for innovative developments will come from the federal government and a small part will come from the state or private foundations. This in turn, implies increased federal involvement, direction, and influence in programs or school experiences. This is not to suggest that there will be a national curriculum, but federal involvement will reduce the wide variations in quality of programs. By 1985 the nationalizing forces will have generated counterthrust by state agencies. The design of state adaptations of the reforms recommended by nationally based and financed commissions for refurbishing the content of various disciplines will be evident by 1985. Nonetheless, the price of federal involvement in program development will be greater consideration of public education as an instrument of national social and economic policy.

A massive reworking of the substantive knowledge in various fields, creation of new programs, and development of new instructional formats on a fairly frequent basis between now and 1985 will demand equally massive retraining programs for teachers, administrators, and supervisors. University, school district, and professional educational organization study programs for the continuing professional growth of all educational personnel will be institutionalized by 1985. Local school district and university budgets for staff development will be at least ten times higher than the present levels. Once again federal funds will be needed. By the middle of this decade, the federal counterpart of what is now called EPDA (Education Professions Development Act) will be expending $500 million annually for retraining programs.

By 1985 school health programs will include treatment of student health problems on an outpatient basis. This means going far beyond the present emphasis on diagnosis and referral services in schools as well as the more traditional health education concerns. The tremendous number of drug abuse problems found among those of high school age, and to a lesser extent among those of elementary school age, encouraged schools to act on the drug abuse problem and to generalize from it to other health concerns. The revelation through examination of pupils enrolled in Job Corps and similar programs of the 1960s of the inadequate dental and medical attention available to most children and youth in poverty areas will prompt national and state officials by 1985 to approve medical care for children ("childcare") and youths ("youthcare"). The significance of medicare for the aged will aid inauguration of similar medical programs for the young as well.

The school is to be tapped as the institution in society most readily able to implement a broader range of health services for children and youths. In this respect history will probably record that United States schools were slow to meet the total health needs of children and youths. Schools in Canada and other countries will likely provide student health treatment as well as diagnostic services, including treatment of dental and health problems, long before 1985.

There will be a greater contribution of cultural institutions to complement and extend the educational experience in schools by 1985. "Schools without walls" and schools located in the heart of the largest urban communities or in the most isolated of retreats will be common. Although, the superintendent of schools will not become a "superintendent of culture," there will be closer working relations between public libraries, museums, and public recreation programs with the institution of public education.

As suggested earlier the format as well as the substance of the curriculum will be different in 1985. In addition new instructional organization patterns will be generated. By 1985 it is projected that new instructional organizational patterns will be implemented to replace or at least modify substantially the traditional graded pattern that began over 100 years ago. The search for better ways of relating experiences, instructional media, instructional personnel, space, and time to promote more effective and efficient learning opportunities at what are now called the middle and senior high school levels is a never-ending one. Individually guided education programs such as the multiunit school pattern may well dominate instructional configurations by the middle of the 1980s. Recreation will at long last gain importance as part of the "worthy use of leisure time" objective and as ways of gaining personal and physical renewal. Year round recreation programs of varying degrees of sophistication will be designed for people of all ages.

The educational institution will touch and interact with all other agencies that concern themselves with children, youths, and adults. These interactions may well be the first steps toward a re-thinking and redefinition of the overall missions and programs of what are presently known as educational institutions. Conceptualization of the child, youth, or adult as a whole rather than in terms of intellect will project the educational institution in directions undreamed of in 1970.

EDUCATIONAL STRATEGIES

By 1985, the learner will be expected to acquire more knowledge in a shorter period of time and demonstrate a greater mastery in knowledge use. A higher degree of skill will be demanded in an environment where the pace of change will far exceed the present rate. To meet these expectations, new instructional or learning strategies (or if you prefer, "methods of teaching") will have to be designed. Present strategies are criticized for failing to meet existing pressures on learners. Obviously, what was not adequate in 1965 cannot possibly satisfy the pace and demands for learning in 1985. The hope for more productive educational strategies lies in a shift as well as an extension of professional preparation approaches to take fuller advantage of the technology that emerged during the 1960s and 1970s and hopefully will have been perfected to a high degree by 1985 and adapted to educational purposes.

New Strategies and Personnel Needs

Professional preparation for instructional personnel will be extended in 1985 to at least six years of collegiate level work; a large number will have earned a doctorate before entering practice. This preparation will focus on acquiring greater sensitivity to human relations, value systems of various cultural groups, societal stresses, and conflict resolution, as well as the relevant technical instructional skills and a deeper understanding of the updated substantive knowledge in many fields. The extended period of study will allow the new concerns to be learned without sacrificing knowledge of subject matter to be taught; human growth and development, or use of media and technology in designing instructional strategies. Significant differences will also be noted in the manner in which professionally prepared instructors of 1985 will employ sophisticated teaching-learning equipment and resources. Human efforts, even though developed through specially designed professional preparation experiences, may fail to reach full potential when only relatively pedestrian tools and equipment are available. The new technology will overcome these shortcomings and open new educational strategies. There will be a dramatic shift in the mix between human resource and physical capital resource inputs used in the instruction process. A larger percentage of the total school budget in 1985 will be dedicated to physical capital expenditures (computer hardware, instructional systems, etc.) than to salaries for instructional personnel.

In 1970 there were over 2 million instructional staff members in local public schools serving an enrollment of over 45 million. In addition, there were about a million noninstructional staff members. Roughly speaking, one noninstructional staff member was employed in 1970 for every two instructional members. This ratio will change to about 1 to 1.5 in 1985. Many of the noninstructional staff members will be technicians who will care for, distribute, and repair the machine marvels of the 1980s. Others will be a variety of aides assisting the professionally prepared instructional personnel.

The "24-hour school" will be talked of with greater seriousness in 1985. Different time periods for learning will be designed to satisfy the different maturity demands of learners in the same facility. Fuller use of buildings and equipment will come from serving a wide range of age groups rather than from rescheduling the 5 to 19 year old group to spend more time in a school building during a calendar year. By 1985, the concept of the "year-round school" will be realized for other reasons as well, not the least of which will be the greater capital expenditures made for the new technological instruction devices. When investments in hardware and software command 50 percent or more of the total school budget the year-round school becomes economically feasible. The ratio between salaries paid to instructional personnel in 1970 and the cost of physical equipment and space for instructional personnel is no less than five to one and often ten to one. In 1970 over 80 percent of the total school budget was dedicated to salaries for human factors involved in instruction, administration, or some other aspect of operation. This fact combined with the relatively low physical capital investment per instructional person in 1970 meant that schools would have to spend more for salaries and demand even bigger budgets for year-round operation.

The trend toward allocating a greater share of the total resources for physical capital equipment in the instructional process will be triggered by at least two factors. One is the unrelenting upward pressure on school budgets by steadily increasing salaries paid to ever growing numbers (which may exceed 3 million by 1985) of public elementary and secondary instructional personnel to meet expansion in programs and enrollments. Beginning salaries for teachers tripled between 1945 and 1965. A teacher with greater professional preparation in 1985 than his counterpart in 1970 will command no less than $12,000 and probably closer to $15,000 as an annual starting wage. In 1968 the NEA Representative Assembly called for a starting salary of $10,500 for a teacher with a bachelors degree and without experience. If past experience can provide clues to future events, $10,500 will be an accepted beginning salary for teachers in less than ten years.

Higher salaries will generate increased concerns during the 1970s for ways to multiply the productivity and effectiveness of instructional personnel. New ways of deploying professional personnel in combination with aides may be one way of increasing productivity. Productivity may be enhanced by new developments in technology as well. The very high percentage of the school budget (in the 60 to 70 percent range) allocated for instructional salaries alone may make some computer-based or laser-based instructional systems economically competitive with the live teacher during the late 1970s. Decreasing unit costs of sophisticated instructional gear is a distinct possibility within a decade as heavy research and development costs are amortized. In short, economic analysis will show that sometime before 1985 there will be an important point where the cost of traditional instruction with a live teacher will rise to intersect the declining cost curve for sophisticated and computer-based instructional systems.[10]

It is not implied that physical capital in the form of the glamorous offshoots of the new technology will be justified primarily on the grounds that "it will save money". A more significant contribution of the technology will be an improvement in the effectiveness of instruction. The largest economic benefits will accrue from a gain in the productivity of the highly skilled and professionally prepared manpower component. In short, a live teacher capable of adapting the new technology to instruction will be a more effective and more productive professional.

The Computer and Instruction

Specifically, the computer will be further refined, so that by 1985 it will be a commonly used tool in the learning process. In the late 1960s, computer-assisted instructional (CAI) devices were in the embryonic stage and simply demonstrated the feasibility of presenting information to pupils on a computer-activated cathode ray tube.[11] Relatively little data were generated during the 1960s on what types of pupils learn more via CAI or what kinds of instructional concerns are presented best via CAI. What is called "individualization" is better described as "individualized pacing," with some degree of branching to provide additional exercises for those who need it. It is not individualization in the sense of using the instructional strategy that is most appropriate to the talents, interests, or background of the learner. Presentation of the printed fact, question, or answer on a cathode ray tube is not too much different from presenting printing on a piece of paper. At present, only bits and pieces of learning sequences are in the tutorial, much less simulation, mode of the computer. The number of CAI experiences is growing, but an additional investment of several billion dollars will be required before 1985 to eliminate the bugs in the audio component of computer-assisted instruction, to reduce extended delays in audio responses, and to translate most knowledge or information from written format into computer format. Practically all aspects of the curriculum will have been programed into machine-usable form by 1985. These devices, particularly when designed for the simulation as well as the tutorial mode and coupled with the appropriate instructional strategies, will help students come closer to achieving their own level of potential as well as to individualizing their studies.

By 1985 the computer will also have assumed much of the burden of instructional classroom management such as pupil progress reporting, attendance and general information keeping, and other record keeping. The teacher will be able to place inputs such as pupil and instructional data into the school's computer via a remote input-output console in each classroom. The same console will enable the teacher to retrieve data or generate more meaningful reports almost instantaneously. Other computer consoles will be reserved for pupils' use in drills, exercises, or exploration experience.

Many of the routine and sophisticated tasks of school administrators will be facilitated by the computer. By 1985 the computer will be the "solid state middle management" specialist, that is, it will organize information required for prudent decisions that is now prepared manually by directors and assistant superintendents. This will be of particular significance for educational administration. The question asked in 1985 will not be whether the school district has a computer, but how many and what capabilities they have. A single general-purpose computer will not be adequate to the challenges.

Computer technology will have been developed to a point in 1985 where programming will be very similar to ordinary written instruction; the key punch operator will be obsolete. Optical scanners will facilitate the task of programming instructional computers, giving teachers tremendous flexibility in adapting the tutorial mode of the computer to individual classroom requirements. The same degree of flexibility and quick response will be available to administrators. There will be a large variety of specialized data banks for supplementary instructional and administrative purposes. What is lacking in 1970 to enhance the dialogue between the professional educator and a computer system is easy access. As Fano indicated "the computer should be easily accessible to people, both physically and intellectually."[12] Physical access demands a terminal device within reach of every teacher. Intellectual access calls for the creation of a computer language similar to human conversation. The access problem will be resolved by 1985.

The Laser and Instruction

Kahn and Wiener suggested the possibility of self-programming for computers and the increasing tendency for them "to perform activities that amount to 'learning' from experience and training."[13] For computers to be an effective individualized teaching aid for pupils at all levels of maturity a tremendous amount of information must be stored. The computer was invented to solve the problems of mathematicians and researchers. The scientists put the emphasis on rapid computational skills. Educators require a device that can easily store and quickly retrieve large volumes of information rather than speedy computation. Kahn and Wiener indicated the potential of lasers in handling large data storage problems. They reported that "IBM has already developed a memory-storage system using an eight-colored laser beam to store as many as one hundred million bits of information on a square inch of photographic film." Of no less significance is the fact that an Air Force scientist used a laser beam to reduce an entire library of 20,000 volumes to an "8-by-10-inch piece of nickel foil, thus storing in one inch what would go on ten miles of magnetic tape."[14] What is even more impressive, is that it could be done "some twenty times cheaper than the cost of many storage systems."

"Laser-assisted instruction," with its fantastic data storage and retrieval characteristics, may well supersede computer-assisted instructional systems by 1985. The communication capabilities of laser beams suggest an added plus in designing dissemination systems within schools.

Three-Dimensional TV and Films

Holography, with or without lasers, may do to visual image reproduction what lasers will do to data storage and computers have done to data processing. Holograms (special kinds of pictures) were originally developed as an application of electron microscopy and were generated when "electron interference patterns were illuminated with ordinary light whose wave lengths are almost a million times greater." Kahn and Wiener declared that "the applications of holography that excite the greatest attention are three-dimensional television and motion pictures." The projection of three-dimensional visual images will revitalize the "audio-visual education" thrusts by 1985. It is estimated that the quality of cameras and TV picture tubes required for this application of holography will be available at a reasonable cost by that time. A further application may be in copying documents. Thus, copies of holograms can "be reproduced cheaply—twenty-five cents a piece for the first thousand copies. . . ." Holography, relatively unknown in educational circles in 1970, may be among the most promising instructional media by the end of the present and subsequent decades.[15]

Facilities, Equipment, and Supplies

The configuration and operational characteristics of learning centers, presently called attendance units or schools, will be notably different in 1985. The many reasons behind this change were discussed previously: the movement toward "womb-to-tomb" educational programs, new technology that will open new vistas and generate new and exciting learning strategies, and the reconceptualization of the teacher's role within the centers. Related to these is the fact that the computer will be as common in the home in 1985 as a television set is today. Computer utilities will supply computer services to homes in a pattern not unlike that for electricity, telephone, gas, and other utilities. A more complete electronic link between home and schools will open a number of new options for the design of learning centers that were not practical before 1985.

The period following the end of World War II will be recognized as the golden age of school architecture in the United States. The basic design of spaces for learning was developed during the past 25 years, as well as a more precise definition of balanced visual, acoustical, thermal, etc., environments for schools. It was a creative period with significant accomplishments that overshadowed all previous efforts in school plant design and construction anywhere in the world. The construction of some poor imitations should not be permitted to detract from the major accomplishment of establishing a more relevant link between space or environment and educational purposes, programs, and strategies.

It is projected that new and exotic materials and new breakthroughs in special forms (*e.g.,* geodesic domes) created by more sophisticated architectural engineering will find their way into school facility design and construction throughout this and subsequent decades. In addition the design of instructional, study and special service spaces in schools of the 1980s will show the impact of the great variety of electronic teaching-learning gear such as computers, lasers, and holograms. In short, the internal arrangement of spaces and external appearance of the school facility in the 1980s will depart even more radically from present configurations than 1970 designs did from those produced in 1920. The size and complexity of increasingly specialized learning facilities will encourage the development of independent clusters of educational units rather than one all-purpose building.

Learning is a social process as well as an intellectual endeavor. Were it not for the social dimension, there would be less need for bringing the learner to a learning center. The alternative future suggesting that the school plant where students are concentrated will disappear by 1985 or 2000 is rejected for a variety of reasons. The alternative to clustering learners in a school facility is directing learning experiences into the home, or in some cases, to the place of work or another social institution. This option need not preclude the existence of a formal learning center with specialized equipment that cannot be placed, because of economics or optimum use, in each home. Not all learners will have to come to a school plant, but most will. The home may be an extension of, but will not be a replacement for, the formal school centers. Many futurists speak of the diminishing influence of the family on groups and society. The living or interaction problems in many homes, particularly in ghetto areas, also suggest that the home may not be the ideal locus for all learning activities. The Job Corps, as a residential educational institution of the 1960s, was designed purposely to remove some learners from a home environment that did more to bring on failure than promote success.

Greater prominence will be attached to a new type of educational facility called the "Central Instructional Development and Dissemination Center." It will electronically beam instructional materials to either school plants or homes at various hours throughout the district. Electronic hookups between the home computer, the educational electronic beaming center, and data banks (known popularly as libraries) will be close to reality in 1985. In short, opportunity to learn at home with access to information previously available only in school or library will be extended greatly. Reaching pupils confined at home or in hospital will be less of a problem. It is emphasized that this will enable learning at home to reinforce what is started at a formal facility rather than to replace the school as a social institution.

Interaction among pupils, particularly those in the early and late adolescent age levels, will continue to have a profound impact on the learning and teaching processes. School plants will be designed to extract the educational advantages of this interaction. School scheduling will be less rigid. "Open campus" operational plans will be a part of all secondary level schools by 1985. There will be a greater flow of pupils in and out of attendance centers at all times of the day rather than at fixed starting and ending periods.

Teacher strikes will be less numerous and less effective in 1985 for a variety of reasons. The roles of teacher will be changed. It will be possible to design an instructional system that can operate for short periods with a limited number of administrative and supervisory personnel. Only a relatively small number is needed to beam a variety of video-taped computer-stored information to homes as well as to school centers.

The "electronic" library with quick access to information and less emphasis on bound volumes will be in transition in the 1980s. The schools will place less emphasis on hardbound books and more on special purpose tracts that can be discarded as new knowledge supersedes the old.

Some Far-Out Possibilities

There are some so-called far-out ideas that may be in the early development stage, but not quite ready for implementation as feasible instructional strategies by 1985. Some, like modification of the genetic code, do not warrant much consideration now, but others do. One is direct electronic communication via implanted electrodes that stimulate the brain. The likelihood of developing "electronic thinking caps" by 1985 that could be placed on students to "feed" knowledge electronically into the minds of students is not very great. Electrophysiological techniques are more likely to reach a state of limited applications after rather than before the year 2000. Quartron stated that (1) "scientists are often not exactly sure where electrodes are placed in the brain since they must be implanted with complex stereotactic devices, using bony land marks and 'brain atlases' as guides" and (2) "the mechanism of brain stimulation is not fully understood, and there is some difficulty in producing reliable effects through repeated efforts to duplicate a single phenomenon."[16]

Related to neurosurgical interventions as a method of behavior control is the implantation of radio transmitters in human subjects. These monitoring devices enable one to "know how an individual behaved before and after the application of behavior-control techniques."[17] This approach has tremendous possibilities in direct educational evaluation of learning of objectives in the affective domain. Hidden emotions could be revealed through microphones detecting signals or translating them into visual signal displays on a cathode ray tube. By 1985 the research on calibration and interpretation of signals from a transmitter attached to learners could be completed and ready for implementation. The odds on acceptance of surgical techniques for learning purposes, however, are not great. Monitoring human behavior by electronic devices is more likely to be accepted if the device is worn or taped on the body for easy removal rather than surgically implanted.

The use of drugs (hormones or enzymes) to control the memory and learning of laboratory animals appears to be further along than electrophysiology or other neurosurgical techniques. Much of the present information is derived from the intriguing rat-brain research by Krech and his colleagues who search for a better understanding of the physical basis for memory by examining its chemical, neurological, and anatomical bases.[18] It was discovered that, after treatment with the chemical metrazol, the maze-learning ability of "hereditarily stupid mice" surpassed the performance of untreated but previously recognized "hereditarily superior" mice. The use of drugs or enzymes to assist learning (the so-called get-smart pills, chemical erasers of wrong mental habits or specific knowledge pills) in animals had not been applied to humans by 1970. The entire art is in a rudimentary state of development at present.

Quartron points out that alcohol and similar drugs have been known for years as substances that could influence human behavior. The data, however, were derived empirically and focused on what sedative or stimulant did what. The new thrusts have shifted to clarifying "the role of chemicals as possible transmitter substances used in the actual transfer of information from one neuron to another." This new approach could revolutionize pharmacology and generate new classes of drugs that could enhance learning efficiency as well as alter human behavior in other ways. There are dangers, for as Quartron noted some of the psychedelic or consciousness expanding drugs have escaped "the control of the scientific community and are distributed by sub-cultures within our society." The ease with which drugs can be used, in contrast to neurosurgical intervention or complex electronic gear, suggests "that they will constitute the most common technique for manipulating behavior with full social approval—for instance, increasingly in the handling of behavior deviants."[1 9]

There are many problems in using enzyme-assisted instruction as part of the instructional strategy in schools. The side effects of electronic gadgets may be little more than irritation or boredom. The unknown side-effects of drugs could have more serious consequences for physical as well as mental growth and development. The use of drugs in the schools to foster learning directly or indirectly could either bring medical practitioners and teachers closer together or place instructional personnel into roles with strong medical overtones.

It is highly improbable that by 1985 chemical gases will be released through school ventilating systems to keep pupils and teachers, with or without their knowledge, alert during formal school sessions. It is equally unlikely that school food services will be used as part of an overall instructional strategy to "season" hot lunches with "get smart" chemical substances, such as metrazol-related compounds, to improve educational efficiency. The present and preliminary insights into the pharmacological stimulants of learning will only begin to be defined more sharply by the mid-1980s. It will be some time after 2000 that school boards will begin to think seriously of approving "anti-brown bag" policies and a "closed" noon hour to ensure that all pupils eat noon meals in the school cafeteria. In this way there could be a positive check that appropriate learning-inducing chemicals were included in every pupil's diet. Instead of being castigated, as is popular among educational critics of today, the school cafeteria may emerge after 2000 as one of the most important instructional spaces in the school plant.

One could project a time when pharmacological technology could extend education to the unborn, perhaps sometime after the year 2020. Chemicals injected during intrauterine life would influence the readiness of the newborn for learning. This suggests an era 100 years from now when there may be generations of "womb readers," who spend their first nine months after conception learning to read. Right now it seems so improbable that it sounds somewhat humorous if not ridiculous even to mention it.

It appears more probable as an alternative future that "learning drugs" that can stimulate the human brain performance beyond previously assumed genetic capabilities will be controlled by noneducational agencies. The home, more than likely, would be the primary agency, and the schools' involvement would be supplementary. Parents could introduce the "learning enzymes" desired for children, youths, and adults through special diets, or if greater concentrations are preferred, through pills dispensed with the ever-present vitamins or anticold tablets. The educational institution would, with the permission of parents and under medical supervision, administer dosages neglected in given home situations.

To Summarize Strategies

Educational strategies (traditionally called "methods of teaching" and sometimes "instructional media") in 1985 will bear little resemblance to those practiced and in vogue in 1970. The technological thrusts of computers, lasers, holography, electrophysiology, and pharmacology will combine forces to make an instructional revolution. The growing concern for individualization, new instructional and noninstructional personnel during the 1970s will exert a complementary influence as well. Rising expectations for education, accountability, and the social ferment will reinforce the other forces of change.

Synergism and serendipity will generate breakthroughs in education as they have elsewhere. Kahn and Wiener speak of synergism—the multiplier effect of a number of interrelated innovations that generates a combined impact greater than any single innovation might be expected to have—that made the Polaris missile system possible long before many knowledgeable scientists thought it could be accomplished.[20]

Serendipity is another way of talking about good fortune, that is, the search for one thing or event results in finding something completely unexpected. It is the luck that comes to those who had hoped for other things but have the sense to appreciate the unanticipated. Serendipity produces the completely unexpected innovation or breakthrough. It may be experienced in applied as well as basic research. The combination of synergism and serendipity may help to explain why the rate of technological development increases faster than anticipated.

NEW ROLES AND RELATIONSHIPS

It would be unrealistic to anticipate significant modifications in educational missions, programs, and strategies by 1985 without an accompanying major shift in roles and relationships among pupils, teachers, and administrators within what is called the "educational establishment." Some new roles and relationships were suggested earlier in references to new instructional organization forms and unique staff deployment patterns.

By 1985 the instructor's or teacher's primary roles will be recognized as (1) diagnostician of learning problems and (2) learning therapist. This is a contrast to the present emphasis on being a subject matter specialist or fulfilling the role of purveyor of knowledge to learners by such direct means as lecturing or focusing the direction of discussions. The implication is that for all the new technology that will be adapted to the purposes of education, technology will not eliminate the need for what is now called a teacher, but will redefine responsibilities. Immediately following World War II, the sound film was predicted as the replacement for the teacher, in the 1950s television was thought to be his successor. Neither technological development succeeded. In the 1960s there was talk that the computer would make the classroom instructor obsolete. Perhaps an analogy with medicine can clarify the impact of technology. Technology adapted to medicine was not introduced to replace, but rather to enhance the effectiveness of the medical practitioner. Thus, the invention of the kidney machine did not spell the end of the need for urologists; the wonder drugs did not make internists obsolete. These devices and chemicals were added to the doctor's repertoire of diagnosis and therapy approaches to enable him to succeed where previously he had failed. The medical practitioner continued to perform useful functions because no other device than human judgment could better fulfill the important roles of diagnostician, therapist, and counselor to the ill. The teacher will be better described as a director of instruction, that is, a specialist in learning analysis, stimulation, and development. In 1985 the instructional specialist can turn to technology to enhance his judgments. Therefore, the teacher of 15 years from now will be a better educational practitioner, for with the assistance of printed and other "tests" and sophisticated electronic gear, he will obtain the information necessary to identify learning difficulties quickly and accurately and will be able to assign appropriate experiences to exploit the learner's interests and potential. The teacher, in this sense, is the manipulator of environmental factors to stimulate learning.

Traditional conceptualization has the classroom teacher a hero practitioner performing professional responsibilities in lonely splendor. The fate of the learner rested in the hands of the single professional. Technology, specialization, and new instructional organization patterns will shatter this traditional practice mode by the end of the 1970s. The master or head teacher will be required to oversee the efforts of clerical and instructional aides. Human relations skills may be demanded as well when planning or teaching with a team of peers. There may be a separation of the diagnostic function and the therapy function in the teaching-learning process around the year 2000. This suggests that some important roles of the "teacher" in 1985 will be skillful use of a large number of electronic learning and monitoring devices to stimulate pupil learning progress or to evaluate learning problems as well as the use and coordination of a large variety of learning specialists within the system.

The pupil-teacher ratio was a valid index when the individual teacher was the only instructional resource available to a group of pupils. This ratio will be abandoned as totally meaningless by 1985. Its demise will be hastened by the increase in the number of specialists in physical and mental health, social welfare, evaluation, and remediation who will be teamed with the master teacher at the professional level to promote pupil learning. At the subprofessional level, there will be the paraprofessionals who perform tasks under the direction of the master classroom teacher. One of the major instructional concerns in 1985 will be the "interface problem," namely, coordination of learning subsystems and specialized personnel teamed with the teacher. More than likely, the productivity of the master teacher will be increased to accommodate approximately 200 pupils with a greater degree of effectiveness in promoting learning than can presently be attained with 25 or 30 pupils. Technology will enable the teacher to give more individual attention to 200 pupils assigned in 1985 than could be given to a small class of 25 with the rudimentary instructional technology of 1970. The importance of human relations and administrative skills for teachers working with other adults involved in the instructional process will be greater than ever.

There will be more administrators and supervisors in 1985 and their roles and responsibilities will be changed as dramatically as those for teachers. Administrators will be systems specialists in 1985, with emphasis on planning. The higher the position in the administrative hierarchy, the higher the priority attached to anticipating future conditions likely to confront learners, employed personnel, and the institution in general. In addition the number of administrators, with a variety of specialized functions to be performed within administration, will grow, putting a premium on coordination. A larger number of temporary systems will be designed to facilitate the change agent role. It follows that a deep understanding and a high degree of skill in technology will be most important to administrators in 1985. Administrators will be focusing on new ways of adapting computers, lasers, holography, pharmacology, and electrophysiology to the problems of learning and the management of learning institutions. In short, the 1985 administrator will be less the efficient manager and more the systems specialist, planner, coordinator, change agent, and expert in technological applications to education. The design and implementation of continuing professional development programs for all instructional, administrative, supervisory, and other staff will receive high priority in the top executive's overcommitted calendar. The range of services to learners of all ages will intensify community relations problems.

The problems of school finance will not be any less severe in 1985 than in 1970. The whole area of resource management will become more complex, but fortunately the computer and the laser will be capable of contributing to the resolution of difficulties that present manual and pedestrian approaches cannot solve. The decreasing relevance of experience will prompt the administrator to dedicate his efforts to continuing professional development to keep abreast of new developments.

Use of extensive and sophisticated electronic gear will stimulate the formation of larger and more efficient local school district structure than in 1970. By 1985 there will be no more than 2,000 local school districts, approximately ten percent of the number in 1970. This may be too large an estimate with the figure on number of districts closer to 1,000. In 1971 one of the important characteristics of an effective local district was the provision of educational opportunities from at least grade 1 through grade 12. In 1985, states with separate junior college districts will be facing a district reorganization movement similar to that experienced in 1960 when high school districts separate from elementary districts were reorganized into unified districts. The effective local school district in 1985 will include educational opportunities from nursery school through to the junior college level of grade 14.

The major thrust of district reorganization in the 1940s, 1950s, and 1960s was found in the rural areas and was expressed in the movement to eliminate the districts that were too small for efficient operation. The emphasis will shift in the 1970s; the new locale will be the urban areas, and the new problem will be bigness. Metropolitan school districts will be established by 1985. Educationally defensible as well as politically palatable decentralized units will be defined by the mid-1980s to gain the most from "economy of scale" and eliminate the danger of strangulation of services from too large and unwieldly administrative units.

IN CONCLUSION

No one can predict with certainty what will happen in 1985, to say nothing of the year 2000. There are signs of what could be. In a certain sense the efforts that identify and focus on specific developments may result in self-fulfilling prophecies. By pointing to the new intellectual and machine technology that could be adapted to education, one could stimulate greater study of these thrusts by larger numbers and thereby increase their rate of development.

It will take more than talk, however, to generate the needed new educational missions, programs, and strategies by 1985. Life is not that simple and major changes in life styles are enormously complex to effect. The futurist longs to do something about the "falling wall" syndrome, that is, the propensity to procrastinate until the full weight of a problem falls on us. The time has come to anticipate the challenges early enough so that something might be done, and in a constructive manner. It is easier to destroy or, for that matter, to point to what might happen than it is to dedicate and organize efforts for a more rational attack on future problems. This dedication and organization of talent to obtain a better understanding of tomorrow is perhaps the greatest challenge facing the education profession.

FOOTNOTES

1. Daniel Bell, ed., *Toward the Year 2000* (Boston: Beacon Press, 1969).
2. Ibid., p. 4.
3. Ibid.
4. Ibid., p. 5.
5. Ibid.

6. Ibid., p. 7.

7. Herman Kahn and A.J. Wiener, *The Year 2000* (New York: Macmillan Co., 1967), pp. 51-55.

8. Ibid., pp. 56-57.

9. Peter Pipe, "Putting Behavioral Objectives to Work," mimeographed (National Academy for School Executives, 1201 - 16th N.W. Washington, D.C., 1970).

10. See S.J. Knezevich and G.G. Eye, eds., *Instructional Technology and the Administrator* (Washington, D.C.: The American Association of School Administrators, 1970), pp. 92-107.

11. Ibid., pp. 57-69, and Commission on Instructional Technology, *To Improve Learning: A Report to the President and Congress of the United States* (Washington, D.C.: Government Printing Office, 1970).

12. Robert M. Fano, "Computers in Human Society—For Good or Ill?", *Technology Review* 72, no. 5 (March 1970): 25-31.

13. Kahn and Wiener, op. cit., p. 90.

14. Ibid., p. 100.

15. Ibid., p. 104.

16. Gardner C. Quartron, "Deliberate Efforts to Control Human Behavior and Modify Personality," *Toward the Year 2000*, ed. Daniel Bell (Boston: Houghton Mifflin Co., 1968), p. 212.

17. Ibid., p. 214.

18. David Krech, "Psychoneurobiochemeducation," *Your AASA in 1968-69* (Washington, D.C.: American Association of School Administrators, 1969), pp. 91-105.

19. Quartron, op. cit., p. 210-211, 217.

20. Kahn and Wiener, op. cit., pp. 67-69.

Walter G. Hack

4

Governance of the Public Education in 1985

The temptation to contemplate the nature of policy decisions and the system of governance that will characterize public education in 1985 is indeed compelling. When one considers the predictions of the American environment for that year and the education program demanded by it in the public schools, the need for substantial changes in policy and policy implementation is apparent. The phenomenon of governance, for the purpose of this chapter, will be defined as decisionmaking in the areas of policy formulation and operation in the public schools.

A rationale for an anticipatory look at the governance of public education in 1985 was articulated by Daniel Bell, Chairman of the American Academy of Arts and Science's Commission on the Year 2000. He stated the premise of that commission as "an effort to indicate now the future consequences of present public policy decisions, to anticipate future problems, and to begin the design of alternate solutions so that our society has more options and can make a moral choice, rather than be constrained, as is so often the case when problems descend upon us unnoticed and demand an immediate response."[1] The theme of proaction, which embodies much of the thrust of this book, is very much present in Bell's statement.

If one interprets Bell's first point in the context of the governance of public education, one can find substantial evidence of the dysfunctionality of present public education policies and the future consequences of these. As Masters[2] addressed himself to political problems involved in educational planning, he reiterated Conant's observation that in a majority of states, educational policies were sanctioned through the dictates of pork barrel politics. Thus one can question both the process of enactment as well as the substance of the policy enacted. It is clear that future consequences of inadequate public education policies of today can only create more dysfunctionality. Accelerating social change will result in a snowballing effect in terms of the cumulative impact of inadequate policy development. Unless either new remediation capability or more "fault free" policy (or both) is developed by 1985, social institutions are likely to become mired in dysfunctional policy. Problems and crises will proliferate faster than solutions.

The nature of future problems is visible just below the surface of the sea of changes suggested in the two preceding chapters. Severe problems for the administration of school systems will spring from environmental change and the resultant programmatic demands in the educational institution. The predicted change in family structure will have a significant impact on one of the key inputs to a school system: the pupil. When the input to this subsystem changes there is little doubt that the school as a mediating agency will have to change also. Programmatic demands springing from an input change might include a modification in the school's custodial function in that it might be required to diagnose, prescribe, and administer services and/or pharmaceuticals for learning stimulation or behavior modification.

The third point of the commission's premise is that of designing alternate solutions in order to provide the society with more options and to better enable it to make a moral choice. In this point one can sense the primary challenge of the governance of education: the creation of a broader range of options to upgrade the making of a moral choice. The upgrading of technical and conceptual capabilities in the near future is probably the primary factor in broadening the range of options rather than any sharp shift in a moral code per se. In all probability there will be some change in public mores such as widespread acceptance of birth control, abortions, and more flexible marital relationships. However, options will be increased primarily because many of the hypothetical or "dream" alternatives of the 1970s will become real or feasible alternatives by 1985.

Martin Shubik conceptualized the basic problem of governance in the future by pointing out the obsolescence and/or inadequacy of the conventional wisdom surrounding the contemporary context of public policy formulation. Shubik attributes this problem to the inadequacy of our "implicit models of man as a rational, informed individual and as a decision-maker with an important freedom of choice. The rational utilitarian man, the Invisible Hand, and the democratic vote may be regarded as forming a trinity for an economic and political faith in a free-enterprise democracy."[3]

According to Shubik, complexities in the information system of the future will limit the applicability of this concept. An increasingly complex and expanded society makes the individual's share of the knowable markedly less. Man's information will be highly incomplete; he will not know how to evaluate many of his options. Further, he will not be even aware of many of them.

The aggregation of individual wants and powers into social wants and powers is one of the central problems of political science, economics, and sociology. We are currently in the position where we need to, and may be able to, answer certain fundamental questions concerning the possibility of constructing institutions to satisfy desired properties for the relation between the individual and his society.[4]

Shubik articulates a challenge in governance of public education in 1985 if we interpret in a collective sense what he perceives to be the problem for the individual decision maker of the future.

[We will need to rethink] some of our models of political and economic man so that they fit the pattern of the uncertain decision-maker acting under severely restricted conditions of information embedded within a communication system upon which he is becoming increasingly more dependent. His freedom of scope is limited by the powers of others; as these powers become more numerous and technology permits quicker communication, his actions become more deeply entwined with those of others.[5]

When one relates the Shubik thesis to Bell's notion of increasing the capability of designing alternative solutions to produce more options and in turn make a moral choice, one can sense a new kind of equilibrium in the future. Those involved in the governance of public education will have a broader range of choices and hence broader decisionmaking powers, but at the same time will feel a new set of constraints—those of being dependent on others for information and its communication. Thus powers are both broadened and narrowed simultaneously.

Despite the admitted inadequacy of establishing simplistic classifications of the components of the highly complex and interrelated phenomenon of governance in public education, the writer now proposes to examine the making of policy decisions in public education from three vantage points. These three views are:

(1) Major shifts in the locus of governance;
(2) Major changes in the process of governance; and
(3) New substantive characteristics

THE LOCUS OF GOVERNANCE IN PUBLIC EDUCATION

In considering the locus of educational decisionmaking on governance, several major characteristics appear to have some support as prognoses for 1985.

Special purpose governmental bodies and/or activities (including public education) appear to be moving toward absorption into general government. Schnore and Fagin observed this as one of two current but seemingly paradoxical trends.[6] Norton E. Long spelled out the eminent logic of the movement toward general government at the local level under the powerful influence of the federal government. Washington, he said, is deeply concerned with coordinating the impact of its programs to resolve physical problems of air and water pollution, transportation, and general land use as well as the social problems including equal education opportunity. Long declared:

> Having for long acted piecemeal through a variety of state and local unifunctional agencies, the federal government has come to realize the importance of overall local coordination if its resources are to have their desired effect. The political logic of a nation leads to a thrust to create a nationally appropriate system of local governments. Such a system, by setting up local governments responsive to the range of problems and the mix of population that are nationally salient, would provide a superior counterpart local government to the present agents of the status quo.[7]

Even today alternatives and proposals along this line are being developed. The Committee for Economic Development spoke to this concern in one of its statements on national policy, *Modernizing Local Government*. The task force preparing the document identified three alternative courses that might be followed:

> FIRST, recent trends toward "functional government" might go on indefinitely, as in highway administration. This would imply an extension of federal standard-setting, decision-making, and administrative controls—with heavier transfusions of federal funds directly or through state channels. In theory, the present system of local governments could then endure without major structural change or modernization. Functional fragmentation under federal auspices discourages local planning and management on any unified, integral basis. In practice, federal efforts to use *existing* local governments as administrative agencies in executing national policy have already disclosed such serious faults that success cannot be expected within the present framework. Sole reliance on this approach would probably lead to (a) an increase in direct federal management of local affairs, (b) assumption by state governments of a larger share in administrative operations, (c) continued neglect of vital local issues, and (d) excessive costs for the services they render.

SECOND, the 50 states might expand their administrative mechanisms to supersede local authorities, gradually perhaps, in function after function. This might be done through regional or district centers, in order to relate state action more directly to local situations. Such an alternative would not be endorsed, however, by those who have found their state capitals consistently unresponsive to local needs, whether these are universal or vary from locality to locality.

THIRD, existing patterns of local government can be drastically revised, to encourage local policy decision-making and to permit effective management of local affairs. This will not be easy, for major structural adjustments are required if we are to preserve the fundamental values in local self-government. But competent local units, responsive to the requirements of an enlightened public, can serve two primary purposes. They can identify local problems and opportunities, and then plan and execute programs with optimum effect. They are also needed to serve in an effective partnership with state agencies, and with the federal government in its expanding fields of activity.[8]

If the concept of creative federalism is to be taken seriously, the third alternative course could very easily subsume a capability to implement nationally appropriate programs as well as programs indigenous to the locality.

Brickell predicted that by 1980 there will be a serious reexamination of the school district as a special purpose governmental unit separate from municipal government and relatively independent from other branches of state government. He, too, recognizes that the centrality of its public function requires it to be more closely related to general government. Thus, school districts might evolve into governmental units with formal interactive relationships with local, state, and federal general governance structures.

Haskew and Hensen recognize the probability of dramatic increases in federal participation in educational policy decisions by the 1980s.[10] Much of the substance of educational policy will be in a national context, and state and local agencies will assume more roles in implementing programs designed to benefit the national welfare.

Goldhammer predicts that the pattern of decisionmaking in public education will be changed.

Policy-making within the schools and between the school's instruments of administration and the public, will become matters of mediation and negotiation, of coordination and allocation, of planning and evaluation. The school board and local administration will be called upon to effect policy through the implementation of mandated state programs and permissive federal programs— but the problems will be such that there will really be no alternative for the school district but to accept federal subventions in order to more effectively provide for educational needs. In return for some loss of independent and discretionary decision-making, the local authorities will be the recipients of larger federal and state subventions.[11]

It is likely that by 1985 one will see a more positive and comprehensive role being played by the federal government. Manifestations of public skepticism about the relevancy and effectiveness of public education at the local and state levels constitute some evidence that the public takes its expectations seriously. When performance at these levels is seriously questioned, it appears that there will be a demand to move authority to a higher level to assure performance more in keeping with popular demand. With accelerating demand for public accountability, there will be more reform, and the direction of the responsibility for that reform seems to be moving toward the federal level.

The character of reform also appears to have a broader governance base. As education is recognized as a key component in the 1985 life style, it will be viewed as a major instrument in assuring the general welfare of the nation's people. The federal government, having assumed responsibility for providing adequate and equal educational opportunity throughout the nation, will use general governmental units to implement this program. The federal government commitment to educational policy formulation will roughly parallel its commitment to full employment as embodied in the Employment Act of 1946. Thus federal educational policy will stimulate the mobilization of general state and local government resources through general aid or block grants to these units. Thus centralized and complementary governmental efforts will maximize program impact and at the same time expedite accountability and cost-benefit analysis.

There is considerable support for the prediction that the governance base of public education will be widened to include elements of the private sector. Not only will schools as operational educational units be conducted as "mixed" units, but also there will be considerable private influence in the governance of these units. Grant McConnell predicted that

in the next few decades private and non-governmental associations will be important factors in our common social and political life . . . in recent years, for example, we have turned to firms like Xerox, Litton, and IBM not just for office machines and electronic devices but for the objectives of social improvement as well. Each of these firms operates schools for job training under the poverty program; the assumption is that they will do this better than ordinary schools run by public bodies.[12]

By 1985 the mix of private-public sector involvement in both governance and operation of public education will be visible and accepted. Not only will private enterprise contract and operate in the public school system, it will also be an active participant in policy formulation and governance. The authority of expertise in their areas of specific competence will grant them entree into this process. However, a more compelling rationale will be found for private sector involvement in governance by virtue of the recognition of the relationship of education and economic development as it pertains to the general welfare.

The locus of public education governance in 1985 will also be shifted because of the influence and the interrelation of subsystems within the whole system. The subsystems will be not only more general than special, but also more closely and formally integrated. Baker and Johns both cite the necessity for a more closely integrated system subsuming interacting federal, state, and local subsystems.[13]

Johns states: "Each of these social systems—the federal education agency, the state educational agencies, and the local education agencies—will be in continuous interaction with the decision making systems in their environment." It appears that the phenomenom of exchange of energy among the subsystems and other parts of the environment will become more formalized among the education units.

There are varied predictions about the degrees and areas of centralization of educational governance. Elazar sees the emerging federal, state, and local governing units as being in the great tradition of noncentralization.[14] He predicts considerable emphasis on improving administration and coordination with the burden falling on all three levels of government.

One can anticipate that intense and prolonged attention will be directed toward the integration of government and the decentralization of school authority as local school district reorganization is being contemplated. Bellweather developments along this line have been metropolitan school districts like Louisville and Jefferson County in Kentucky and Nashville and Davidson County in Tennessee. Despite the fact that not all these attempts will produce instant success, the metropolitanism thrust will continue on a broken front. In all probability new models will be developed, tried, and in some cases rejected.

Separate layers of federal, state, and local educational programs with discrete measures of both responsibility and concomitant authority will be the exception rather than the rule by 1985. Instead a systematic integration of federal, state, and local educational functions, funding, and accountability will have emerged. Thus program decisions made at one level may be funded primarily at a second level, and operated at a third level.

The nature of the policies enacted will also characterize the future in educational governance. Moynihan identified forces that will continue to move policy making toward a more central locus.[15] In projecting his thinking to the year 2000, Moynihan believes that American government will be much like it has been in the past. However, several developments will probably add stability to the federal system and none of these appears to generate disequilibrium. Among these developments will be nationalization of public policy accompanying the development of a genuinely national society. National issues will be settled in national terms at the national level. Other developments include the federal domination as a source of revenue for public expenditure, federal grant-in-aid programs as principal forms of federal support of domestic programs, and increasingly complex government as a result of increased citizen participation.

The Campbell-Layton conceptualization of "thrust and counterthrust" provides a specific illustration of the centralization-decentralization paradox.[16] It is anticipated that more national influence will be exerted, but it will be accompanied by greater state and local influence as well.

Elazar has made specific projections to 1980 and beyond for the American governmental partnership that conducts public education.[17] In these he predicts growth of government participation in education but with constant proportions of governmental expenditures. He sees state and local governments retaining their present level of influence, *providing* that these latter units continue to strengthen themselves through extended cooperation.

The combined federal, state, and local effort on behalf of public education will not be harmonious and stable by 1985. The roles of all three levels will continue to be in a state of dynamic tension as each is redefined by the others and by environmental demands that continue to change. Each level will continue to search for new organizational mechanisms to expand its power and autonomy. Each new coordinative decision will shift the power center within the triad.

THE PROCESS OF GOVERNANCE IN PUBLIC EDUCATION

In considering the process of governance of public education, the author suggests that the way in which policy decisions are made for this segment of social activity will be radically altered by 1985. The inexorable tides of change can already be felt. The future consequences of present policy suggest that individuals and groups who are currently dissatisfied with their traditional roles in policy making will indeed change the mode of governance. The primary change in process of governance appears to be a reconceptualization of representation.

Brzezinski observed that the concept of representation

seems to be moving increasingly in the direction of functional representation, the generalized theory of representation based largely on the predominance of lawyers and generalists giving way to technological, functional specialization. This, in turn, will fundamentally alter the pattern of legislation. Legislation will cease to be a cancelling out and a balancing of interests, and will become something far more abstracted, involving the weighing of interrelationships within the society and within the technological processes.[18]

Brzezinski goes on to say that this weighing will have to be done by a body other than the one involving functional representation. He suggests some kind of computing and planning agency outside the legislative process—thus the process will have to adjust to these changes, which in turn suggest changes in the behavior of the executive. This suggests that by 1985 we will have planning bodies to provide guidelines for determining national priorities and implementing programs involving federal, state, and local governance units. This activity will stimulate general government within the three levels as well as general governance among them.

A functional example of a planning body may be drawn implicitly from the basic thrust or mission of this book. A given governmental body might employ a group of "futurists" to ascertain, describe, design, and cost a set of alternative futures for that body over a given period of time. If the body were the future counterpart of today's city board of education, state board of regents, or United States Office of Education, it might very well include the considerations addressed in this book *i.e.,* the futures environment, programs, governance, organizations, and administrators. The planning group would develop not only the alternative futures, but also a capability of planning. This would avoid the trap of "selecting" the wrong alternative future and having difficulty in redirecting the institution's activity.

If one applies Brzezinski's thinking to governance and policy making in education, it is no pipedream to predict that the representative of professional personnel will occupy a formal chair on deliberative bodies formulating educational policy rather than merely having the lobbying privileges previously afforded them.

The changing character of representation as it is embodied in educational governance in 1985 will reflect a general acceptance of antecedent models being developed today. The "town meeting" democracy model with simple majority rule will give way to a functional representation model. The crucial functions antecedent to naming the functional representatives will be identified on the basis of governmental priorities. Today's priorities—problems related to poverty, unemployment, inflation, etc.—will change. The priorities of 1985 might instead include problems related to the economics of affluence, absence of individual privacy, and wholesome urban ecology. Thus, specialists in these functions will be representatives on the governance bodies.

Another type of representation determined by national priorities is that of the "unequals" in the distribution of the general welfare. As priorities are established to resolve problems of the society, those who bear the burden of unequal treatment will be represented in bodies charged with the responsibility of developing remedial action. Thus, groups denied equal educational opportunity will be represented in governance units designing programs to resolve the problem.

By 1985 this model, already being tried in 1971, will show an uneven pattern of shifting along the separate-cohesive continuum. Some diverse and unique social groups will press for self-identification and eventual representation within the larger society. Others, having already achieved this, will seek to establish autonomy and governance over their own affairs. Still others, who have moved through the second phase, will have achieved sufficient integrity and political power to enable them to move back into the larger society because of the ability to formulate coalitions that enable them to attain the benefits previously denied them.

Functionality in representation might very well be demonstrated in the emergence of relatively small specialized policy-making bodies serving particular interests. One can observe what might be a trend in the governance of local programs undertaken on behalf of the national welfare. The character of representatives has been redefined, and the character of participation has dramatically changed; the focus of interest has shifted from providing jobs and communication to the policy-making functions of the neighborhood boards. In other words, the poor who were to benefit from the program are now running it.

THE SUBSTANTIVE CHARACTER OF
PUBLIC EDUCATION GOVERNANCE

In considering the kind of policy questions the system of educational governance will entertain in 1985, several general types of prognoses are represented in the literature.

Implementation Policies

Daniel J. Elazar anticipates, for the immediate future, a period of implementing the new programs initiated in the recent past, which he perceives as a reform period. At the same time, Elazar also predicts that the 1980s will see the extension of the traditional principles of intergovernmental collaboration. There will, however, be calls for reforms in policy pertaining to the nature and method of the intergovernmental collaboration. He predicts that considerable emphasis will be placed on improving administration and simplifying coordination through multilevel governmental planning.[19]

Thus, the new programs proposed and even initiated in the 1960s and 1970s will be the major business of government, but considerable emphasis will be placed on designing the governance machinery to ensure that the objectives of the programs are met.

Planning Policies

Schnore and Fagin in the preface to their work *Urban Research and Policy Planning* note the recurrence of several themes suggesting that public planning has taken two seemingly divergent directions.[20]

They note a trend toward specialization with program proliferation, but at the same time a trend toward centralization and integration of policies that interact. The current emphasis on systems development suggests a variety of component decisions within unified and comprehensive frameworks. Doland suggests that planning or developmental policy making has shifted goals from maintaining an orderly pattern of growth to trying to produce change in the basic economic and social structure of the great urban areas.[21] For public education this implies a whole new order of policy decisions that will relate the school system to the larger community in many complex relationships.

In looking ahead to 1977, Max Ways defined one problem of governance as the incapacity of the old bureaucratic model to innovate and generate change as demanded by the new environment.[22] He suggests a new style of public planning that can help develop in the public mind the means of making more intelligent choices among competing values.

In pursuing Way's reasoning, Culbertson asks whether future historians might view the present decade as a time when we began to use new approaches to planning large and complex educational institutions.[23] Responding to his own question, he has developed a strong case for concluding that an important shift in attitudes toward problem solving and planning may now be taking place in American society.

Culbertson joins many others in predicting the wide use of the PBS approach in planning and implementing policy decisions in education. However, if the thrust toward planning in education does occur, there are powerful implications for governance of public education.

If planning is to be effective, a different kind of political behavior will be required. Undoubtedly, there will be some conflict between: (1) the more traditional patterns of compromise, bargaining, informal agreements, and private communications where the deciding values in legislative decision making are often implicit, and (2) the emergent patterns of weighing the costs and benefits of a given legislative proposal, arriving at decisions based upon carefully developed data, and systematically engaging in open and public discussion during the decision process. *This means that there may be substantial conflict at times between planners and responsible representatives of the people.*[24]

By 1985 the role of the planner will be at the heart of the most crucial problem of the century's fourth quarter. Shall a major function of governance be that of incorporating planned disequilibrium in order to precipitate change in governance itself?

SUMMARY

In considering alternate futures in public education in 1985, one becomes aware of the presence of several recurring themes. First, this relatively short-range look at the future suggests that educational governance will develop within itself alternate solutions for the problems emerging from a rapidly changing society. These alternative solutions will make available more options for moral choice. Thus, educational institutions will be forced to look at themselves and their functions as they never have before. Decisionmaking within the governance structure will be both broadened and restricted. It will be broadened by virtue of the fact that there will be more options to choose from. It will be restricted by the availability of much more information supplied by individuals and agencies outside the educational organization.

The locus of governance will move toward the federal level.[25] However, upgraded programs, support, and decisionmaking at the state and local levels will prevent a functional domination by Washington. Increased planning and coordination will move toward a complementing rather than competing federalism. Increased interdependence of the three levels will promote a heightened sensitivity. Probably a more visible dynamic tension among the three levels will be observable in the future.

The process of governance will be characterized in 1985 by a new definition of representation. The traditional "town hall democracy" model will give way to a functional representation model. Governing bodies will have representatives who are particularly qualified to speak to the needs and issues of the time. Participants in the institution's activity and those who are directly affected by the body's decisions will be parts of the governing body.

Some of the substantative policies that are likely to dominate the legislative docket in 1985's educational affairs are likely to be related to implementing the reforms proposed in the 1960s and 1970s. In the author's eyes the most significant type of educational policy likely to be developed is that related to planning. It appears that a most crucial policy will be that of implanting a planning capability to project, coordinate, and create alternative futures to ensure a parallel development of humanistic institutions in our economic and technological affluence.

FOOTNOTES

1. Daniel Bell, "The Year 2000—The Trajectory of an Idea," *Daedalus* 96, no. 3 (Summer 1967): 639.

2. Nicholas A. Masters, "Some Political Problems Involved in Education Planning," in *Planning and Effecting Needed Changes in Education* Designing Education for the Future, no. 3 (New York: Citation Press, 1967), p. 143.

3. Martin Shubik, "Information, Rationality, and Free Choice in a Future Democratic Society," *Daedalus* 96, no. 3 (Summer 1967): 771.

4. Ibid., pp. 774-775.

5. Ibid.

6. Leo F. Schnore, and Henry Fagin, eds., *Urban Research and Policy Planning* (Beverly Hills, California: Sage Publications, 1967), pp. 11-12.

7. Norton E. Long, "Political Science and the City," in *Urban Research and Policy Planning* (Beverly Hills, California: Sage Publications, 1967), pp. 254-255.

8. *Modernizing Local Government* (New York: Committee for Economic Development, 1966), pp. 14-15.

9. Henry M. Brickell, "Local Organization and Administration of Education," in *Implications for Education of Prospective Changes in Society*, Designing Education for the Future, no. 2 (Denver, Colorado: January 1967), p. 224.

10. Laurence D. Haskew, "What Lies Ahead," and Kenneth H. Hansen, "Planning and Change: Design-Decision-Action," in *Cooperative Planning for Education in 1980*, Designing Education for the Future, no. 4 (New York: Citation Press, 1968) pp. 22, 54.

11. Keith Goldhammer, "Supplementary Statement," in *Implications for Education of Prospective Changes in Society*, Designing Education for the Future, no. 2 (Denver, Colorado: January 1967), p. 240.

12. Grant McConnell, "Non-Government Organizations in American Political Life," in *Prospective Changes in Society by 1980*, Designing Education for the Future, no. 1 (New York: Citation Press, 1967), pp. 124-125.

13. Robert L. Baker, "Supplementary Statement," in *Planning and Effecting Needed Changes in Education*, Designing Education for the Future, no. 3 (New York: Citation Press, 1967), p. 107; R. L. Johns, "State Organization and Responsibilities for Education," in *Implications for Education of Prospective Changes in Society*, Designing Education for the Future, no. 2 (Denver, Colorado: January 1967), p. 263.

14. Daniel J. Elazar, "The American Partnership," in *Prospective Changes in Society by 1980*, Designing Education for the Future, no. 1 (New York: Citation Press, 1967), pp. 107-110.

15. Daniel P. Moynihan, "The Relationship of Federal to Local Authorities," *Daedalus* 96, no. 3 (Summer 1967): 801-808.

16. Roald F. Campbell, and Donald H. Layton, "Thrust and Counter-Thrust in Education Policy Making," *Phi Delta Kappan* 49, no. 6 (February 1968): 290-294.

17. Elazar, op. cit., pp. 101-119.

18. Zbigniew Brzezinski, "Alternative Futures," *Daedalus* 96, no. 3 (Summer 1967): 671.

19. Elazar, op. cit., pp. 106, 108-109.

20. Schnore and Fagin, op. cit.

21. Robert T. Doland, "Public Administration and Urban Policy," in *Urban Research and Policy Planning* (Beverly Hills, California: Sage Publications, 1967), pp. 496-499.

22. Max Ways, "The Road to 1977," *Fortune*, January 1967, pp. 93ff.

23. Jack Culbertson, "State Planning for Education," in *Planning and Effecting Needed Changes in Education*, Designing Education for the Future, no. 3 (New York: Citation Press, 1967), p. 266.

24. Ibid., p. 284.

25. It should not be assumed that all federal influence will be centralized. Despite proposals for centralizing all educational concerns in one or a few areas (such as Health, Education, and Welfare), many federal agencies will continue to influence educational policy and programs.

Conrad Briner

Gerald Sroufe

5

Organization for Education in 1985

Futurists claiming vision of more than ten or fifteen years offer startling descriptions of forthcoming education programs. While compelling, many of the futures are all but unimaginable to us as we reflect on an education system made up of approved texts, black or green boards, teachers, principals, and mimeograph machines. Unfortunately, the futurists seldom address themselves to questions about patterns of organization that will be necessary to enable and support education in the future. When they do reflect on the organization requirements of technologically-impacted forecasts, their suggestions are often simplistic and nearly always lacking in the futurists' characteristic creativity. In sum, education futurists have announced a radical new education era characterized by technological breakthroughs that must be taken seriously, but they have often been satisfied to impose these exciting ideas on an existing pattern of organization that cannot be taken seriously. Our present ritualistic concepts of education organization will not enable us to seize the opportunities of the future.

One may suggest three reasons for our relative unconcern about future organization: (1) Technological breakthroughs deal more immediately with the heart of education—the learner and his environment—and are most readily sought out to illustrate what will be different about education in the future; (2) the most developed forecasting techniques are especially useful in identifying technological futures and are less successful in dealing with questions of values and structures; and (3) much of the education public, including futurists, see organization as an essentially negative pattern of social interaction, inimicable to enhancement of a creative, self-fulfilling society.

This chapter presents a future for organization in education that seeks to incorporate fully what we regard as the dominant value of the next 15 years—increased individual fulfillment—and totally rejects the notion that organization will be of secondary importance to technology in providing the education of the future. The chapter draws on understandings of the future that are developed by others in the book. It seeks to build a model for the organization of education that is in keeping with other observations about the future through the extension of some embryonic organization developments now on display in different parts of the country. The organization patterns and capacities we have tried to outline will be questioned by some and resisted by many; they are unlikely to occur on a large scale without conscientious and extensive effort. However, without adoption of organization patterns similar in essential characteristics to those we have tried to describe, the awesome beauty of the education experiences illustrated in works such as *Education and Ecstasy*[1] will suffer the same fate as overhead slide projectors, language laboratories, and movable walls. Moreover, without substantial movement toward the organization patterns suggested, the school system will become increasingly at odds with the dominant press of the society it seeks to serve.

THE DIRECTING PHILOSOPHY OF EDUCATION ENTERPRISE IN 1985: INDIVIDUAL FULFILLMENT

We anticipate that the basic principle of organization in 1985 will be preoccupation with individual freedom and fulfillment that are unknown today except in the dreams of visionaries such as George Leonard, P. W. Jackson and A. S. Neill. This concern for human dignity and integrity in formal education systems will be attained not at the expense of organization, but as a result of alternative understandings about the possibilities of organization. Many assume that education organizations are necessary to achieve the ends of education (usually expressed in degrees or hours of credit achieved), and that the individual freedoms of the faculty, students, and even administrators are necessarily curtailed as a cost of organization. We anticipate development of an understanding of organization for education that promises even greater achievement of individual freedoms and self-fullfillment than would be attainable outside the organization and that will, of course, succeed in achieving the goals of education.

The Traditional Role of Schools

The character of education organization has been shaped by traditional understandings of the relationship between the individual and state. In brief, schools and school administrators have inherited concepts of education organizations designed to perpetuate the ideology of an ominiscient state providing for docile and mindless students. It is obvious that education has been the province of the state for at least a century, and one is compelled (or condemned) to be educated in our society. However, it appears that the dominance of political reactionism is being forcefully challenged by concerns for the quality of human life in education.

For many years compulsory education has seemed practical and desirable. The state has explained to each student, usually without his consent, how his society, his body, his car, and his universe worked, and even more important it explained to the student what to do with his body and his soul as he became a citizen of the state. Ultimately, both the individual and educational organizations, such as schools, became the arms of the state. All was well until a great number of individuals began to question the authority and moral position of the state at all levels and to assert that they as individuals had the right and the duty to make choices the state had previously made for them. Implicit in this observation are questions about the propriety of compulsory education, the meaning of academic freedom, and the services schools must supply.

Examination of the traditional role of administrators illustrates how completely we have adopted the view that the individual and education are functionaries of the state and suggests the potential failings inherent in that view. In the United States the common school, to the best of our knowlege, has always been conceived as an institution for the perpetuation of the values and customs of the United States. A review of education literature prompts the conclusion that education is inhabited almost solely by functionaries who define education as having something to do with telling children the truths of the race. Unfortunately, the following statement is unusual only in its forcefulness:

But if you will enter the lists in dead earnest, if you will take once again the interest in education that your grandfathers and grandmothers took, if you will support in every positive way those who are trying to break the bonds of pragmatic and permissive progressive education throughout this country, then education will in absolute truth assume its ancient role in this great land as the mentor and handmaiden of the American way of life.[2]

This behavior exalted by Max Rafferty as the only honest purpose of education, is defensive, ceremonial, and largely irrelevant because it seeks only to preserve what is or what was. The admonition is continuously directed to administrators as well as children but usually disguised by a vocabulary of order, efficiency, and duty.

The Administrator as Ritual Chief

Traditional education writers suggest that the principal is an important man who takes care of virtually everything in an orderly way.

The *principal* should be recognized as an instructional leader, staff officer, and as the dean of his faculty. He also has line functions in that he is the administrative officer to whom all teachers are directly responsible.[3]
There is no basic difference except in scope of authority and specific responsibilities between the superintendent and the principal. However, primarily for reasons of accounting, budget classification, and also in imitation of commercial or army organization, the superintendent, deputy, associate, and district superintendents are considered *general* officers, while the building principals are classified as *field* or line officers.[4]

On closer inspection, however, we discover that the principal is usually a man who is delegated all responsibility, but no power to fulfill it. The principal's position is quite hollow and, like a priest, he is only the defender of higher authority. Being thus, dependent, his eyes are ever cast upward and are little concerned with those around him.

General supervision of all teachers, clerks, custodians, cafeteria managers and helpers, other certified and non-certified members of his staff [is the duty of the principal]. Except when engaged in teaching a class he shall devote his entire time to the general administration and supervision of the school. . . As a representative of the Superintendent and the Board of Education, *he is expected to support and carry out the decisions and policies both in letter and in spirit. All disputed questions in matters of discipline, classification, grading, etc., shall be referred to the Superintendent, whose decision shall be final.*[5]

The dilemma of the principal reflects the larger problem of the social institution of education: As presently organized and managed, formal education is mostly irrelevant to the individual in terms of his intrinsic worth. Rather, formal education is ritualistic—an extended Bar Mitzvah, but less effective perhaps, because the student experiences little sense of passage. Particularly at present, students and administrators alike are the victims of antiintellectual and antihumanist forces in the school community. Charles Silberman's devastating and justly renowned passage is an all too accurate description of our circumstance.

Because adults take the schools too much for granted, they fail to appreciate what grim joyless places most American schools are, how oppressive ₂nd petty are the rules by which they are governed, how intellectually sterile and esthetically barren the atmosphere, what an appalling lack of civility obtains on the part of teachers and principals, what contempt they unconsciously display for children as children.[6]

Only in rare instances is public education truly intellectually stimulating or, more important, emotionally satisfying for the parent, student, teacher and administrator. Few know what education in America is really about because it is a patchwork of everything we have tried; administrators therefore are in the position of justifying its vagaries by the almost unlimited, specialized rhetoric of the bureaucracy.

The major fault is that education is treated ritualistically, the administrator being ritual chief charged with yielding to community pressure, setting a social example, performing trivial tasks, enforcing the roles of other staff members, and concentrating on rules rather than people. He represents a system that outlines the sacred cows, socializes the child to accept authority and a sense of his own insignificance without question, and "prepares" him to "make a living." Thus, in 8, 12, 16, or 20 years we "produce" citizens who observe rituals and may discuss topics analytically, but who are spiritually and emotionally dead. Our schools provide little opportunity for emotional learning, all social-democratic and pseudoliberal humanitarian talk to the contrary, because this kind of education does not fit in with our national beliefs in efficiency or traditional ideas about organization.

The principal is as much a victim of this system as the child because his role is the incarnation of the problem. As an individual he is practically powerless because he is subject to anonymous authority on all sides. His tasks are largely menial and in the long run not very important. One often hears staff members remark: "What does the principal *do,* anyway?" Obviously, few men of vitality will be attracted to this position; the nature of the job decrees that a principal be a cipher. Take for example, the year-end memo of a principal at a California high school. It declared that if any teachers allowed students to leave classes early, the teachers would be penalized a day's salary. The memo suggests either mindless behavior or the principal's fear of disorder and uncertainty about what to do if it should arise. The memo reveals, too, the principal's means of influence: fear and repression, the same means used to control students. The principal usually does not have the authority to enact such a threat, but he, alone or in the habit of his office, is reinforcing the mindless fear of which he is himself a product. This traditional role is thus nonintellectual, nonemotional, defensive and hence self-justifying, powerless, and unrewarding. It occupies the weakest of all ethical positions, the preservation of the status quo, and can offer neither enlightenment nor sustenance in a time of change. In this sense it is positively dangerous to the welfare of society.

Individual Fulfillment: Implications for Education Organization

What are the possible alternatives? One radical possibility is suggested by Ivan Illich: "The New World Church is the knowledge industry, both purveyor of opium and the workbench during an increasing number of years of an individual's life. De-schooling is therefore at the root of any movement for human liberation."[7] A more appealing possibility, equally unconventional, seeks to exploit the creative possibility of education organizations rather than simply to decry mass society. Clearly, we must begin to view education as an existential experience that does not end with formal schooling. On the other hand, we must also begin to organize education institutions so that existential experiences that are both intellectual and emotional are fostered rather than discouraged.

Modern industrial society does not resemble the tribe, the family, pre-industrial society, or agricultural society. It is largely anonymous and functions smoothly in most ways. Its major characteristics in individual terms are perhaps loneliness and alienation. Clearly, there is little in the education bureaucracy that nourishes the inner life of the individual. But it is the inner life that determines the quality of existence, and, if ignored, no amount of affluence can take its place. Only fulfillment of life's basic needs—love, acceptance, and self-expression—ensures the quality of life. To the extent that education ignores these needs (and they are all important to the process of education as society becomes increasingly sterile and bureaucratized), the individual, while more knowledgeable, will be less able to deal with society.

In other words, education organizations must fit into the relationship of the individual, family, and state. As the family disintegrates as a source of inner nourishment and until alternatives, such as collective communities based on choice (extended families) are more fully realized, the school will take on a different function in order to meet the needs of individuals. Our students seem to be suffering more from loneliness than from lack of books, more from the desire to talk to someone and have someone take an interest in them than from "permissiveness" or the results of "progressivism". Education organizations must more adequately fulfill the inner needs of the individuals being served. Repression in the schoools, which is now condoned, and even encouraged, does more to contradict the belief in freedom of the individual than any alternative institution might.

Probably future organization will be based on a "free" system, the generic principle of which A.S. Neill calls self-regulation. The obvious implication of this principle is, of course, the elimination of compulsory education. The school as an organization would then become a place where individuals meet by choice and with a common purpose, and would not be, as it is now, a regulatory, and in many cases, penal, institution. Discipline problems would largely be solved by members of the school themselves, so that the staff would be immediately relieved of one of its traditional duties. Once education becomes noncompulsory, it no longer needs to be apologized for, and each educational community can then work to solve its own problems. The issue of academic freedom would not arise in the form it now does because as individuals sense that they have the power to run their own lives, they are not fearful of ideas different from their own. Moreover, once education does not have to be justified by invoking classical beliefs, customary organizational purposes and functions can be drastically changed. The usual bureaucratic hierarchy will be eliminated or sharply reduced in favor of an organizational rationality based on individual freedom.

ORGANIZATIONAL PATTERNS IN 1985

In operational terms, the organization of the school of the 1980s will express two characteristics: (1) An arrangement by which individual schools are differentiated from centralized uniformity to become "creatures" of their various communities, and (2) A resource capacity to sense and respond effectively to educational problems and opportunities affecting schools. These characteristics actually are logical projections of available understanding of the workings of formal organizations and the various management technologies as applied to education. The beginning sights and sounds of these characteristics are evident today when reorganization efforts, especially those focusing on decentralization, are being used to stimulate and guide new conceptualization and development of organizations in education.

School Differentiation

The first characteristic is differentiation. Differentiation will render the "headship" explicated in Chapter 6 applicable to the local school as well as the central authority. Differentiation of subunits will also facilitate development of the headship concept among central administrators. Individual schools will become functional units unto themselves. Schools now are uniform and conforming expressions of educational purposes and functions. They are collectively a unit to be administered by across-the-board district- or state-level financial formulas, pupil-teacher ratios, personnel classifications, courses of study, instructional materials, and physical arrangements. Such administration supposedly assures economical and efficient operations, assures quality educational opportunities and performances, and makes administrative routine and bureaucratic organization possible. The justification, more political than functional in nature, is the uniform achievement of program and financial standards, but rarely do all schools succeed in their mission as a result.

School differentiation is not the equivalent of usual definitions of organizational decentralization. In differentiation, program definition and resource allocation are intended to facilitate localizing the educational effort within each school. In the usual decentralization, subunit organizational structure is modeled after the centralized structure. The form of structure is closer to the school, but the quality of life in the school and especially the conforming force of ritualistic socialization is not lessened. Therefore, subunits seldom acquire distinctive administrative integrity. Direction of function emanates from the top of the bureaucratic hierarchy. Essential decisions about personnel, budget, and instructional practices are made centrally for the entire school district, thus generating little actual variation among schools.

Differentiation will produce qualitatively independent school programs. Schools will be somewhat like satellites out in space on their own. The programs and administration in each school will reflect the interests and competencies of each school community including the parents, staff, and students they serve at any point in time. Both the community and the school will be interdependent variables in determining the educational purposes to be emphasized and the functions necessary to realize these purposes. Functional criteria in calculating the adequacy of community-school organization will include: quality education, representation, accountability, integration, cost, and implementability. The application of these criteria in planning and developing community-school organization will facilitate accomplishing intellectual and emotional education purposes. The responsibility for providing, inventing if necessary, the instructional and learning opportunities requisite to each student's optimum development will rest squarely on the shoulders of community representatives and school staffs. They will be accountable to each other for realizing fully the purposes for which their school is geared.

School staffs will interrelate and be interdependent with other school staffs to share expertise and resources and to coordinate and articulate instruction and administration among communities and schools (*e.g.,* curriculum coordination, school placement of pupils). School staffs will maintain continual contact with area or central services and with government and business (*e.g.,* teaching-learning packages, multi-media centers, transportation) as desired and as services are needed to identify and solve problems or identify and exploit opportunities to facilitate the functioning of individual schools (*e.g.,* planning and implementing career education programs, staff development, reading skills task force). This autonomy will be reality rather than rhetoric in the school of the 1980s.

School staffs will relate with their communities and be accountable to them for the quality of instructional and community service mutually defined. Articulated in the relationship will be descriptions and explanations of programs offered or not offered (*e.g.,* remedial reading, speech therapy, nongraded instruction), weaknesses and strengths of programs, expertness of personnel and nature of other resources available and needed, limits of understanding of teaching and learning problems, and realities of expectations for instruction and community service held by various publics including students and parents. Communication with a school's clientele will move toward the seminar model, away from the public relations model. Area or central office staffs will relate likewise to larger communities of parents, businessmen, and government officials at both state and national levels.

Schools will compete with each other for resources and approval of staff, students, and community members. The single salary schedule will not exist. Competition will expose competence and success and thereby facilitate articulation of education programs within and among schools. The prime benefit will be that each student is known by relevant educational characteristics and accommodated as he works within schools and moves among them. Differentiation will require an open market for personnel and other resources according to the mission and performance of each school in the context of democratizing local school policy making and administration.

Capacity to Sense and Respond

The other characteristic of future school organization, already inferred somewhat, is community and centralized administrative service to schools. Special types of problem solving and quick response resources, such as budget and personnel, will back up schools by helping chart and work through problems and opportunities. A teacher or teachers who are not succeeding with a student or students will be helped by a teaching assistant, by a consultant, or by a problem-solving task force quickly called on from a community resource and staff personnel pool. Likewise, the principal will be helped in his activities with students, teachers, and members of his school community. An entire school staff will be helped to avert and overcome crises. We should imagine a task force or cadre taking over a school or initiating a special program for certain students within a school on a "turn-key" basis as dramatic efforts to improve instruction. Such centralized services will be integrated with school activities and thus help to follow through problems and opportunities.

A startling feature of centralized resources is an organizational capacity for quick response. This can mean institutionalized advocacy for continually questioning the status quo and sensing emerging problems and opportunities. It can also mean that decision discretion will be exercised mainly by parents, teachers, principals, and resource directors to formulate and try unusual as well as usual instructional efforts—a decision path that will mainly involve only the school. Action taken in accordance with broad policy and central administrative guidelines will be stressed, rather than continued referral to a board through central administration. Central boards as they might exist in the future will be legislative in nature, not administrative. Parents, teachers, principals, and students will decide how to organize their schools, how to group and place students, how to define and deploy teachers, how to concentrate and spread out the allocation of resources, in short, how to maximize efforts to realize truly individualized instruction. Organizational purposes and structures will necessarily have to be time-definite to assure a dynamic rather than static character of organization.

The educators will not solely determine operational control in administering differentiated schools. Parents, students, and others will help rationalize organizational purpose and structure. The "man on the street" knows and cares about educational problems and opportunities because of reading newspapers and news magazines, and generally he regards education as important to the quality of life. Some know a great deal about education and read analytical magazines such as *Saturday Review, Harpers,* and *Fortune.* This increasing sophistication suggests a heightening of the vital relationship between the political and educational institutions. The freedom for educators to administer education organizations will be delegated by political process. It must always be remembered: the goals, finances and structures of organization can be determined absolutely by political and governmental action. It is within the political and governmental culture, as it should be, that voices presently are clamoring for schools that fully accommodate individual students—schools that are relevant to serving contemporary society. This political basis for education is an opportunity for educators to earn their way into increased social status and professional responsibility by participating in the political culture with rational reports of accomplishments, failures, and proposals for improving schools. Political control by enlightened citizens will mean professional opportunity to achieve education in the fullest sense.

The social ethic and professional commitment underlying these organizational characteristics of differentiation and special resources is that schools shall not fail in their social responsibility. Students, parents, and staff will be assured of success in education. The form of organization must assure, therefore, decision and instructional arrangements that are relevant to various publics and to each student. This ethic will originate with and be sustained by both the education profession and the political culture at large. As a result, higher levels of educator professionalism will be achieved based on rational expressions of decision and instructional efforts. Evidence and communication to the fullest extent will prevail in school-community relationships. For parents and staff alike, new understandings of function will develop from continuous curiousity and doubt about usual educational methods. Determining and testing alternative ways of getting instructional and administrative jobs done better will be prevalent features of teaching and administration. Experimentation and evaluation will be necessary tools of justifying teaching and administration practices. In this regard, new management technologies depicted in Chapters 2 and 3 will be heavily used. A system of information will continuously track student development and the effectiveness and cost of various teaching and administrative activities. Full communication to parents, teachers, and others about the functioning of schools will be possible and necessary. The information system will make possible independent audits of practices, and will institutionalize advocacy about the adequacy of practices, proposing of alternative practice, and anticipating need for new practices. Two startling implications should result.

(1) Competition among alternative practices (including contracting for instruction and administration in both public and private sectors) will provide a basis for compensating staff on merit. The insidious single salary schedule aspect of organization will be phased out.

(2) Time-definite provision of organizational purposes and structures will assure flexibility and adaptive practices.

Fluid Organizational Structure

In order to achieve the capacity to sense and respond that will characterize education organization in the future, rigid and hierarchical forms necessarily will be replaced with more fluid structures.

For example, organization charts will not be useful to describe positions and functions. Teaching and learning will be explainable only in terms of what people are doing at the moment. Rigid formal structure as we now know it will be minimized in favor of opportunity for informal and fluid communication and decisionmaking. Teachers, students, parents, principals, and others will be continuously assessing their schools' successes and failures. Necessary changes will occur quickly; no aspect of structure and function will be free from scrutiny and criticism. Structure will be especially changeable, always in a state of flux or potential flux. An observer would have to watch people at work to describe and understand definitively the organizational structure at any point of time.

Fundamental to this expectation for "changeability," of course, is the assumption that fluid organizational structure will facilitate goal achievement. This assumption probably holds true up to some undefined point. The expert competence of teachers, parents, administrators, and other consultants deserves freedom of expression in determining education programs rarely known today. However, some formal structure is necessary to any organization. We shall have to learn what freedom is workable. What functions and responsibilities will finally get delegated to schools and what concomitant implications for continuing structure will have to be invented?

We expect the school district as we now know it will disappear in favor of schools going it alone but able to draw on a bank of resources as desired. Time-definite provisions for the resource bank will prevail too. Job expectations for persons competent to exploit the new technology will be reviewed systematically along with the application of new learning strategies.

Periodic measurement and evaluation of programs will be required to facilitate program budgeting and ongoing planning to further develop instruction and learning. The organizational dynamics involved include continuously updating instructional programs, setting program priorities to ensure appropriate allocation of what will always be scarce financial, personnel, and time resources.

The tradition of proliferating administrative layers in the organization as it grows in size and multiplies in function will disappear. An emphasis on fluid structure, one characterized by informal decisional relations, will mean less hand work and more machine work. The quill pen and certain people will be replaced by machines. New data and management technologies will be instituted, including data systems that keep track of individual students and schools as well as complexes of schools. Individual student development will be charted regularly and will become the basis for program decisions.

CAREER JEOPARDY

One of the oldest traditions in education administration, that of managing the schools and school districts by the common application of district-wide standards of behavior and routing procedures, will no longer be possible because of the differentiated structures. Probably school administrators will be most shaken by this change. Probably, too, administrators will openly resist this development. We have been comfortable accounting for and allocating resources according to certain-sized spaces, the time of the year, and uniform formulae. It has been convenient to justify assigning whole or parts of administrative assistants, counselors, secretaries, custodians, etc., as required by the handbook of "Modern Management." (These handbooks and other administrative aids are prepared by prominent management consultants to absolve the administration of personal responsibility.) It has been simple to allow the calendar to regulate requisitioning, budgeting, and employment procedures. In sum, it is for the convenience of the administrator that schools and school districts have been run by applying simplistic accounting concepts. In this sense, school administrators have been important to education organizations as comptrollers rather than leaders or "headmen". They have spent a lot of time on their jobs with quill in hand. Consequently administrators have been positioned to run organizations not develop them; their role has been that of organizational maintenance men rather than of advocates and guarantors of change. A change to the latter role will be required according to the governmental structure of the future envisioned in Chapter 4.

In 1985 standards of behavior and administrative procedure will be calculated to be relevant to the particular population and program of each school. Administration then will not be simple; it will be complex. Chancellors, principals, and other administrators will be accounting for the quality of each school—keeping track of and directing the functioning and development of each school. Most important, they will be ever adapting the school to the environment. This responsibility will necessitate devising the means of describing and explaining to the board and community members the differences among schools as positive attributes. The individual school as a basic unit of analysis will undergird all organizational purposes and structures either implicitly or explicitly.

Finally, the traditional reluctance and sometimes refusal to evaluate learning, teaching, and administration will be overtaken by the organizational need to account for how well the schools are realizing the purposes for which they exist. Fundamental to differentiating individual school administration and marshaling necessary resources is knowledge about the extent to which any instructional program is succeeding or failing to facilitate learning. It is self-evident that essential to provision of personnel, materials, facilities, time, and even parental and legislative approval, is knowledge of what is working, what is not working, what is needed, and why. The latter question will be answered in political arenas, but only in relation to measurement made possible by future technological breakthroughs and evaluation communicated openly to the public. Otherwise, schools will only exist, and educators will only play at educating students.

FOOTNOTES

1. George B. Leonard, *Education and Ecstasy* (New York: Delacort Press, 1968).

2. Max Rafferty, *What They Are Doing to Your Children* (New York: New American Library, 1963), p. 9.

3. Calvin Grieder, Truman Pierce, and William Everett Rosengtengel, *Public School Administration* (New York: Houghton Mifflin, 1940), p. 288.

4. Arthur Moehlman, *School Administration: Its Development, Principles, and Future in the United States* (New York: Houghton Mifflin, 1940), p. 288.

5. "Principal's Handbook" (San Diego, California: San Diego Unified School District, n.d.), p. 3.

6. Charles E. Silberman, *Crisis in the Classroom* (New York: Random House, 1970), p. 10.

7. Ivan Illich, "Schooling: The Ritual of Progress," *New York Review of Books* 15, no. 10 (December 3, 1970): 24.

6

The School Administrator in 1985

INTRODUCTION

Predicting the form and character of school administration in 1985 is likely to be hazardous to one's professional health. The appropriate snakebite kit in this instance is the following set of limiting assumptions.

School systems will become exceedingly complex. Specialization in position and role will continue with a significant increase in the number of specializations required to form functional administrative teams. Many, if not most of these specializations will require specific and rather narrow training with an emphasis on requisite skills. The traditional trilogy of buildings, buses, and bonds together with such new areas of administrative concern as computers, community action, and collective bargaining requires staff with intensive but specialized training. It is recognized that the maintenance of the system will depend more and more on trained specialists organized in administrative teams, headed by a "comprehensivist" administrator.

As the problems confronted by teams of specialists become more complex, team composition will become increasingly interdisciplinary while team organization will become increasingly ad hoc and temporary. The "comprehensivist" role, therefore, will assume a new importance in the continuity of effort needed to solve complex problems and achieve multiple organizational objectives.

This chapter is limited to an analysis of the "comprehensivist" headship role in educational administration. Headship in this context is defined as that focal role through which responsibility and accountability flow and continuity of effort among specializations and temporary groups is maintained. The functions of headship are essentially process in form. The analysis, therefore, proceeds from the concept of administration as a process, a concept serving not only as a major focus of current research on administrative behavior, but one that is likely to continue as a major focus for future research as well.

ADMINISTRATION AS PROCESS

Administration as a process is probably the most accepted of the current views of the nature of administration. The field of administration in general and educational administration in particular in 1985 is most likely to derive from current conceptions of process and further conceptual development in the study of administration as a social system, as a process of planning, as a process of goal setting, and as a process of conflict resolution. Each of these processes has received considerable explication in the literature. The conceptual forms of these processes will continue to develop in sophistication and usefulness as analysis, testing, and synthesis occur. In this chapter processes of planning, goal setting, and conflict resolution will be examined briefly. In addition, it will be argued that a future central task of the educational administrator or administrator of professional personnel is the process of engaging members of the organization in research and development of the nature and processes of the organization.

Each process is treated using the phenomenon of paradox to provide the structural analysis from which predictions may be made or inferred.

Administration as a Process of Planning

The notion that administration is centrally the process of planning is, of course, as old as the first efforts to treat administration as a rational process. Fayol's concept of prevoyance, the process of foretelling the future and planning for it, first suggested the centrality of planning in administration.[1] Yet according to Starr: "The term planning has many meanings and little substance. It is an omnibus word . . . whose significance may have succumbed to generality."[2] And as Friedman has pointed out, planning as an abstract model of perfect rationality in decisionmaking turned out to be unsatisfactory.[3] The assumption of perfectable rationality behind traditional planning models, exemplified by the aphoristic textbook principle that planning is a process of defining objectives, selecting procedures, and evaluating outcomes is being questioned. Simon has pointed to the fact that, while organizations are the most rationally contrived units of human association, an organization of perfectly rational human beings is very nearly a vacuous theory.

It is only because individual human beings are limited in knowledge, foresight, skill and time that organizations are useful instruments for the achievement of human purpose; and it is only because organized groups of human beings are limited in ability to agree on goals, to communicate, and to cooperate that organizing becomes for them a problem.[4]

Simon treats the rationality problem by proposing a principle of bounded rationality, which, he asserts, "lies at the very core of organization theory and at the core, as well of any 'theory of action' that purports to treat of human behavior in complex situations." The principle of bounded rationality is defined as: "The capacity of the human mind for formulating and solving complex problems is very small compared with the size of the problems whose solution is required for objectively rational behavior in the real world—or even for a reasonable approximation to such objective rationality."[5]

Organizational complexity is considerably greater than the assumed simplicity treated in traditional principles and practices of administration. This complexity has been well defined in Beer's analysis of a relatively simple system.[6] If we think of a system with only seven related elements, the system has forty-two relations within itself. If the state of this system is defined as the pattern produced in the network when each of these relations is either in being or not in being (a simple on-off relation), then there will be 2^{42} different states of the system or more than four trillion states.

Similarly, Schwab has pointed out that the minimum factors involved in dealing with problems in educational administration is upward of 4,500 with a more likely estimate of 50,000.[7] He notes also, that there is an astonishingly high degree of interdependence and interaction among the classes of factors and concludes that the school or school system as an administered entity is a stochastic series of an especially complicated kind.

Organizational complexity becomes a black box problem of considerable consequence to administrative behavior. It introduces such factors as ambiguity, unknowable and unknown information, indeterminate analysis, and satisfying rather than optimal rationality, into the decisionmaking process. Future administrative rationality must include ways of handling the unknown as well as the known in determining and selecting courses of action. Thus a paradox emerges in which rationality confronts and must consider the black box of complexity with its unknowable and seemingly probabilistic component.

The reality of the paradox is apparent in the context of intended rather than real rationality. As Simon has pointed out, the intended rationality of an administrator requires him to construct a simplified model of the real situation in order to deal with it.[8] If he behaves rationally in respect to this model, his behavior is not even approximately optimal with respect to the real world. In order to understand and predict an administrator's behavior we must understand how this simplified model is constructed, and its construction will certainly be related to his psychological properties as a perceiving, thinking, and learning animal.

The emerging paradox in planning is fueled by a number of recent theoretical and technical developments in the discipline. New planning process methods include systems analysis, operations research, Program Evaluation and Review Technique, Program Planning Budgeting System, and developments in computer science. Each has been touted as the answer to the limitations of the administrator as a rational planner. However, the relatively few critiques of these new planning processes suggest that the planning paradox continues.

Gross argues that the definition of PPBS is a source of disagreement and confusion.[9] He suggests that there is a "gentlemen's agreement" among the technical specialists and other parties that the basic terms need never be defined. *System, output, planning,* and *programming* have become fad words used with a false sophistication. He proposes that the spirit of PPBS—a marriage between program planning and budgeting—is more important than the letter and that there is no one system but rather a large variety of PPB-type systems.

Despite his criticism of the "state of the art," Gross sees constructive potential of great significance through an approach that puts people and institutions—with their motivations, divided interests, and unpredictabilities—into system models. He foresees the development of multidimensional models of people and resources—the development of complex sociotechnical systems as a major thrust in future planning.

The increment in planning rationality made possible by the new planning tools and the capability of the computer to store and treat large amounts of data needed for planning in complex systems has several consequences that sharpen the planning paradox. Michael has pointed out that while the computer may relieve top management of routine decisions and reduce the number of clerks and middle managers needed to run the organization, it will enormously increase the demands on them to wrestle with the moral and ethical consequences of the policies they choose and implement. Management will confront the necessity of making decisions and plans that transcend those included in a purely rational approach. The administrator will have to be a perpetual student, not only of the techniques of rationalized decisionmaking but even more of the humanities.[10]

A further complication lurks in the question of whether there is one rationality or many. Churchman addresses the question through a view of system reality in which "facts" are themselves decisions based on a way of viewing reality, *i.e.*, the larger system. He goes on to say that a strong interactive relation between manager and systems analyst may reinforce a biased view of reality that emphasizes decision, control, planning, and implementation.[11]

Similarly, Michael argues that, with the computer as the core and dominant guide to rationalized processes, attempted solutions to social problems will be statistical solutions. Problem solvers will be those who will define the problem (because of their techniques) as a statistical problem, emphasizing the aspects of reality the computer can deal with just because it can deal with them. Boguslaw calls the system designers and computer professionals the new utopians. He argues that the tasks set for computerized equipment systems prescribe behavior patterns within a social system. Behaviors not specified are more than illegal, they are impossible. The large scale industrial, military, and space systems the age of computers has thrust on us are the new utopias, lacking only the humanoid orientation of the classical forms.[12]

Quantitative, computer-formed rationality is only one of the rationalities appropriate to a complex administrative problem. Political rationality, economic rationality, the valuing process, or human relations concerns, may be equally appropriate "rational" approaches to the same problem. Friedmann considers this question in his development of a conceptual model for the analysis of planning behavior.[13] He distinguishes four planning modes—developmental, adaptive, allocative, and innovative—and two kinds of thinking that he classifies as rational and extrarational. Rational thought is further classified as bounded or nonbounded with bounded rationality further classified as functionally or substantively rational. He asserts further that these kinds of thinking are decisive in influencing both the prevailing styles of planning and the actual behavior of planners. In a philosophical postscript to his model Friedmann puts the issue in context.

If planning is accepted as the attempted intervention of reason in history, then it is clear that such intervention cannot be immediate and direct, but must be filtered through a series of complex structures and processes to be effective. A definitely anti-heroic picture of reason emerges. It is not the great mind that intervenes, but a multitude of individual actors, each playing his role in a collective process that he does not fully comprehend because he is involved in it himself and lacks perspective.[14]

A further dissonance contributing to the rationality paradox is identified in Argyris' provocative analysis of the impact of a specific set of organizational values on the behavior of its members.[15] He argues that an intensive emphasis on rationality, in conjunction with other values, will decrease interpersonal competence and increase conflict. The relation of rationality to conflict has been supported by a number of observers. The continued application of narrowly viewed systems analysis to social and institutional problems is likely to exacerbate the extralegal, extrapolitical, nonrational revolts of a growing postindustrial intelligentsia currently located in institutions of higher education. It may be no accident that a counter-culture is emerging at this time.

In summary, the abstract model of perfect rationality implicit in traditional views of planning is only partially adequate both as a base for research and for use in intervening in the flow of reality. As rationality increases through new tools and techniques for data treatment and problem solving, extrarational considerations become increasingly insistent and central. Planning at the headship level may be as much intuitional as rational, as much an art as a science, as the unknowable and nonrational components of a complex system become more clearly identified. The conflict in this paradox is suggested by Gross in his summary description of planning: "an exercise in conflict management rather than only a sober application of technical rationality. Any real life planning process may be characterized as a stream of deadlock or avoidance and occasional victories, defeats and integrations."[16] Administrators of the future will find no easy solution in better rational planning techniques. Instead, a developing paradox will force some integration of rationality and purpose, planning and risk, cognition and affect.

Administration as a Process of Goal Setting

Conventional views of planning and current planning models accept purpose and goals as undefined terms. The dictum, define your objectives, is the conventional starting point. Yet to view goal definition as a simple process of formulating and agreeing on statements and to accept goals as an undefined element in organizational structure ignores the complex nature of goals. Gross, Simon, and Ohm have argued for the position that goal setting is a complex and partially indeterminate process.[17]

Goals are statements that depict a variety of desired states of the organization and serve a number of system functions such as adaptation, pattern maintenance, and integration, as well as end state definition. The multifunctional, multidimensional nature of goals permits goal statements to be categorized as defined parts of the structure of an organization. In addition, in the process of interaction, goals may emerge that did not exist before the action. These emergent goals are generally a function of the strategies of competing individuals and groups for scarce resources. Thus planning may not necessarily begin with the process of goal definition, as is assumed in such methods as PPBS, but may include the identification of goals as part of the planning process. Goal definition may be a complex, strategical process over time involving changing, redefining, and emerging goals rather than readily defined statements that initiate a planning process. The implications of goal strategy for planning have yet to be explored.

The standard requirement for clear and specific objectives, touched in quantitative or measurable terms of such planning methods as operations research and PPBS, becomes paradoxical in the light of Simon's view of goals as a set of organizational constraints. He argues that an acceptable course of action must satisfy a whole set of requirements or constraints, and that, while sometimes one of these requirements is singled out and referred to as the goal of the action, it is more meaningful to refer to the whole set of requirements as the complex goal of the action. He concludes that:

> It is doubtful whether decisions are generally directed toward achieving a goal. It is easier, and clearer, to view decisions as being concerned with discovering courses of action that satisfy a whole set of constraints. It is this set, and not any one of its members, that is most accurately viewed as the goal of the action.[18]

The paradox is sharpened by moving Simon's argument to a system perspective in which goals occur not only as inputs or precursors to action but in system transformation and output as well. In the "black box" character of complex organizations, goal definition, particularly in its participatory and pluralistic modes, may well perform an ordering function for the system. Goal setting may be part of the control process of a complex organization. As such, it is possible to view certain goals as outputs that function to relate the system to other systems and in the feedback loops of the system.

The system paradox lies in the question whether goals are best defined by some technical or power elite or through a process in which goals emerge through the activities of competing groups, individuals, and interests. The paradox suggests that the transformation of human purpose into communicable forms for the direction of organizations will become a central administrative task. And since human purposes have been the domain of the humanities for centuries, the administrator of the future will be required to be more and more a humanist, an expert in working with others in purpose definition and goal setting within a pluralistic and conflicted milieu. As Harlow has observed, purpose defining may be the central function of the school administrator of the future.[19]

Administration as a Process of Conflict Resolution

Current and future planning and goal setting processes reflect an administrative environment that is becoming increasingly conflictive. Dissent and militancy are becoming a way of life in professionally staffed organizations. The concept of administration as a process of conflict resolution is again becoming popular. Certainly, a considerable part of a line administrator's work revolves around the process of dealing with conflicting interests, groups in conflict, and conflicts in and with the organization's environment. Handling conflict successfully or constructively is a major administrative problem that has attracted considerable new thought and research. There are three approaches that are likely to influence the nature of administration in 1985.

The first approach emerges from a growing awareness of the incongruence between current conceptions of participatory management and the processes of negotiation, bargaining, mediation, and other manifestations of collective action. The new militancy has brought on a resurgence of administrative concern for the involvement of members of the organization in the decision processes. The older human relations approach takes a current fix on participation as the key to the new administration, as reflected in such recent publications as Likert's *New Patterns of Management.*[20] In the popular and descriptive literature on educational administration, the exhortative, "democratic" leadership approach continues to be prescribed as a principle of administration.

The participatory approach, however, fails to recognize the emergence of collective action processes and continues to refuse to examine the implicit assumptions on which it is based. The participatory approach accepts the centrality of a hierarchical structure. The determination of participative structures and areas and problems suitable for participatory decisionmaking is seen as an administrative decision, a privilege that can be given, changed, or taken away rather than a right. And it is precisely at this point that one set of confrontations is occurring.

Current arguments for the participatory mode in the governance and administration of educational organizations derive from the principles of political pluralism, originally designed for interinstitutional relations, but now applied to intraorganizational government. The drive for representation in administrative processes including the revival of decentralization structures confronts executive power and technical competence as a new form of conflict and dissent. Conflict and dissent imply a desire for change. Change through pluralism confronts the paradox of pluralistic participatory administration involving political as well as rational processes, with bargains and compromises as the prelude to action, and the fact that this method of change is slow and is as likely to support the status quo as it is to move ahead. Increasingly, therefore, administrators will have to work with the paradox of a society having a pluralistic tradition and participative ideology in confrontation with a postindustrial technology and management science elite over how to get change. An increase in conflict, negotiation, bargaining, and consensus is one consequence of the apparent paradox. An involvement in politics and power is a second consequence. In educational organizations, no single source of power is dominant. Instead, each source of power—government, board, administration, faculty, students, and community—can exercise a form of negative power. Any one group can, through collective action, withdraw or choose not to act to a point where the enterprise stops. It is this negative power, implicit or exercised, that leads to negotiation rather than the traditional forms of participation. The administrator of the future will work in a changing, conflictive decision system so complex and sophisticated that the old notions of hierarchy and authority will hardly apply.

As the paradoxes in conflict become more clearly defined, new approaches to the analysis of conflict have and are being sought. One of these approaches is the application of strategical games theories to conflict problems.[21] The rationale has permitted the analysis of the logical structure of a large range of administrative conflict situations to a point where alternative solutions can be identified and consequences examined.

The continuing development of strategical game theory derives from the notion that administrative conflict is generally mixed with a mutual dependence requiring some form of collaboration of mutual accommodation, either tacit or explicit, as a part of the strategy involved in choosing actions or making decisions. In the future, much greater attention will be given to the concept of strategy and administration as a strategical process. The contributions of game theory to strategy will be augmented by developments exemplified by Caplow's theory of coalition formation and the newer forms of bargaining theory.[22] A clearer understanding of conflict will emerge as will an extensive armamentarium of administrative strategies for dealing with conflict. The construction of new organizational forms for the ritualizing of conflict in ways that are therapeutic as well as solution-oriented will be one of the central tasks of the educational administrator of the future.

A new concern, emerging from conflict studies in administration, is the problem of stress and its prevention or alleviation. Continuing conflict is stress producing. Stress has predictable psychological and physiological effects. Administrators vary in their ability to handle stress. Wolfe and Snoek found that role pressures aroused a high level of tension in the role occupant and stimulated a variety of emotional reactions.[23] Coping reactions were often maladjustive and at times seemed to stimulate an intensification of the conflict to the detriment of the organization and the individual.

In an extensive review of studies relating stress to coronary disease, Sales concludes that role overload can contribute to the etiology of coronary disease.[24] Role overload is defined as a condition in which the individual is faced with a set of obligations that, *taken as a set,* require him to do more than he is able in the time available. Where role overload is coupled with low job satisfaction, and considered as a stress factor, the relation to coronary disease is high. Further, certain personality types may seek role overload functions. The aggressive, ambitious, competitive, hard-driving person who strives to meet deadlines and lives under time pressures tends to move to positions that have the potential for role overload. When a personality type and the fact that head positions in educational administration are generally role overloaded are combined, it seems clear that the administrator of the future will need self-insight as well as extensive coping mechanisms for the increase in stress that can be predicted for educational organizations of the future.

Administration as a Process of Research and Training

Under the pressure of rationalizing processes, multiple goals, participatory pluralism, professionalism, and conflict resolution, a new perception of the role and function of the administrator seems to be emerging. The sources of this developing concept are varied. One early source derives from efforts to describe organizational learning. Cangelosi and Dill propose a theory that makes learning in organizations a product of three kinds of stress:[25]

(1) Discomfort stress is the result of the complexity of the environment relative to the time, energy, and the ability that groups can expend understanding it and of the uncertainty in the environment relative to a group's ability to forecast the future.

(2) Performance stress is the sensitivity to, and concern for, success or failure.

(3) Disjunctive stress is a product of divergence and conflict in the ways individuals behave.

When individual and subgroup adaptation produce more divergence and conflict than the organization can tolerate, total system learning is likely to take place. Thus organizational learning is sporadic and stepwise rather than continuous or gradual, and it is not necessarily a product of planning.

From another point of view, organizational learning is a form of output used as a measure of organizational effectiveness. For example, the concept of job enlargement has been extended to include the possibility of an output measure that is the sum of the amount of enlargement for each job, position, or role in the organization. A related measure is the amount of education or training received by members of the organization over some defined period of time. Both measures may be subsumed under organizational learning.

The general concept of organizational learning is augmented by a view of the administrator as an organizational diagnostician making decisions that ensure a healthy organization. The model most frequently offered in support of this concept is the professor of medicine, who unites theory and practice more functionally than any other profession. Schwab argues for this model and suggests that the professor of educational administration and the professing educational administrator are ideally the same. Goldhammer submits that the preparation of the school administrator as the clinical student of organization or the clinical student of society is a far more viable model for the preparation of the educational administrator than the research exposure models of current programs.[26]

The clinician concept is essentially an effort to get some productive consummation in the marriage of theory and practice. However, it falls short in its prescription for the future. The steps or actions beyond effective clinical diagnoses are ignored, and the implication that an organization of professionals is similar to a client or sick patient is somewhat difficult to build explicitly into policies and plans for administrative action.

A more encompassing conception is the proposition that a major task of the chief administrator is the training of members of the organization in the processes of administration and educating them in the nature of organization. The essential expertise of the administrator is applied primarily to instructing others on organizational structure and administrative rationality.

This proposition is supported by the fact that professionals in organizations are increasing in number and level of training. Certainly the problem of administering an organization composed primarily of professionals is a central problem for the educational administrator as well as for administrators of many other types of organizations. Typical hierarchical views of organization do not suffice to depict the design of or explanation of organizations in which professionals predominate. New concepts of organization have just begun to emerge, yet we know very little about organizational design and administrative process for dealing with professionals or even with intelligent, articulate, action-oriented students.

The administrator as trainer involves a continuing relation between theory and practice. The behavioral data of this process derives from the behavior of each member of the organization, individually and in groups. This behavior may be analyzed according to the various rationales and concepts of organization and administration. It is only as organization members become knowledgeable and skilled in organizational activity that they can in fact so perform membership and leadership roles as to achieve both organizational and personal goals.

One implication of the general training proposition is suggested in the authority relation between superior and subordinate. This relation is frequently a source of conflict and of interpersonal as well as personal problems that may not only reduce the effectiveness of the organization but of the individual as well. Individual responses to authority have roots in early parental relations, religious training, and indoctrination to school and classroom. It is not unusual to find evidences of early authority relations in the superior-subordinate dyad of adults in organizations. Infantile reactions in adult situations can cripple individual performance and reduce the effectiveness of both members of the dyad. One task of the administrator, therefore, is to be able to interact in ways that enable subordinates to develop mature responses to authority.

The same authority problem appears at the group level. Mills theorizes that group solidarity may be a function of hostility toward the leader and that the leader, in turn, should handle this hostility by accepting the attack, managing his feelings, and keeping the group goal before the group so that a transfer to group goal is made.[27] A further step may be added to this process by proposing that, in addition to the continuing focus on group goals, the administrator as group leader must also argue for the organizational and administrative rationality of the problem situation and its solution. In short, he must be able to successfully instruct others in the organizational logic of a problem solution to a point where other, more emotional alternatives are seen as having ineffective consequences. Such a process, of course, requires a thorough, penetrating, and sensitive knowledge of organizations in general and of the system for which the administrator is responsible in particular. It is no accident that sensitivity group training continues to be popular with management people. Sensitivity training, however, may be missing an opportunity to increase management effectiveness by concentrating attention on organizational rationalities based on the study of organizations as well as on its traditional concern for group process and self-understanding.

Another administrative instructional or training technique is the use of simulation and games in the analysis of organizational problems and development of alternative solutions or plans for solving problems. Problems can be cast into gamed simulation form with appropriate modeling of the organizational context. Selected members of the organization play the game to a point where a number of alternative solutions are identified and incorporated for further play. In this way alternatives may be tested and player behavior in the simulated context may be recorded for further analysis without the costs or effects of putting a real alternative in action. The technique is particularly useful in long-range planning where errors or mistakes may not appear until it is too late to change direction.

The instruction function is likely to grow into a more complex form as it incorporates such logical extensions as the concepts of administration as a research process and research as an administrative process. This research aspect of the training function is made explicit in Churchman's rationale for a continuing dialogue between managers and PPB analyst. He suggests that management be examined to see in what way it is a "part" of the research function of the organization. He argues that:

Research on organizations can be regarded as a way of managing organizations—managing can create fundamental knowledge about organizations, since every important managerial decision can be regarded as an "experiment". It loses its experimental power, however, if its experimental nature is not evaluated. Thus the [systems] analyst can contribute by looking at many current decisions in an experimental framework.[28]

The managerial decision and the decision series that comprise a plan become a way of conducting research, and, in turn, the debate, interactions, and identification of underlying assumptions that lead to a plan that includes a research component become a way of managing.

The research and education function of the administrator is a way of resolving a set of paradoxes or dilemmas that form the nub of administration. The experimental approach is a way of making decisions in the value conflict arena. The decision to move with one of several equally arguable value-based alternatives can be cast in a research design that can provide data for testing the correctness of the selected alternative to a point where it is shown either that the alternative is the best or that another alternative should be tried.

Administration as the experimental design of key decisions for the resolution of conflict depends on some participant knowledge of the nature of the organization. Membership knowledge of organization is also essential to a further conception of the administrator as the creator of new forms of organizational structure. The future administrator must be able to redefine roles; restructure tasks; create new divisions, sections, committees, units, and groups; and form new subsystem arrangements. Paine calls this process organizational architecture and refers to the open-system administrator as an architect of organization.[29]

If the felicitous phrase, "the administrator as organizational architect," is accepted, the concept includes the idea of the art of administration. Just as architecture can express both art and utility, so administration in the open-system mode is a combination of art and science. Administrators with an open-system mode responsibility will be held accountable for designs of systems that reflect an artistic or aesthetic sense, particularly in the relations among members of the organization. The future will require creative administrators in a more precise sense of the term. Creative performance and product will be evaluated. Style will become an important characteristic in the selection, preparation, and evaluation of administrators. The concept of style will provide a bridge to the art, theory, and practice together.

In summary a concept of educational administration is emerging that considers organizational research, instruction, goal setting, conflict-handling, and creative structuring as basic processes in working with the indeterminate, conflictive, and risk-prone open-system forms of future educational organizations.

FOOTNOTES

1. Henri Fayol, *General and Industrial Management* (London: Pitman & Sons, 1949).

2. Martin K. Starr, "Planning Models," *Management Science* 13 (December 1966): pp. B-115-141.

3. John Friedman, "A Conceptual Model for the Analysis of Planning Behavior," *Administrative Science Quarterly* 12 (September 1967): p. 226.

4. Ibid., p. 199.

5. Herbert G. Simon, *Models of Man*, (New York: John Wiley & Sons, 1964), pp. 10-11, 199.

6. Stafford Beer, *Cybernetics and Management* (New York: John Wiley & Sons, 1964), pp. 10-11.

7. Joseph J. Schwab, "The Professorship in Educational Administration: Theory-Art-Practice," in *The Professorship in Educational Administration*, eds. Donald J. Willower and Jack Culbertson (Columbus, Ohio: University Council for Educational Administration, 1964), p. 54.

8. Simon, op. cit., pp. 199-200.

9. Bertram M. Gross, "The New Systems Budgeting," *Public Administration Review* 29, no. 2 (March-April 1969): p. 115.

10. Donald M. Michael, "Some Long-Range Implications of Computer Technology for Human Behavior in Organizations," in *Computer Concepts in Educational Administration*, ed. R. U. Marker (Iowa City: Iowa Educational Information Center, 1966), pp. 55-66.

11. C. Wesley Churchman, "PPB: How Can It Be Implemented?" *Public Administration Review* 29 no. 2 (March-April 1969):187.

12. Michael, op. cit., p. 66; Robert Boguslaw, *The New Utopians* (Englewood Cliffs, N. J.: Prentice-Hall, 1965).

13. Friedmann, op. cit., p. 229.

14. Ibid., p. 252.

15. Chris Argyris, *Interpersonal Competence and Organizational Effectiveness* (Homewood, Illinois: R. N. Irwin, Inc., 1962).

16. Bertram Gross, "What are your Organization's Objectives?" *Human Relations* 18 (August 1965): 192-215.

17. Bertram Gross, *The Managing of Organizations* (New York: The Free Press, 1965); Herbert G. Simon, "On the Concept of Organizational Goals," *Administrative Science Quarterly* 9 (June 1964):2-22; Robert E. Ohm, "Organizational Goals: A Systems Approach" (Paper presented at the 20th Annual Meeting of the National Conference of Professors of Educational Administration, Indiana University, August 25, 1966).

18. Simon, op. cit., pp. 2-22, 30.

19. James G. Harlow, "The Humanities in the Training of Educational Administrators," in *Educational Administration—Philosophy In Action*, eds. Robert E. Ohm and W. G. Monaham (Norman, Okla: University of Oklahoma, 1965).

20. Rensis Likert, *New Patterns of Management* (New York: McGraw-Hill, 1951).

21. Robert E. Ohm, "A Game Model Analysis of Conflicts of Interest Situations in Administration," *Educational Administration Quarterly*, Fall 1968.

22. Theodore Caplow, *Two Against One* (Englewood Cliffs, N. J.: Prentice-Hall, 1968).

23. Donald M. Wolfe, and J. Diedrich Snoek, "A Study of Tensions and Adjustment Under Role Conflict," *Journal of Social Issues* 18 (July 1962).

24. Stephen M. Sales, "Organization Role as a Risk Factor in Coronary Disease," *Administrative Science Quarterly* 14 (September 1969): 325-338.

25. Vincent E. Cangelosi and William R. Dill, "Organizational Learning: Observations Toward a Theory," *Administrative Science Quarterly* 10 (September 1965):715-203.

26. Schwab, op. cit., p. 65; Keith Goldhammer, "Implications for Change in Training Programs" in *Knowledge Production and Utilization in Educational Administration* (Eugene, Oregon: Center for the Advanced Study of Educational Administration, 1968).

27. Theodore M. Mills, "Authority and Group Emotion," in *Interpersonal Dynamics,* ed. Warren G. Bennis, et al (Homewood, Illinois: Dorsey Press, 1964), pp. 94-108.

28. Churchman, op. cit., pp. 187-188.

29. Thomas O. Paine, "Space Age Management and City Administration" (Paper presented at the 1969 Conference on Public Administration, Miami, Florida).

Richard C. Lonsdale

Robert E. Ohm

7

Futuristic Planning: An Example and Procedures

Futurism can be just an academic exercise, permitting its practitioners the fascination of creating social science fiction as they manipulate alternative futures, scenarios, system breaks, and related paraphernalia of this enticing new specialization. But any partial approach truncates futurism. Carried to its fullest development, futurism is really for the activist who wants to exercise some degree of control over the future and not just let the future control him. Futurism involves a welding of creative forecasting, planning, and action. For the educational futurist, then, this requires (1) the study and development of alternative futures and their supporting scenarios focusing on specific societal areas or institutions, and (2) drawing from these alternative futures, scenarios, and related influencing variables, by inference and deduction, criteria describing the kinds of educational programs needed to meet the projected future conditions. Working from these criteria, the educational futurist develops the broad, long-range plans and the detailed short-term plans through which the futurist study can be translated into educational action programs.

In the sense of this scheme, and to use our own phrase, this book by itself would be truncated futurism—but necessarily so. It goes only part way and can go only part way. Chapters 3, 4, 5, and 6 represent a kind of creative forecasting of the educational future of 1985 for elementary and secondary education. This chapter will give an example of criteria for one kind of educational program that were derived from those projected future educational conditions. It will also outline procedures for long-range and short-term planning in order to translate futurist study into educational action programs. But no general book can set forth the actual plans. That is the proper work of a task force or study team, as suggested in Chapter 1,

109

charged with making plans for a specific institution, such as the Enterprise Public School District or Lafayette State University.

What is new about futurism, therefore, making it different from simply long-range planning that has been with us a long time? One new aspect is the systematic projection of alternative future environments. This embodies the concept of options affording a new sense of freedom in the face of a future subject at last to some degree of influence or even control. A second new aspect is the cyclical evolution from the general to the particular, that is, from a projected future environment to criteria, to plans, and then to action pointed to the future. The sequence is cyclical because the implied purpose of the action is either to accommodate or to modify the projected future environment.

EXAMPLE: DEVELOPMENT OF "CRITERIA FOR SURVIVAL"

The dramatic social changes projected for the future justify doubts about the survival of at least some of the present forms of institutionalized education. For example, whether educational administration as we know it now and present patterns of preparing educational administrators in our universities will survive until 1985 emerges as a critical question from the futurist process used in Chapters 2 through 6. Facing this question led us to develop a set of "criteria for survival." Our implication is that only graduate programs in educational administration meeting these criteria deserve to survive until 1985. Our intent is to stimulate professors and other planners of programs to use these criteria in so redirecting their graduate programs in educational administration as to be worthy of surviving in 1985.

Two classes of assumptions underly these survival criteria. One deals with the expected nature of organization and administration around 1985. The other deals with the expected nature of preparation programs for educational administrators, in general terms, around 1985. Together they provide a tool for evaluating, reconstructing, and further revising preparation programs. Both classes of assumptions derive from a process of drawing out second order projections about administration and preparation for administration form the content of Chapters 2 through 6. The assumptions that follow are representative rather than exhaustive. Those engaged in designing programs will want to generate their own additional assumptions as they apply the futurist methodology to the design problem.

ASSUMPTIONS ABOUT ORGANIZATION
AND ADMINISTRATION IN 1985

(1.) Change within education organizations and the larger society will be the hallmark of the next 15 years. Educational organizations will accommodate themselves to substantial societal changes; this new accommodation will accelerate the general rate of educational change.

(2.) Concern for individuals—both the members of education organizations and their clients— will direct the massing and allocation of resources. Technology, including management technology, will be evaluated in part according to its effectiveness in sustaining attainment of individual goals.

(3.) The educational enterprise will be increasingly characterized by a multiplicity of organizations: public, private, commercial, corporate, industrial, military, church, and governmental. Formal public schooling will be experiencing increasing competition for resources and students. It will be required to engage in a greater number of cooperative, coordinated activities with other agencies.

(4.) The team concept of administration will become increasingly prevalent with teams put together for specific functions and problems. In many instances these teams will be ad hoc or temporary with team membership changing as tasks are accomplished and problems solved.

(5.) With the continuing development of new specializations will come the need for team leaders or "headship" administrators capable of organizing and directing teams of specialists.

(6.) Authority relationships will be sharply modified in the direction of goal-centered collegial relationships; authority will be conceded on the basis of specific expertise and within limited area and time spheres.

(7.) All administrators will need to know the nature of organization and administration well enough to instruct members of their organization and to create situations helping members to learn and function more effectively through the operation of the organization.

(8.) Administrators will need a sufficient knowledge of research on organization and administration and of research design to initiate and coordinate research on the organizations they head.

(9.) The entire staff of a school will be held accountable for the success of each student in relation to specified outcomes. The provision of staff, facilities, and materials in quantity will be expected to produce a guaranteed level of output in a specified period of time.

(10.) Basic research on learning (biological, chemical, physical, psychological, sociological, and anthropological) will create difficult value-based problems and issues for administrators. As the ability to control, program, intervene in, and augment human behavior expands from prenatal intervention, through early childhood conditioning, to adolescent programing, difficult policy issues will arise more frequently with consequences that have greater scope and impact on the individual.

ASSUMPTIONS ABOUT PREPARATION PROGRAMS FOR ADMINISTRATORS

Research Assumption

Some part of every preparation program must be based on a theory of administration and related to a theory of program design with evaluative feedback for program development and improvement. Unless significant parts of a preparation program are cast in research design form, the profession will be unable to shape its future.

Most current programs for the preparation of educational administrators have a pragmatic, eclectic, or empirical design. They reflect varying forms of a system that has evolved over time, is constrained by relations with other systems, such as the agencies responsible for certification and accreditation, and is bound by institutional structures involving course-defined and departmentalized knowledge. Theoretical models of program design are rejected or ignored by implication in favor of a set of notions about program design drawn from tradition and experience. The lack of a general theory of administration tends to support the pragmatic approach. As Schwab has asserted, the pursuit of one sufficing theory of administration is impossible in the foreseeable future.[1] He suggests instead that a sophisticated and cynical grasp of about a dozen separate and distinct bodies of theory is indispensable to good administration, but that such intimacy with these bodies of theory, however sophisticated and cynical, is still insufficient. The lack of one comprehensive theory of administration, however, does not preclude the need for research on program elements.

Subsumed under research design are the essential processes of program planning, definition of objectives, selection of instructional methods, and evaluation of results. The following questions indicate more details of the research assumption:

(1.) What parts of the preparation program are in a research design form?

(2.) Does the research design conform to accepted standards, including a review of past research, a statement of the problem or problems, a methodology for the collection and treatment of data, and a description of the potential contribution of the research to further program improvement?

(3.) To what extent have students participated in the formulation of the research, the collection and treatment of data, and the application of results to program change?

(4.) Is there evidence that the program has been changed as a result of successful research?

(5.) Is the best available evidence from past research being used to develop the parts of the preparation program not presently being subjected to research?

(6.) Are those parts of the preparation program not directly researched subject to a systematic evaluation process?

(7.) What plan is in effect to relate the results of research to program change?

Experience Assumption

Some part of every preparation program must provide students and professors with direct experience in dealing with social problems in a manner that includes some sharing of accountability for results. This assumption derives from a professional and professorial responsibility for the conduct of research and development activity on significant social problems of, or related to, education. The professional school of the future is likely to be directly involved in a number of the intransigent educational problems of the future. Involvement through school surveys, consultant activity, and the like is not new; what is new is the necessity of a form of involvement that includes some sharing of accountability for results.

The following questions indicate the nature of this experience assumption:

(1.) Does the program design include a list of the interinstitutional and interorganizational activities, projects, or programs in which students and faculty members are engaged, with some justifying data on the significance and scope of the problem and the resources committed?

(2.) Can the department describe the forms of student participation for training purposes in each social action project?

(3.) Can the department provide a list of experience opportunities, internships, assistantships, jobs, instructorships, and program-related positions in the constituent communities that contribute to the overall preparation program?

(4.) Is there evidence on the continuing interaction of theory and practice in the preparation program in relation to the conduct of problem-solving projects?

(5.) Is there evidence that in its dealing with social problems the department has clearly shared responsibility not only for plans, but also for resulting action programs and their evaluation?

Instructional Laboratory Assumption

Some part of every preparation program requires a laboratory approach to instruction. Without laboratory data drawn from group processes, simulations, T-groups, and laboratory exercises, much of the value of course instruction or of administrative and organizational theory would be lost. In addition, the kind of disciplined thought required in laboratory exercises involving the modeling of organization units or modeling for simulation purposes is difficult to achieve in any other way.

Some appropriate questions related to this assumption are:

(1.) To what extent are the department, college, and university used as laboratories in support of course activity?

(2.) How is student experience generated to produce laboratory experience for theoretical analysis related to course content?

(3.) To what extent are students systematically confronted with the value systems, including their own, involved in making administrative decisions?

(4.) What group processes are used to develop insight, tolerance of stress, and sensitivity to others?

(5.) Are laboratory performance units defined and sequenced to provide appraisal data on students?

(6.) Are students involved in the development of simulation models?

SPECIFIC SURVIVAL CRITERIA

From the content of Chapters 2 through 6 and from the foregoing assumptions may be drawn a number of specific operationalized survival criteria pertaining to content and process in a preparation program in educational administration. A set of these critieria is given below. The writers make no claim that these statements are comprehensive or complete. Instead, they assume a variety of programs could be developed in part from the five chapters describing futurism and the nature of educational administration in 1985. Therefore, no single set of specific criteria will be applicable to all programs that will survive. Rather, the criterion statements below will have to be used by university personnel to revise existing preparation programs for school administrators, or to devise new ones, to survive in the societal and educational environment of 1985.

To provide a link with the present, the designations of contemporary program components are used, namely, purposes, organization, program, faculty, students, alumni, facilities, and funds. The specific criteria are listed under these headings. The statements include both concepts and values. Since the preparation program may be seen as an open system within the larger system of a university and a total system of education, criteria may be seen as pertaining to input, mediating, and output variables, and are so designated in parentheses after each statement. The specific criteria listed under each component might be classified elsewhere, since the several categories are not mutually exclusive.

Purposes

1. Faculty, students, practitioners of educational agencies and institutions, and others interested in preparation programs in educational administration shall share in setting goals and in continuous, systematic long-range planning for and evaluation of the program. Periodically, they shall analyze the purposes to be inferred from present program elements and the extent to which these inferred purposes are desirable and relevant. (Input)

2. The preparation program shall give balanced or intentionally distinctive emphasis among the several phases in the knowledge transfer chain along which knowledge is converted into action. These phases are the production of knowledge through research, and its development, dissemination-diffusion, and application-use. (Mediating)

3. The preparation program shall give balanced emphasis among the social and behavioral sciences, the humanities, mathematics, and the natural sciences. There shall be an explicit rationale for the inclusion of concepts and other content. (Input mediating)

4. The preparation program shall reflect changing societal and educational conditions and new knowledge. (Input)

5. The preparation program shall demonstrate concern for the opportunity of faculty and students to live rich, varied lives, as well as to be professionally productive. (Output)

6. The preparation program shall give attention periodically to alternative societal and educational futures. Scenarios should be extracted from the literature or developed originally describing these alternative futures and the steps or developments by which they might be achieved. Selection of one or more of these futures or of compatible elements from among them should constitute planning goals for the preparation program with a clear linkage shown between these planning goals and program elements of the preparation program. (Input)

7. The preparation program shall give students experience in general administration across such other fields outside education as general government, business and industry, health, and social work. (Mediating)

8. The preparation program shall devote as much attention to helping students become sensitive to emerging role expectations and to training them for emerging roles as to training them for existing roles. (Input)

9. The preparation program shall include continuous programs of research focused on the preparation program itself. Therefore, the program should always include some experimental elements paralleling regular elements, with systematic provision being made for the evaluation of these experimental elements. (Input, output)

10. The preparation program shall include the assembling and training of administrative teams to constitute the core of an administrative staff for an educational institution. (Input)

11. The preparation program shall prepare students for leadership in a pluralistic society by providing each student at least one intensive experience in a culture or subculture markedly different from the culture in which he was reared. (Mediating)

12. The preparation program shall develop in potential higher level administrators the skills of community-societal leadership that will prepare them to share with administrators from other fields in broad kinds of socio-economic-political leadership involving other fields of activity, as well as education. Students shall have an opportunity to share in efforts to change the social system through the electoral and legislative process. (Mediating)

13. The preparation program shall prepare administrators for uncertainty and discontinuity. (Input)

14. The preparation program shall provide for an analysis of input-output cost-benefit relationships to determine the appropriate nature and quantity of inputs to optimize the nature and quantity of outputs. (Input, output)

Organization

1. The preparation program shall be provided within an organization marked more by collegial than by hierarchical relationships. (Mediating)

2. The preparation program shall show evidence of flexibility of organizational structure to meet new needs and conditions. There have been significant shifts in the organizational structure within the past five years. (Mediating)

3. The preparation program shall give students the opportunity to observe and participate in periodic changes in organizational structure within the department, school, university, and/or other unit of organization. For instance, there should be experiments with "adaptive, rapidly changing, temporary systems." (Mediating)

4. The preparation program shall give opportunity for the application of organizational theory to the immediate and long-range problems of the program and of the institution and of other educational programs and institutions. (Input)

5. The preparation program shall constitute an open instructional subsystem linked to a group of other related subsystems. These shall include other subsystems within the parent university and possibly within other universities, one or more public school systems or units within public school systems, one or more private school systems, one or more marginal emerging educational institutions (of which a 1970 illustration would have been the Harlem Preparatory Academy or the New York Urban League's Street Academies, both in New York City), one or more education industry components, (perhaps a "performance contractor"), and one or more professional management associations. The university shall coordinate the relationships with the other subsystems. In addition, the preparation program shall have a variety of other relationships with professional and nonprofessional agencies, such as public and nonpublic schools; professional associations and unions; other programs of administrative training; research and development centers and institutes; governmental and nongovernmental local community agencies; industry; state, regional, and federal governmental agencies; and international educational and noneducational agencies. Included should

be participation in programs, meetings, committees, and study teams. (Input, mediating)

6. The preparation program shall provide joint training of educational administrators with at least one other group of administrators in such fields as general government, health, social work, or business and industry. (Input)

7. The preparation program shall give students the opportunity to share as equals with faculty members and administrators in the decisionmaking and evaluation pertaining to departmental or institutional purposes, organization, program, admissions, facilities, and funding.

8. The preparation program shall give students experience in functioning in a variety of temporary, short-term task forces operating within or outside the permanent organizational structure of the preparation program. (Mediating)

Program

1. The preparation program shall provide a planned program of socialization to the profession. This shall be a socialization designed not to make the individuals satisfied with the status quo, but dissatisfied with what is happening and motivated to improve existing conditions. (Mediating)

2. The preparation program shall give evidence of continuous change in the program through the frequent establishment, modification, and abandonment of courses and other units of learning experiences. (Input)

3. The preparation program shall provide individualized learning experiences to the extent of at least one-third of the entire program. No course shall be formally or subtlely required. (Mediating)

4. The preparation program shall provide distinctly identifiable, but not necessarily completely separated, programs for those planning to specialize as researchers, developers, disseminators, or practitioners in the field of administration. Programs for practitioners shall be further differentiated to provide for administration of educational programs in unique organizational settings. (Mediating)

5. The preparation program shall provide at least one major intensive experience as an alternative to the conventional doctoral dissertation, as known around 1970, and of equivalent intellectual challenge. (Mediating)

6. The preparation program shall include a variety of social interaction experiences in which students and faculty members can become acquainted informally. (Mediating)

7. The preparation program shall give special attention to the learning process, including the variety of ways in which humans learn at all ages and under many social conditions; the variety of ways in which teachers can motivate, stimulate, and facilitate learning; and the ways in which administrators can assist other members of an organization to learn the nature of organization, to learn the processes of administration, to learn more mature responses to authority, and to learn such organizational processes as goal-setting, decisionmaking, and conflict management. (Input, mediating)

8. The preparation program shall emphasize instructional excellence by giving special attention to the quality of instructional procedures and to the development and use of a wide variety of instructional materials. These materials should be prepared by both students and faculty members and should be tried out experimentally and systematically, with frequent revisions. (Input, mediating)

9. The preparation program shall provide first-hand knowledge of and experience with the latest instructional technology, including information-storage and retrieval systems, other uses of computers, television, and other audio-visual devices. (Mediating)

10. The preparation program shall provide career counseling and planning, including the possibility of dual or multiple careers in a lifetime. (Input)

11. The preparation program shall give students experience in using computers for instruction, administration, and research. (Input)

12. The preparation program shall give students training in complex decisionmaking processes, such as network analysis, (e.g., PERT and CPM), systems analysis, gaming, and operations research. (Mediating)

13. The preparation program shall give students knowledge and understanding of other agencies and means of education, such as museums, libraries, public recreation programs, and educational travel. Students shall be given experience in working with representatives of those other agencies and means of education. (Mediating)

14. The preparation program shall provide an opportunity for students to have an intensive experience as a member of an administrative team in a nonacademic, non-middle class situation, such as a narcotics rehabilitation program, a halfway house program for

former mental patients, a prison program, or a program for the amelioration of poverty conditions. (Mediating)

15. The preparation program shall provide opportunity for experience with teaching teams and other arrangements for differentiated staffing. (Mediating)

16. The preparation program shall give opportunities for the development and trial of organizational designs using fluid organizational structure, time-definite provisions for the establishment of certain positions, resource allocation responsiveness, and school unit differentiation within a school district structure. (Input)

17. The preparation program shall provide for "flying squads" of professors and students making themselves available to troubled schools to institute, help administer, and evaluate proposals for dealing with current educational problems. These experiences should also constitute opportunities for generating and testing hypotheses for the creation of new knowledge. (Input, mediating)

18. The preparation program shall give students and faculty members opportunities better to know themselves and their impact on a skill in relating to others through sensitivity training, psychiatric counseling, and other kinds of experiences. This and other social-psychological dimensions of the program (e.g., developing values and a sense of mission) shall be given equal weight with the cognitive aspects of the program. (Mediating)

19. The preparation program shall give opportunities for cross-cultural experiences, ranging in duration from about a month to about a year, either in the United States or abroad, providing for real-life interaction with individuals of varying cultural backgrounds and with kinds of formal organizations different from standard "establishment" organizations. (Mediating)

20. The preparation program shall give students experience in constructing alternative futures and assessing their educational consequences, in inventing future educational programs and educational roles. (Input)

21. The preparation program shall prepare administrators for uncertainty and discontinuity by confronting students with simulated system-break experiences such as the accidental death of a superintendent, the destruction by fire-bombing of a high school, a two-month teachers' strike, the defaulting of a municipality on its bonds, or the destruction of a community's water supply. (Mediating)

22. The preparation program shall include a one-year, full-time internship experience in at least two of the following: an established

educational organization, a noneducational government agency (such as a court, welfare agency, or law enforcement agency), a private social service organization, or an organization in a foreign country. The internship in the established educational organization shall give at least some students experience at each of the levels of education from nursery school through higher education and adult education. (Mediating)

23. The preparation program shall incorporate subprograms for persons in client and supporting systems, such as policy-making boards, community leaders, and special interest groups. (Mediating)

Faculty

1. The preparation program shall have a faculty made up of specialists in the major social and behavioral sciences and in the humanities and of interdisciplinary generalists, as well as of specialists in educational administration. At least some of the specialists in educational administration should have had experience at local, state, and national levels of education and other governmental activity. The faculty should be large and diverse enough to justify and demonstrate extensive role differentiation and specialization. For instance, there should be clear differentiation among researchers, developers, and disseminators. (Input)

2. The preparation program shall have a faculty recruited from a variety of institutional and occupational backgrounds. (Input)

3. The preparation program faculty shall include representatives of minority groups in at least as great a proportion as the groups represent in the elementary-secondary school populations of that region of the country. (Input)

4. The preparation program shall show a concern for the opportunity of faculty members to live rich, varied lives, as well as to be professionally productive. The program shall show a recognition of personal needs of faculty members and other employees as equal in importance to the achievement of the purposes of the institution. (Input)

5. The preparation program shall provide a work load for faculty members which leaves them time and energy to be creative people. (Input)

6. The preparation program shall provide administrative personnel in the program with sufficient assistance to prevent their becoming submerged in detailed managerial tasks. (Input)

7. The preparation program shall provide a reward system recognizing varied faculty contributions to the production, development, dissemination, and application of knowledge. (Output)

8. The preparation program shall provide incentives, opportunities, and experiences for the continuing professional development of all faculty members to qualify them to contribute to emerging program demands. This should include a cycle of quadrennial (not sabbatical) exchanges between professors and practitioners, and between professors in this program and professors in other kinds of administrative preparation programs. Upon their return to campus, professors shall be requested to evaluate existing program elements and to provide new program inputs. (Input)

9. The preparation program shall provide a plan of compensation for the faculty commensurate with that provided those in the practice of administration and in other fields of administrative training. (Input)

10. The preparation program shall provide for a system of monitoring faculty performance and productivity in contributing to the objectives of the program. Particular attention should be given to the quality of instruction offered by the faculty. Video tapes of actual instruction in progress will be used as one means of analyzing quality of teaching. The creation and effective use of a variety of instructional aids will be a criterion of the quality of instruction. This monitoring of faculty performance and productivity will be part of a system of rewards in which compensation will be related to quality of performance. (Output)

Students

1. The preparation program shall be a part of a nationally coordinated system of student recruitment and selection in which the number of students admitted to doctoral programs, and even lower levels of training, is related to estimates of future likely vacancies for educational administrators in local, state, regional, and national agencies of education. (Input)

2. The preparation program shall recruit students from a variety of regions and cultural backgrounds who show the best potential for meeting the goals accepted by the faculty. (Input)

3. The preparation program shall incorporate experimental student selection procedures and make continuous evaluation of these procedures. (Input)

4. The preparation program shall have differentiated programs for full-time and part-time students. (Mediating)

5. The preparation program shall recognize a variety of career patterns, including the possibility of dual and multiple careers in a single lifetime. This should include admission of students to the program who have reached the midcareer point in other occupational fields. (Input)

6. The preparation program shall test applicants for divergent versus convergent thinking, open versus closed mindedness, and other elements of creativity, and give admissions preference to those whose scores show higher creativity. (Input)

7. The preparation program shall include a continuous evaluation of the performance and potential of students. There shall be evidence that some students have been counseled out of the program at various points in their experience in it. A student's record should include performance appraisals and test scores on such dimensions as conflict tolerance, culture shock, and future shock. These evaluative data shall be used in modifying the program. (Output, input)

Alumni

1. The preparation program shall provide for systematic follow-up of its graduates periodically to assess their career development, administrative style, and other aspects of administrative performance. These data shall be incorporated in a suitable record for each alumnus. They shall also be analyzed and used as feedback data for the purpose of assessing program purposes and their achievement, criteria of admission and completion, specific program elements, and cost-benefit aspects of the program. (Output)

2. The preparation program shall make use of alumni in planning and evaluating the program and shall use them as resource consultants to the students in the program. (Input)

Facilities

1. The preparation program shall have facilities permitting the full use of a wide range of relevant technologies and methodologies, including computers, the latest audio-visual devices, lasers, and the like. (Input)

2. The preparation program shall be housed as an integrated unit where appropriate space is provided for full-time and part-time students, faculty members, and various consultants and where there will be suitable laboratory space and social rooms. (Input)

3. The preparation program shall provide for facilities outside the university, such as a jet plane for frequent use of student travel groups. (Input)

Funds

1. The preparation program shall have sufficient financial support that it will not be unreasonably constrained by a lack of funds. Yet the program should always be generating more fiscal demands than can be met at any one time. (Input)

2. The preparation program shall provide fellowships and assistantships in sufficient number and of a sufficient financial value to support a substantial corps of full-time students. There shall also be support for a range of independent and group program costs for students, such as internships, travel, and special materials. (Input)

3. The preparation program shall make use of an appropriate form of planning-programming-budgeting system relating program costs to program purposes in order to determine the most effective use of existing funds and justify the possible need for additional funds. Such a process should also help to generate knowledge sufficient to develop a theory for the rational acquisition and allocation of economic resources to fund the program. (Output, input)

SOME GENERAL PROCEDURES FOR
FUTURIST PROGRAM PLANNING

In the introduction to this chapter, we pointed out the cyclical evolution in futurist program planning from the general to the particular. We noted the stages in that evolution proceeding from the description of a projected future environment, to criteria guiding program development, to program plans, and then to action pointed to the future either to accommodate to it or to modify it. Most of this book has been confined to the first two of these stages. In this concluding section we can supplement the "guidelines for the application of futurism in education," set forth in Chapter 1, to conclude the book with a discussion of some general procedures for futurist program planning. It will help to be as specific as possible. Therefore, we shall direct these recommendations to a "futurist program planning task force" such as might be established by a school district, private school, college, university, or other educational agency.

1. The board of education or board of trustees or head administrator should appoint the task force and set the objectives for it. This will give the project the status it deserves and needs. Program development, all too often, is accorded a relatively low priority, especially in higher education. The reward system tends to favor research, writing, and even teaching above program development.

This is partly because so much program development, in elementary and secondary education as well as in higher education, has been abortive; either the necessary committee work has been carried out halfheartedly or the recommendations of the committee have had little impact on the instructional program. Top level stimulation and support are needed, therefore, to overcome the negative image that program development activity has acquired and to give the work of a futurist program planning task force the importance it should have.

2. The futurist program planning should be based on an assumption of uncertainty. This is in contrast to the assumption of stability that has underlain so much long-range planning. So often in the past it has seemed as if long-range plans were based either on things remaining essentially as they were or on growth and change proceeding in a smooth projection. If a more careful study of history could not dispel this notion, futurism should, for the methods of futurism reject surprise-free projections and have a built in allowance for uncertainty and discontinuity. This same allowance, correspondingly, should be built into the plans emanating from the proposed task force. One way this can be done is to identify certain contingency points in a long-range plan, points where there would be branching in the sequence of decisionmaking, with alternative courses of action laid out at each fork in the road. As with the illustrations of "system breaks" given in Chapter 2, these contingency points might be either positive or negative. Thus, for a college or university a system break might be a substantial bequest left by a prominent alumnus or, in similar fiscal terms for a school district, a substantial revenue increase resulting from the passage of a federal revenue-sharing plan. Negatively, it could be a natural calamity, such as the severe earthquake in Los Angeles County in early 1971 or a disastrous flood or fire. Less sudden discontinuity would be the adoption by a school district of a system of differentiated staffing or the decision of a college to enter a "university without walls" program. The challenge of the task force is to develop long-range plans in which the institution will be at home with uncertainty.

3. Appropriate to our "temporary" society with its adaptive, rapidly changing, temporary systems, appointment to the task force should be, ideally, a full-time rather than a part-time assignment. A work pattern marked by meetings after school, after class, at the end of the day, in evenings, or on weekends is neither consistent with the status the work of the task force merits nor with the productivity expected of it. At least those members of the task force who are

under some degree of control by the institution, such as teachers or professors, administrators, and students, should be relieved of all or of a major part of their regular responsibilities in order to devote all or most of their working time to the objectives of the task force.

4. The most effective futurist program planning will make use of specific short-term plans coupled to broad long-range plans. For example, in 1967 a team of professors developed a long-range plan for a 15,000-pupil suburban school district in one of the outer rings of the New York Metropolitan Area.[2] In a chapter on "Strategies for Educational Planning and Change" in that report, the survey team recommended that a long-range planning committee be appointed every three years to function for a semester or, at most, a year. Its first task would be to advance the original 15-year plan by another three years, taking account of new developments and updating the projections. Its second task would be to make a new three-year, specific, short-term plan, laying out the details of program objectives, program content, staffing needed, facilities needed, and financing. A plan such as this is recommended in connection with the futurist program planning task force being proposed here. In effect, the long-range plan charts the course while the short-term plan gives the day-to-day operating details.

5. The task force should make use not only of the conventional techniques and tools of research and planning, but also of appropriate ones among the special techniques and tools of research in futurism. As mentioned in Chapter 2, these would include the Delphi technique and cross-impact analysis, various kinds of trend extrapolation and other types of forecasting, dynamic modeling, simulation/gaming, expert position papers, and, especially, scenario building. Weaver stresses the use of the Delphi technique as a planning tool in investigating the priorities held by various members of an organization.[3] The Delphi technique would thus be an effective way to involve students, faculty members, administrators, and laymen in certain aspects of the work of the task force. Likewise, others outside the membership of the task force can be involved in its work by being invited to try their hands at the development of alternative futures and their related scenarios.

6. The task force should keep in mind the interaction between their institution as a system and other systems, subsystems and suprasystems. Thus, the future development of a school district will be affected by the development of its community, region, and state. Likewise, a school within a university is obviously affected by the development of its component divisions and departments. There is

clearly a limit to how far the futurist program planning can go in making projections for coordinate systems and for suprasystems. Some of those future conditions simply have to be left as uncertainties. Another tack, however, is to realize that in some instances it will become important for the task force to propose political action bringing to bear the institution's influence or political power on other systems, including legislative bodies, in order to effect certain changes in the other systems or to secure desired legislation. Our clear intent is to emphasize the need for an increasing political role for educational institutions in taking appropriate action to influence their own educational and societal environment. This is simply a logical result of one of futurism's main reasons for being: proaction to help shape or influence the future rather than simple reaction.

Conclusion

Educational futurism is a new field of specialization, and no one can claim any great degree of expertise in the specialization yet. But it is an area of high promise and great potential significance for education, as well as for other fields. New knowledge must be developed through the use of new and improved techniques of research and planning. In this book we have tried to sketch something of the nature of futurism; some of the possibilities for education in about 1985, including its governance, organization, and administration; and some of the procedures that can be used in applying futurist planning to specific institutions in the field of education.

The future has always been and always will be the universal frontier. Futurism provides the means for probing that frontier so that we can not only prepare for what lies ahead but also try to determine the shape of things to come. Futurism offers intoxicating possibilities tempered by sobering responsibilities.

FOOTNOTES

1. Joseph J. Schwab, "The Professorship in Educational Administration: Theory—Art—Practice," in *The Professorship in Educational Administration*, eds. Donald J. Willower and Jack Culbertson (Columbus, Ohio: University Council for Educational Administration, 1964).

2. Richard C. Lonsdale, director and ed., *A Fifteen-Year Educational Projection, 1967-82: A Long-Range Plan for the Ramapo Central School District No. 2, Spring Valley, Rockland County, New York* (Center for Field Research and School Service, School of Education, New York University, December 1967).

3. W. Timothy Weaver, "The Delphi Forecasting Method," *Phi Delta Kappan* 52 (January 1971): 267-272.

Appendix: Essential Reading for the Future of Education

CONTENTS

I. INTRODUCTION

This selected bibliography represents a very tentative and subjective judgment of the literature most relevant to the future of American education. It covers an immense area, including futures methodology, trends, possible developments, and alternative futures that are being increasingly prescribed from all quarters. To define the scope in four very basic questions: (a) How and why do we look at the future? (b) What is happening now? (c) What might happen? (d) What ought to happen?

Such a scope may seem incredibly broad to one who is accustomed to a specialist's niche. But as our society becomes more complex, and linkages more diverse, it becomes conceptually necessary to develop holistic frameworks. This is especially so for the rapidly emerging field of educational policy research, and this bibliography attempts to sketch broadly the parameters of the field, not only for the specialists and generalists within the field, but for the diverse "outsiders" who, hopefully, will be aided in policymaking, as well as research and teaching.

The "cream" presented here is part of a larger effort (see item 197) to upgrade previous work,* with the following rationale: Simple listing of titles can be helpful, and doubly so if well-categorized. A line or two of explanatory annotation can perhaps double the value, and a paragraph of intelligent annotation can double the value once more. The value is perhaps doubled again if the annotation is critical, pointing out virtues and faults of the document at hand.

The exploration of the literature has thus proceeded with the ideal of critical annotation in mind. But the product falls considerably short of this ideal: many of the critical comments are superficial, and it has often been the case that there has been no capacity to make any comment. Even the "objective" annotations vary in length and quality, and it has occasionally been necessary to paraphrase reviews or cite publisher's advertisements as a temporary annotation.

It is felt that an information system such as this is particularly suited to a broad and rapidly emerging area of critical concern, where

---

*Michael Marien, *Shaping the Future of American Education: A Preliminary Annotated Bibliography of Educational and General Futures* (Syracuse: Educational Policy Research Center, May 1969; Supplement, August 1969 [539 items total]); *Essential Reading for the Future of Education* (Syracuse: EPRC, September 1970 [146 items]).

knowledge must be diffused widely and quickly. It is assumed that every reader of this bibliography is inundated by the information explosion. The necessary response to this system overload is to establish priorities and to develop holistic frameworks so that more information can be meaningfully accommodated. This selected bibliography of 200 items attempts to suggest priorities and to point out the holistic literature that may facilitate a broader understanding. The irony, of course, is that this bibliography contributes to information overload, not only as another document to read, but through its urging of still more reading.

For the reader who is new to this entire realm, several general books are especially recommended: Michael (item 1), Brzezinski (21), McHale (24), Ferkiss (36), Toffler (37), Bennis and Slater (38), Drucker (39), Mead (78), and Coombs (81). Although there is an overlap, each of these syntheses provides a distinctive approach to explaining what is happening in our society. There is an important similarity to the images of The Unprepared Society, Technetronic Society, Planetary Society, Technological Man Super-Industrial Society, The Temporary Society, The Age of Discontinuity, Pre-Figurative Culture, and The World Educational Crisis proposed respectively by each of the authors. Indeed, nearly 40% of this bibliography is devoted to works that do not deal solely (if at all) with education, for it is increasingly necessary to understand the societal context in order to understand the future of education.

Cautions

Although a selected transdisciplinary bibliography may be appealing, it is essential that the limitations to this effort be kept in mind. This is strictly a one-man project, with all the advantages and drawbacks that such an effort entails. The cautions should therefore be made explicit:

1. *Ignorance.* Although there is an awareness of about 1400 documents that are considered to be relevant, the universe has by no means been covered, especially with respect to journal articles.

2. *Inconsistency.* The literature has been considered in varying degrees, from a thorough reading, to a quick skimming, to a glance at the table of contents or the book jacket, to a simple knowledge that an item exists. Moreover, a document read a year ago may not be judged in the same light as one read at the present. Consequently, the full bibliography may contain many items that, if fully considered, would merit promotion to a "selected" status, perhaps replacing some of the literature that is recommended.

3. *Bias.* Any selection exhibits a bias, whether or not one wishes to admit it. There is, of course, a cultural bias, with most items written by U.S. authors for U.S. audiences. In general, a preference has been shown here for competent but imaginative scholarship, as opposed to timid but "respectable" works that are divorced from what is considered as emerging realities. If this particular selection is found to be slanted, it might stimulate counter-bibliographies.

4. *Obsolescence.* In that about 60% of this selected bibliography involves items published in 1969-1971 (with more than 90% published between 1967 and 1971), there can be little doubt that there is a considerable amount of "essential reading" that is presently in galley proofs or typewriter carriages. If subsequent bibliographies are issued, say on an annual basis, one can anticipate that one-fourth to one-third of the items will be new publications. If such a selected bibliography can be taken as a rough approximation of the field of educational futures research, then it must be concluded that the rate of knowledge turnover in this field is considerably higher than elsewhere. (In engineering, for example, it is commonly stated that 50% of the relevant knowledge becomes obsolete over the period of a decade.)

Despite these cautions, a start must be made. As pointed out by Drucker (item 40) and Platt (item 148), we are entering an era in which priorities in knowledge must be established, not only because of the ever-growing quantity, but even more so because of pervasive social problems requiring knowledge for their solution. It is hoped that this selected bibliography will stimulate the reader's thinking about policy priorities, as well as priorities in research and teaching. Indeed, one might confront the painful question as to whether this literature (or any such approximation of "essential reading") enters the curriculum of schools and colleges in any manner. If not, in an age when many students are flailing about for "relevance," can there be little wonder that many resort to drugs, disruption, and dropping out?

The Classification of Items

The citations are *not arranged alphabetically,* for such classification is considered to be mechanical. Its only benefit—that of convenience—is easily provided for by the author index supplied here. Rather, there has been an attempt at "heuristic juxtaposition," arranging items so that there is some logical flow or clashing contrast, so that a group of, say, five or six documents may be compared together. Although this has been attempted, there are many cases where there is little or no relationship, and the user is therefore cautioned against reading too much meaning into the arrangement, which in some cases is arbitrary. In general, the attempt has been to lead from the broad to the narrow, and the more valuable to the less valuable.

The categories have attempted to distinguish between methodology, trends, descriptive futures, and prescriptive futures or policy proposals. Although the literature has been placed in these categories, there is nevertheless a considerable overlap, and it is not uncommon to find a book discussing methodology, supplying evidence of trends, extrapolating into the future or suggesting several possible futures, and making a judgment as to what the future *ought* to be like (*e.g.,* Johnson, item 106). Indeed, many ostensibly descriptive futures are to some degree an "objective" mask for the future that is preferred by the author. Items have been classified under the category that they most strongly suggest, although a more thorough analysis could warrant a reclassification, *e.g.,* from prescriptive to descriptive. The literature of trends and descriptive futures has been found to be similar enough to warrant a joint category, as distinguished from two separate categories in the May 1969 bibliography.

II. SELECTED BIBLIOGRAPHY

A. Methodology

1. *Background to Contemporary Futures Studies*

1. MICHAEL, Donald N. *The Unprepared Society: Planning for a Precarious Future.* Foreword by Ward Madden. The John Dewey Society Lecture—No. Ten. N.Y.: Basic Books, 1968. 132 pp. $4.95.
   An excellent introduction to explaining the need for looking at the future, who does it, how it is done, and problems encountered. The final chapter, "Some Challenges for Educators," discusses implications for education, *e.g.,* "We must educate so people can cope efficiently, imaginatively, and perceptively with information overload." (p. 108)
2. DROR, Yehezkel. *Public Policy-Making Re-examined.* San Francisco: Chandler, 1968. 370 pp.

An authoritative work discussing contemporary policy making and proposing an optimal model characterized by rational and extrarational components. See Chapter 17, "Changes Needed in Knowledge" (and especially notes on policy science, pp. 240-245); also discussion in Chapter 19 on organizations for policy analysis. Excellent biographic essay, pp. 327-356.

3. MARTY, Martin E. *The Search for a Usable Future.* N.Y.: Harper & Row, 1969. 157 pp.

An eminent theologian reviews contemporary thinking among futurists and theologians, and argues "for an approach which retains the ambiguity of history and yet which motivates action and prevents paralysis" (p. 73)—a future with hope. "The sense of a useless past . . . is not to take a nihilist's view of historical life but rather to point to the creative possibilities of the moment." (p. 12) The volume goes on to point out how various approaches to the future of man and society affect the actions of people.

4. ARMYTAGE, W.H.G. *Yesterday's Tomorrows: A Historical Survey of Future Societies.* Toronto: University of Toronto Press, 1968. 288 pp.

"The rise of . . . 'conflict models' of prediction out of what might otherwise be regarded as a welter of futuristic fantasies is the theme of this book. It tries to show how, out of the long process of preparatory daydreams, imagined encounters, wish-fulfillments, and compensatory projections, a constructive debate about tomorrow is emerging, providing us with operational models about what tomorrow could, or should be. This debate (dialogue is perhaps the more fashionable term) is increasingly becoming part of the modern self whereby man is enabled to maintain his equilibrium." (p. x) An excellent survey not only of utopian literature, but of modern scientific efforts. Although no attempt is made at an orderly bibliographic presentation, about 500 titles are mentioned in the notes (pp. 222-265), and several hundred additional titles are sprinkled throughout the text. (For a chronological listing of about 550 Utopian writings, see Miriam Strauss Weiss, *A Lively Corpse.* Cranbury, N.J.: A.S. Barnes, 1969.)

5. CUBBERLY, Ellwood P. *Changing Conceptions of Education.* Boston: Houghton-Mifflin, 1909. 70 pp.

This item is included to remind readers that attempts to adapt education to a changing society are not new.

After reviewing Changes in the Nature of our Life and Changes in the Conception of the School, Cubberly contends that "We are standing on the threshold of a new era in educational progress." (p. 52)

"To convey to the next generation the knowledge and accumulated experience of the past is not (the school's) only function. It must equally prepare the future citizen for the tomorrow of our complex life . . . There are many reasons for believing that this change is taking place rapidly at present . . ." (p. 54) Needless to say, the glowing optimism has proved to be unwarranted.

6. KILPATRICK, William Heard. *Education for a Changing Civilization.* Three Lectures Delivered on the Luther Laflin Kellogg Foundation at Rutgers University, 1926. N.Y.: Macmillan, 1936. 143 pp.

We must often remember that what appears to be new may not really be so. Even though conceived nearly half a century ago, these lectures by an eminent "Progressive" are in many respects not unlike the prescriptions advocated by today's reformers. (It is not that present writers have been influenced by Kilpatrick, but rather that an anticipation of change leads to similar educational prescriptions.)

Observing that "Our young people face too clearly an unknown future" (p. 41), and "Our youth no longer accept authoritarian morals" (p. 50), it is recommended that "We must free our children to think for themselves." Older education is seen as pretending that the future will be like the present, but "no longer can one generation bind the next to its solutions. On the other hand, our young people must learn such general and flexible techniques as promise best to serve them in that unknown future." (p. 85)

But rhetoric and reality become confused when it is asserted (similar to Cubberly) that "Our schools are already changing" (p. 89), based on scattered impressions of "less group precision and straight line marching," more individual movement, school as a place where "actual experiencing goes on" and the fact that "the better schools now favor student participation in school affairs." (p. 107) Does this all sound familiar?

2. *General Futures*

7. DE JOUVENEL, Bertrand. *The Art of Conjecture.* Translated from the French by Nikita Lary. N.Y.: Basic Books, 1967. 307

pp. (First published by Editions du Rocher in 1964.)
An authoritative discussion of "the customs of the mind in its commerce with the future," covering predictions, ways of conceiving the future, and quantitative predictions. The last chapter advocates "a surmising forum" as "a necessary response to a growing demand for forecasts."

8. JANTSCH, Erich. *Technological Forecasting in Perspective.* Paris: Organisation for Economic Co-Operation and Development (OECD), 1967. 401 pp.

Extensive discussion of a framework for technological forecasting and related techniques. Of even greater importance are the two annexes. Annex A lists "Technological Forecasting Activities in Non-Industrial Environments," including 17 forecasting institutes and consulting firms (13 American), military and national planning in various nations, and forerunner activities in look-out institutions (9 of 13 listed are American). Annex B contains an annotated bibliography of about 420 items divided into 14 categories. Despite comprehensiveness in the area of scientific and technological forecasting, there is no mention of writings on educational futures or of organizations listed having such a concern. (For a more current listing of American researchers, see McHale, item 200.)

9. DE BONO, Edward. *New Think: The Use of Lateral Thinking in the Generation of New Ideas.* N.Y. Basic Books, 1968. 156 pp. $5.95.

This slim and simply written volume is easily as important as any of the ponderous tomes on rational methodology, which de Bono characterizes as "vertical thinking" or digging the same hole deeper. "Lateral thinking is based on biological information processing principles which differ from the physical information processing principles of mathematics, logic, and computers." (p. 1-2) It is not a magic formula, but an attitude and habit of mind. It is not a substitute for vertical thinking, but a complementary process. It is not simply creative thinking, which often requires a talent for expression, for it is open to everyone interested in new ideas.

The principles of lateral thinking involve the recognition of dominating ideas, the deliberate search for alternative ways of looking at things (which is not considered to be natural), relaxing the rigid control of vertical thinking, and the use of chance. Many examples are given from the hard sciences and from stage magic, which "takes advantage of people who use high probability or vertical thinking." Although no examples are given as to lateral thinking about society, education, or the future, this book is nevertheless quite appropriate to such concerns. (Also see Edward de Bono, "Zigzag Thinking," *The Futurist,* IV:1, February 1970, pp. 29-31.)

10. WEAVER, W. Timothy. *The Delphi Method.* Syracuse: Educational Policy Research Center. Working Draft, June 1970. 160 pp. mimeo.

A three-part report with an extensive analysis of the experimental research that has proceeded and accompanied the development of the Delphi method, and its use as a device for technological forecasting and educational forecasting. Many reservations are made, and it is concluded that "Although Delphi was originally intended as a forecasting tool, its more promising educational application seems to be in the following areas: (a) a method for studying the process of thinking about the future, (b) a pedagogical tool which forces people to think about the future, and (c) a planning tool which may aid in probing priorities held by members and constituencies of an organization."

11. ROCHBERG, Richard, Theodore J. GORDON, and Olaf HELMER. *The Use of Cross-Impact Matrices for Forecasting and Planning.* Middletown, Conn.: Institute for the Future, IFF Report R-10, April 1970. 63 pp.

"A cross-impact matrix is an array consisting of a list of potential future developments and two kinds of data concerning these developments: first, the estimated probabilities that these developments will occur within some specified period in the future, and, second, estimates of the effect that the occurrence of any one of these events could be expected to have on the likelihood of occurrence of each of the others.

"In general, the data for such a matrix are obtained by collating expert opinions derived through the use of methods such as the Delphi technique. Such a matrix is analyzed in order to revise the estimated possibilities of occurrence of each development in light of the expected cross impacts of other events on the list, (and to) discover how a change in the probability of occurrence of one or more events (by virtue of a technological breakthrough, a social change, a policy decision) might be expected to change the probabilities of occurrence of other events on the list." (p. 1)

The possible benefits of such an approach are the prompting of meaningful questions, serving pedagogical purposes, comparing the plausibility of scenarios, providing a predictive device in areas in which exact causal relationships are extremely difficult to discern, and providing a method of simulating certain policy actions.

This technical report of ongoing methodological development will probably be of interest only to specialists in forecasting. (Also see items 44 and 45 concerning IFF applications of the Delphi technique.)

12. BAIER, Kurt and Nicholas RESCHER (eds.). *Values and the Future: The Impact of Technological Change on American Values.* N.Y.: The Free Press, 1969. 527 pp. Bib., pp. 472-512. 17 essays aimed "toward the discovery of ways of guiding social change in directions which are at the least not incompatible with the realization of our deepest values, and perhaps even helpful to it." (p. v) Some groundwork is laid for a new profession of "value impact forecasters," especially via methodological pieces by Rescher, Gordon, and Helmer. The other essays are largely focused on economics, and the editors readily confess the weakness of excluding views by anthropologists, sociologists, and psychologists. There are two bibliographies: the first lists 300 uncategorized items on technological progress and future-oriented studies; the second offers about 500 categorized items on theory of value.

13. U.S. Congress. House Committee on Science and Astronautics. *Technology: Processes of Assessment and Choice.* Report of the National Academy of Sciences. Washington: USGPO, July 1969. 163 pp. 75 cents.
"Technology Assessment" describes "what occurs when the likely consequences of a technological development are explored and evaluated. (The) objective is ... to foster a more constructive evolution of our technological order." (p. 3) This authoritative report includes chapters on existing processes of assessment and decision, formulation of objectives, problems and pitfalls, and approaches and recommendations. It is concluded that new assessment mechanisms are needed with a broader and less self-interested viewpoint. To this end, "the panel urges the creation of a constellation of organizations, with components located strategically within both political branches, that can create a focus and a forum for responsible technology-

assessment activities throughout government and the private
sector . . . such organizations must be separated scrupulously
from any reponsibility for promoting or regulating technological applications . . ." (p. 117)

14. U.S. Congress. House Committee on Science and Astronautics. *A
Study of Technology Assessment.* Report of the Committee on
Public Engineering Policy, National Academy of Engineering.
Washington: USGPO, July 1969. 208 pp. $1.25.
A summary of findings and commentary about the concept and
practice of technology and assessment, with three experiments
and an analysis of the methodology employed. Of particular
interest is the first experiment, Technology of Teaching Aids,
where alternative strategies of using ETV and CAI in higher
education and their impacts are explored. (pp. 37-76) Although
these experiments are preliminary, they indicate the scope and
direction of future efforts. It is concluded that technology
assessments are feasible, and that they can help to alert the
nation to future benefits and to future problems, if produced in
an environment free from political influence or predetermined
bias.

15. Educational Policy Research Center at Stanford. *Toward Master
Social Indicators.* Menlo Park, Calif.: Stanford Research Institute, Research Memorandum EPRC 6747-2, February 1969. 52
pp.
A discussion of social accounting, with particular emphasis on
deriving master indicators (critical and aggregative indicators in
hierarchical schema), relating indicators on individuals and
social systems, and attaining "a comprehensive system of
national social data capable of generating descriptive social
reporting, projective social trending, and predictive social
accounting." (p. 46)

3. *Educational Futures*

16. ZIEGLER, Warren L., with the assistance of Michael MARIEN.
*An Approach to the Futures-Perspective in American Educa-
tion.* Syracuse: Educational Policy Research Center, May 1970.
103 pp.
A synthesis of the attempts to define alternative educational
futures in the U.S., discussing the idea itself and the various
methodologies in the macrosystem context of the educating
domain, or "the education complex" (which includes the

"periphery" of adult education, suppliers to educating institutions, and organized beneficiaries—especially students). Five planning models are discussed: the future-as-the present, the future-as-an-extrapolation-of-the-past, the single alternative future, the technological future, and the comprehensive future. Problems in the polity, in policy-formulation, and in planning are discussed, and the document is concluded with two critiques by outsiders.

17. HIRSCH, Werner Z. and Colleagues. *Inventing Education for the Future.* San Francisco: Chandler Publishing Co., 1967. 353 pp. 19 articles arising from the 1965-66 Educational Innovations Seminar at UCLA. Largely concerned with methodology of planning and future-casting, and methods of introducing change.

18. FURSE, Bernarr and Lyle O. WRIGHT (eds.). *Comprehensive Planning in State Education Agencies: A 7-State Project.* Salt Lake City: Utah State Board of Education, 1969. A compendium of reports from six states [Utah, Colorado, Texas, Iowa, West Virginia, Connecticut] and Puerto Rico, as developed under Section 505 of Title V, E.S.E.A.

19. MAYHEW, Lewis B. *Long Range Planning for Higher Education.* Studies in the Future of Higher Education, Report No. 3. N.Y.: Academy for Educational Development, May 1969. 221 pp. An authoritative assessment of statewide coordination systems for higher education and resultant master plans, voluntary coordination, and long range planning of individual institutions. "Only 10 states have no master plans, higher education studies with the attributes of a master plan, or definite activities designed to result either in a master plan or some form of coordinating agency." (p. 1) But, although "the movement towards planning seems inexorable" (p. 1), of the ten non-planning states, "all seem unlikely, for a wide variety of reasons, to produce master plans." (p. 101) There is a great similarity among the states that plan and the unquestioned assumptions that plans are based on. Mayhew aptly questions a number of these assumptions, but not in terms of alternative future states of society. Rather, in his final chapter on "The Future of American Higher Education," "the outlines of American society for 1980 are reasonably clear." (p. 172) Clarity is provided by extrapolation of various demographic trends, and a scenario of relatively little change in higher education.

1. *General*

a. Global Overviews

20. SNOW, C. P. *The State of Siege.* The John Findley Green Foundation Lecture, Westminster College, November 1968. N.Y.: Charles Scribner's Sons, 1969. 50 pp.

This mini-book provides an excellent (albeit disturbing) introduction to future-study through a consciously pessimistic overview that juxtaposes the present world-wide malaise ("We are behaving as though we were in a state of siege") with critical future problems of population growth and famine. Although serious local famines will occur, a large-scale famine will not appear before 1980—but a major catastrophe is expected before the end of the century. To avoid this, population restriction and large-scale aid from the developed nations is required, but the eventuality of either is doubted. "To stint ourselves to avoid a disaster in twenty years—what body of people would even do it? Right." (p. 38) Three scenarios are offered, along with an assessment of their probable occurrence.

21. BRZEZINSKI, Zbigniew. *Between Two Ages: America's Role in the Technetronic Era.* N.Y.: Viking Press, 1970. 334 pp. $7.95. A broad perspective of global trends by a leading scholar of international relations. The U.S. is seen as the "principal disseminator of the technetronic revolution" (p. 24) and as "a society that is both a social pioneer and a guinea pig for mankind." (p. xv) ("Technetronic" has been coined by the author to connote the pervasive influence of technology and electronics.) Under these unprecedented conditions, there is an "age of volatile belief," leading to a worldwide condition of crumbling religions and ideologies. The Soviet Union is seen as steeped in "dull social and political orthodoxy," and, among five alternative paths for Soviet development (p. 164), the most probable short-term outcome is viewed as a balance between oligarchic petrification and technological adaptation. America is left to lead the way, despite problems with the New Left ("an essentially negative and obsolescent force" —p. 231) and doctrinaire liberals, and the future is optimistically seen as a combination of more social planning, participatory pluralism, rational humanism, and a community of the developed nations.

The distinguishing feature of "The Third American Revolution" that is creating three Americas in one (technetronic, industrial, and pre-industrial) is that it "simultaneously maximizes America's potential as it unmasks its obsolescence." Unfortunately, Brzezinski is overly preoccupied with "The New Left Reaction" and "The Crisis of Liberalism" (each meriting a full chapter), while failing to seriously address the problems of American obsolescence (which are teasingly mentioned in passing throughout the volume). Despite such imbalance, this volume should be important.

22. KAHN, Herman and Anthony J. WIENER. *The Year 2000: A Framework for Speculation on the Next Thirty-Three Years.* N.Y.: Macmillan, 1967. 431 pp.

A widely known and respected volume—perhaps inordinately so, considering the focus on international politics and the possibilities of nuclear war, with little or no mention of ecology, communications, transportation, education, and the global economy. Nevertheless, it is a modern classic (for the present, at least). Especially see the discussion of "The Basic, Long-Term Multifold Trend" (pp. 39-64), various scenarios, and the excellent final chapter on "Policy Research and Social Change."

23. LUNDBERG, Ferdinand. *The Coming World Transformation.* Garden City, N.Y.: Doubleday, 1963. 395 pp.

A broad and sophisticated assessment of basic social trends, in many instances seen within the span of the next 150 years. The second chapter provides a good history of future study, and the third chapter discusses various aspects "toward a general theory of social prediction." Major attention is given to population, economics, government, and education, with the final chapter paying briefer attention to the prospects of marriage and the family, the city, recreation, religion, medicine, the sciences, the judiciary, and the future of prognostics (which is seen as practically certain to become a regular university discipline).

The most noteworthy attribute of this overview is the major attention that is paid to learning needs and brainpower as a matter of national survival, so much so that a meritocracy is seen, with the 21st century as "the era of the savant," and continuing adult higher education for the elite as the largest segment of the educating system. This "entirely new mentally different governing class" will be selected by IQ (a measure that is disputed at present). "The New Upper Labor Force" (pp. 256-264) discusses trends in various specialties.

Western government will become a gigantic social service institution, and in the U.S., government will be completely centered
in the national capital. "The pressure of overpopulation against
resources in the backward countries makes it certain that the
prospects for the spread of liberal government in the world are
extremely dark." (p. 119)

24. McHALE, John. *The Future of the Future.* N.Y.: George
    Braziller, 1969. 322 pp. $7.95.

    A wide-ranging overview aided by scores of charts and photo-
    graphs, with particular emphasis on ecology, technology, and
    planetary resources. Chapter 1 provides a good summation of
    future-study in the context of a transition toward a world-man
    image, and Chapter 5 continues with a discussion of individual
    futurists and organizations studying the future (a continuing
    interest of McHale). The final chapter discusses various aspects
    of the emerging planetary society, concluding that "we must
    understand and cooperate on a truly global scale, or we perish."
    (p. 300)

25. PECCEI, Aurelio. *The Chasm Ahead.* N.Y.: Macmillan, 1969.
    297 pp.

    An Italian industrial manager lucidly assesses the macro-
    problems of our time with particular emphasis on the growing
    cleavage across the Atlantic brought on by the technological
    gap. "The gap, in effect, is between the GM age and the IBM
    age." (p. 64) Although Americans criticize their education
    system, in world perspective it is seen as far ahead: "a solid case
    can be made for the claim that education supports the very
    underpinnings of the technological gap of the future." (p. 50)
    To facilitate "Global Dimensions to Our Thinking," a New
    Approach called Project 69 is proposed to serve as "a multi-
    nationally sponsored feasibility study on systematic, long-term
    planning of world scope." (p. 219)

26. WAGER, W. Warren. *The City of Man: Prophecies of a World
    Civilization in Twentieth-Century Thought.* Boston: Houghton-
    Mifflin, 1963. 310 pp. Bib., pp. 293-302.

    A comprehensive, scholarly, and highly readable "biography" of
    the vision of cosmopolis throughout history, as it has appeared
    in the East and West, in ancient Greece and Rome, in the
    Middle Ages, and in the present. Prophetic thinkers using
    various approaches are analyzed: the biological approach of
    Huxley and Teilhard de Chardin, the historical approach of
    Toynbee and Sorokin, and the "lines and spirals" approach of

Hocking, Jaspers, Mumford, and Kahler. In contrast to these independent thinkers, various doctrinaire views are explored. The prospects of synthesis in philosophy, religion, knowledge, government, culture, and economics are dealt with in separate chapters, with a brief consideration in the final chapters of what might happen after a world civilization is attained. Annotated bibliography of about 100 "recent books on world order."

27. JUNGK, Robert and Johan GALTUNG (eds.). *Mankind 2000.* Oslo: Universitetsforlaget; London: Allen & Unwin, 1969. 368 pp. $14.90.

Papers presented at the First International Future Research Conference, Oslo, 1967. The first array of writings from the international "invisible college" of professional futurists. The second IFRC was held in Kyoto, Japan in April 1970. The 65 English language papers (to be subsequently published) may be ordered separately at 50 cents each, or $31.50 + $4.00 postage from IFRC, Kyoto International Conference Hall, Takara-Ike, Sakyo-Ku, Kyoto.

28. FULLER, R. Buckminster. *Utopia or Oblivion? The Prospects for Humanity.* N.Y.: Bantam Books, Matrix Editions, December 1969. 363 pp. $1.25.

Twelve papers based on talks or articles prepared over the past several years, providing a good overview of Fuller's thought. Especially see instructions for The World Game, and the explanation of the 14 dominate concepts unique to Fuller's philosophy: universe, humanity, children, teleology, reform the environment (rather than man), general systems theory, industrialization, design science, world service industries, ephemeralization and invisible commonwealth, prime design initiative, self-disciplines, comprehensive coordination, and world community and sub-communities of world man. (pp. 309-342) In the Epilogue written for this book there is a good summation of Fuller's wildest ideas: two-mile high tower habitations, tetrahedronal floating cities, 10,000 passenger aircraft, domed-over cities, sky-floating geodesic spheres, and mobile habitats.

In summation, "The comprehensive introduction of automation everywhere around the earth will free man from being an automaton and will generate so fast a mastery and multiplication of energy wealth by humanity that we will be able to support all of humanity in ever greater physical and economic success anywhere around his little spaceship Earth. . . . My intuitions foresee (man's) success despite his negative inertias. This means things are going to move fast." (pp. 362-363)

Another recent book by Fuller, *Operating Manual for Spaceship Earth* (Pocket Books, November 1970. 127 pp. $1.25) is hardly a manual but possibly a preface to one.

29. STULMAN, Julius. *Climbing to Mankind Solutions*. N.Y.: World Institute Council (777 UN Plaza), *Fields Within Fields . . . Within Fields,* 1:3, 1968. 120 pp. $1.00.

A one-man periodical promulgating globalism and the integration of knowledge. A pot-pourri of imaginative ideas, including proposals for an Executive Brain Center, Cargo City (a city within a city to enhance distribution), and Urban Distribution Satellites. The hospital of the future is advocated as a brain center rather than a bed center, and "the medical student should be goal-oriented with the attitude that everything he has been taught is to be considered already antiquated by the time he receives it." (p. 93)

"Only through a totally new method of approach such as that offered by the World Institute which maximizes man's knowledge in a constant flow, cross-catalytically across all the disciplines, breaking it down more nearly to underlying principles, and new common denominators, ultimately we believe to pulsing fields, in systems, in the 'methodology of pattern,' can he hope to cope adequately with his problems." (p. 17)

Also see an inspiring anthology edited by Stulman, *Man's Emergent Evolution* (*Fields Within Fields . . .* 3:1, 1970); especially "Alternate Futures and Habitability" by Willis W. Harman and "Towards a Humanistic Biology" by Abraham H. Maslow.

b. National Overviews

30. U.S. Department of Health, Education, and Welfare. *Toward a Social Report*. Washington: USGPO, 1969. 101 pp. 55 cents.

The first attempt by the federal government to systematically measure the social well-being of the U.S. and an important preliminary step toward a regular system of social reporting. Seven areas have been selected for initial study with the aid of existing data: health and illness, social mobility, physical environment, income and poverty, public order and safety, participation and alienation, and learning, science, and art. In the latter category, it is tentatively concluded (on the basis of limited data) that children are learning more than in the past, but that we could do much better. It is pointed out that *The Digest of Educational Statistics* "has virtually no information on how much children have learned" (the National Assessment of Educational Progress may soon supply some data to this end). A concluding appendix discusses "How can we do better social reporting in the future?" with comments on the deficiencies of existing statistics, the need for new social indicators, and the development of policy accounts (or meaningful integrations of social indicators).

31. GROSS, Bertram M. (ed.). *Social Intelligence for America's Future: Explorations in Societal Problems.* Boston: Allyn and Bacon, Inc., 1969.

A collection of authoritative articles on social indicators and the need for additional indicators. This volume is the hard cover marriage of the two volumes of *The Annals of the American Academy of Political and Social Science* entitled *Social Goals and Indicators for American Society.* (Vol. 371, May 1967; Vol. 373, September 1967.) Especially see Wilbur J. Cohen, "Education and Learning" (Annals, Vol. 373), which provides an excellent overview of education, introduces the concept of "the learning force," and points out the many areas where new educational indicators are needed.

32. SHELDON, Eleanor Bernert and Wilbert E. MOORE (eds.). *Indicators of Social Change: Concepts and Measurements.* N.Y.: Russell Sage Foundation, 1968.

An authoritative work by and for sociologists. Especially see Daniel Bell, "The Measurement of Knowledge and Technology" (pp. 145-246) and Beverly Duncan, "Trends in Output and Distribution of Schooling" (pp. 601-672, 32 tables). The Bell article, a far-ranging essay covering implications of knowledge growth in a post-industrial society, is especially recommended.

33. BELL, Daniel (ed.). *Toward the Year 2000. Work in Progress.* N.Y.: Houghton-Mifflin, 1968. 400 pp. Originally published by American Academy of Arts and Sciences in *Daedalus,* Summer 1967.

Deliberations of the Commission on the Year 2000. Five of the 22 articles involve education and education-related topics, while four others discuss futures methodology. Although well publicized, these essays do not appear to be especially superior to those of any other anthology on the future. But this is "Work in Progress," foreshadowing a series of 8 volumes that will appear over the next 2-3 years, starting with Harvey Perloff (ed.), *U.S. Government in the Year 2000.* Other volumes will cover Values and Rights (Fred C. Ikle), Intellectual Institutions (Stephen Graubard), The Life Cycle (Kai Erickson), The International System (Stanley Hoffman), The Social Impact of the Computer (Robert M. Fano), Science and Society (Franklin Long and Robert Morison), and Business Institutions (Martin Shubik). Some of the volumes will be by a single author, while others will include contributed papers and discussions.

34. KOSTELANETZ, Richard (ed.). *Beyond Left and Right: Radical Thought for Our Time.* N.Y.: William Morrow, 1968. 436 pp. $7.95.

An excellent anthology that defines "radical" in the innovative sense, rather than the political sense. A good introduction to futures is provided through a provocative selection of articles by Boulding, Fuller, Kahn, Wiener, McLuhan, Bell, and others, as grouped in the categories of man and his future, technology and society, enterprise and remuneration, architecture, people and resources, education, defense, and redesigning society.

35. THEOBALD, Robert (ed.). *An Alternative Future for America II.* Revised and Enlarged Edition. Chicago: Swallow, May 1970. 199 pp. $6.00; paper $2.00.

Two-thirds of the book incorporates new material, including a "working appendix" listing various organizations studying alternative futures. Education (pp. 157-182) is defined as "the process of providing each individual with the capacity to develop his potential to the full." Four levels of learning are viewed: the first level is the simple perception of a fact; the second occurs when two facts are interrelated; the third (to which present systems of education are geared) makes it possible to improve our level of performance within our present perceptions of the state of the universe. "We are beginning to perceive the need for fourth-level learning—learning which permits us to change our perceptions about the nature of the world in which we live . . . the styles which make possible fourth-level learning are profoundly contradictory to those needed in third-level situations.

36. FERKISS, Victor C. *Technological Man: The Myth and the Reality.* N.Y.: George Braziller, 1969. 352 pp. Bib., pp. 295-327.

A political scientist looks at the vast changes transforming society and attacks "the myth of the future," which focuses attention on what is to come rather than what is. (pp. 10-16) He concludes that "Technological man is more myth than reality . . . Bourgeois man is still in the saddle . . . At the same time, an existential revolution is under way that may destroy the identity of the human race, make society unmanageable and render the planet literally uninhabitable. Bourgeois man is incapable of coping with this revolution. The race's only salvation is in the creation of technological man." (p. 245) To survive, a new philosophy is required, involving the new naturalism, the new holism, and the new immanentism. (p. 252)

Chapter 4, "The Prophets of the New" provides an excellent critique of prominent writers such as Ellul, McLuhan, Teilhard de Chardin, Skinner, Landers, and Marx. The unannotated bibliography lists about 500 books and 400 articles on technology, social change, and the future.

37. TOFFLER, Alvin. *Future Shock.* N.Y.: Random House, 1970. 505 pp. $8.95. Bib., pp. 461-483.

Future shock is the disease of change, "the dizzying disorientation brought on by the premature arrival of the future . . . culture shock in one's own society . . . the malaise, mass neurosis, irrationality, and free-floating violence already apparent in contemporary life are merely a foretaste of what may lie ahead unless we come to understand and treat this disease." (p. 13)

The sources come from increasing transience, novelty, and diversity. Transience involves the throw-away society, the new nomads (or the declining significance of place to human life), modular man (who has modular relationships with many, rather than holistic relationships with a few), the coming post-bureaucratic ad-hocracy, and the obsolescence of information. The novelty ratio (altering the relationship between the familiar and the unfamiliar) is growing, due to science, an economy geared to the provision of psychic gratification, and new family relationships. Diversity has led us to overchoice, a surfeit of subcults in the world of work and play, and a diversity of life styles enabling serial selves. This accelerating pace leads to serious psychological problems, obsessive reversion (both right-wing and left-wing) and super-simplifying.

Numerous strategies for survival are proposed for individuals (personal stability zones, crisis counseling, half-way houses, enclaves of the past, and enclaves of the future), technological control, social futurism (including comments on the collapse of technocratic planning and the need for social futures assemblies to salvage the system of representative politics) and education, which is seen as "a hopeless anachronism." Although education is admittedly undergoing rapid change, "much of this change is no more than an attempt to refine the existent machinery, making it ever more efficient in the pursuit of obsolete goals." (p. 359) Toffler advocates a Council of the Future in every school and community, provision for lifelong education, and developing common skills of learning, relating, and choosing while extending super-industrial diversity.

This challenging overview at times appears glib, especially with its zippy chapter headings and sub-headings. It is written for a broad audience, but backed up by considerable research, including a bibliography of 359 items. And it raises some very important questions.

38. BENNIS, Warren G. and Philip E. SLATER. *The Temporary Society*. N.Y.: Harper & Row, 1968. 147 pp.

Six separate essays by one or both of the authors "to force into view certain changes affecting vital aspects of our key institutions: organizational life, family life, interpersonal relationships, and authority." In the first essay, democracy is seen as inevitable—the necessary social system of the electronic era. In the second essay, Slater looks at change and the democratic family, noting that "experiential chasms between age cohorts serve to invalidate parental authority." (p. 24) The topics that follow concern the new style organizations beyond bureaucracy, social consequences of temporary systems, new patterns of leadership for adaptive organizations, and in the final chapter on the temporary society, the necessary education is prescribed for the art and science of being more fully human: how to get love, to love and to lose love; how to enter groups and leave them; how to attain satisfying roles; and how to cope more readily with ambiguity. "For the most part we learn the significant things informally and badly, having to unlearn them later on in life when the consequences are grave and frightfully expensive, like five-day-a-week analysis." (p. 127)

39. HAUSER, Philip M. "The Chaotic Society: Product of the Social Morphological Revolution," *American Sociological Review*, 34:1, February 1969, pp. 1-19. Based on Presidential Address, American Sociological Association annual meeting, August 28, 1968.

Contemporary society "is realistically characterized as 'the chaotic society' and best understood as 'the anachronistic society.' " (p. 1) The cause of the contemporary chaos is seen as "the social morphological revolution," which consists of increased size, density, heterogeneity, and tempo of change.

40. DRUCKER, Peter F. *The Age of Discontinuity: Guidelines to Our Changing Society.* N.Y.: Harper and Row, 1969.

An important book focusing on four major discontinuities: new technologies, the world economy (including a chapter on "The Global Shopping Center"), a society of large organizations (including a chapter on "The New Pluralism"), and the changed position and power of knowledge such that we are becoming a knowledge society— "the greatest of the discontinuities around us." This final section on knowledge (Chapters 12-17) is of immense importance to educators.

Drucker forecasts that the knowledge industries will account for one-half of the total national product in the late 1970's (p. 263), and argues that knowledge, rather than agriculture and mining, has now become the primary industry supplying the essential and central resource of production. Under these circumstances, "It is not that we cannot afford the high costs of education; we cannot afford its low productivity" (p. 334) and economic necessity will therefore force a revolution. "In a knowledge society, school and life can no longer be separate." (p. 324) The diploma curtain is seen as a problem, as is the prolongation of adolescence by the schools and the inherent conflict between extended schooling and continuing education. Because of our knowledge needs, "We face an unprecedented situation in which we will have to set priorities for new knowledge" (p. 365) and the existing disciplines will not remain appropriate for long, if knowledge is to have a future.

41. HACKER, Andrew. *The End of the American Era.* N.Y.: Atheneum, 1970. 239 pp. $6.50.

A pessimistic view of the disintegration of social cohesion in the United States, and the declining quality of scholarship.

42. HUXLEY, Aldous. *Brave New World.* (Many editions, first published in 1939.)

A classic anti-utopia that still provides a plausible scenario of an undesirable future condition. Especially relevant for our time are the observations on the use of "soma." George Orwell's *1984* (first published in 1949, also with many editions), although an obvious classic, lacks the wit and subtlety of Huxley.

43. Educational Policy Research Center at Stanford. *Alternative Futures and Educational Policy.* Menlo Park, Calif.: Stanford

Research Institute, EPRC Memorandum Report, January 1970. 43 pp.

Tentatively summarizes the findings of a preliminary set of alternative future histories prepared at EPRC/Stanford, and suggests implications for educational policy. Of some two score future histories (ranging from Manifest Destiny and Exuberant Democracy to Authoritarian Recession, "1984"/Theocracy, and Collapse), "there are very few which manage to avoid one or another kind of time of serious troubles between now and 2050. The few that do, require a dramatic shift of values and perceptions with regard to what we came to term the 'world macroproblem.' This macroproblem will be the predominant concern of the foreseeable future, for all the alternative paths. It is the composite of all the problems which have been brought about by a combination of rampant technology application and industrial development together with high population levels." (p. 6)

"The overall message is clear. It is not yet time to redesign education for ecstatic individuals in a carefree world. To the extent that one believes that the analysis of the roots of the 'world macroproblem' holds up, to that extent he will believe that the paramount educational task for the nation is the development of a sense of purpose and unity. To that extent, also, it will seem essential that we re-examine all our present educational institutions, practices, and commitments to determine how their priority is altered in view of these future outlooks." (p. 42)

44. GORDON, Theodore J. and Robert H. AMENT. *Forecasts of Some Technological and Scientific Developments and their Societal Consequences*. Middletown, Conn.: The Institute for the Future, IFF Report R-6, September 1969. 98 pp.

The Delphi method involves a questionnaire mailed to a panel of experts who, after several iterations, tend to produce a converging group consensus—in this instance, on important prospective events, when they might take place, societal consequences and the degree to which they are likely to be beneficial or detrimental, and the degree to which intervention appears feasible.

The panelists ruminated on 32 physical events, including the following (median date of 50% chance of occurrence in parentheses): central data storage facility with wide public access (1980), language translators (1980), sophisticated teaching machines responsive to student's physiology (1980), individual portable two-way communication devices (1990), and 3-D television (1990). Similarly, 44 biological events were considered, including cheap non-narcotic drugs for producing specific personality changes (1980), laboratory creation of artificial life (1980), relatively inexpensive techniques to increase the world's arable acreage by 50% (1990), the ability to stimulate maximum cognitive growth of pre-school children (1995), and chemical control in the aging process (2015).

In addition to the elaboration of consequences for each of these events, 3 scenarios are constructed by the authors of the technological world in 1985, 2000, and 2025. The overall conclusion is that "Taken together, the forecasted events, the expected consequences, and the suggested strategies which might be employed in manipulating them, tell of a changing world in which man is gaining more precise control over his environment, his information, and himself; a world in which the new control techniques will increase comfort, eliminate some human misery, increase military power, and increase knowledge, but which will concomitantly bring political and social problems of unprecedented dimensions; a world in which the techniques for coping with these problems will not be much more advanced than they are today." (pp. 7-8)

These forecasts, however, should not be taken as Revealed Truth. (See Weaver, Item 10 for qualifications to the methodology.) Nevertheless, this broad array of possibilities should be considered, if for no other reason than as a compact listing of scientific aspirations circa 1969.

45. DE BRIGARD, Raul and Olaf HELMER. *Some Potential Societal Developments, 1970-2000.* Middletown, Conn.: The Institute for the Future, IFF Report R-7, April 1970. 134 pp.
Unlike IFF Report R-6 (above), which has precedents back to the original Gordon and Helmer RAND study of September 1964, this report concerns the first attempt to employ the Delphi method in forecasting societal developments. Adding to this lack of scientific precedent is the inherent difficulty of accurately gauging social matters in the present, let alone the future.

Nevertheless, the authors have forged ahead, providing substantial qualification to their effort. Potential developments are assessed in major categories of urbanization, the family, leisure

and the economy, education, food and population, international relations, conflict in society and law enforcement,
national political structures, values, and the impact of technology on government and society. In some instances, convergent opinions were obtained (e.g., inexpensive and uncompli-
cated mass contraceptive devices will be available, education
will become much more decentralized and diversified), while in
other instances there was wide disagreement (e.g., the alienation
and impersonality of urban life will increase, widespread famine
will occur). At the end of each of the ten sections, there is a
brief but valuable discussion of "some policy issues raised by
the preceding expectations." In the final section of the report,
the panelists estimated to the year 2000 the course of 46 statistical indicators such as GNP, divorce rate, expenditures for
education, life expectancy, income levels, overseas travel, etc.

Being an initial effort, this panel was limited to 34 members—hardly enough, in light of the multitude of topics
explored, to focus a balanced array of expert opinion on any
one question. Aside from providing a substantial listing of
largely unconnected events, the chief value of this document is
as an exercise in futures methodology that may serve to
influence future applications of the Delphi technique.

c. Technology and Society

46. MESTHENE, Emmanuel. *Technological Change: Its Impact on
Man and Society.* Harvard Studies in Technology and Society.
Cambridge: Harvard University Press, 1970. 124 pp. $4.95;
N.Y.: NAL Mentor Books, 1970. 127 pp. $1.25. Bib., pp.
96-124.

An overview of the ongoing research of the Harvard Program on
Technology and Society, woven into three chapters on social
change, values, and economic and political organization. The
opening comments quickly dispose of "three inadequate
views": the optimistic view of technology as a virtually
unalloyed blessing, the pessimistic view of technology as an
unmitigated curse, and the complacent historical view that
technology is not worthy of special notice. Rather, technology
is seen as outstripping traditional categories of thought and
established values and institutions, and necessary responses are
suggested. The volume is concluded with a well-annotated bibliography of 70 items.

47. MULLER, Herbert J. *The Children of Frankenstein: A Primer on Modern Technology and Human Values.* Bloomington: Indiana University Press, 1970. 431 pp. $10.00.

A balanced, "informal" volume by a well-known "nonprofessional historian" (presently a Professor of English and Government), who addresses "the general reader." The view of technology is that the consequences have been "profoundly, thoroughly mixed," in contrast to Ellul, whose totally negative view is rejected as over-stated and over-simplified. After providing historical background, the impact on society and culture is explored in separate chapters on war, science, government, business, language, higher education, natural environment, urban environment, mass media, the traditional arts, religion, and people. The chapter on higher education observes the consequences of specialization and "the spell of scientific methods," with a view that "most college graduates—whatever their specialty—have too limited an understanding of our technological society for potential leaders." (p. 230) The final three chapters are under the heading "Toward the Year 2000," examining utopian writers of the past, the individual papers from the Commission on the Year 2000, and Kahn and Wiener's *The Year 2000.* A concern for human nature and recurrent human values is expressed throughout, and it is concluded that the Brave New World of Huxley "looks like a real possibility, considering the nature of technological man and affluent man in America." (p. 405) As suggested by the sub-title, this volume should serve well as a primer, despite some rambling, a reticence to forecast, and some curious notions, e.g., "most middle-class teenagers appear to be basically satisfied with themselves and their prospects, by no means alienated from their society." (p. 364. This may have been truer in 1968 when written, than in 1970 when published.)

48. BURKE, John G. (ed.). *The New Technology and Human Values.* Belmont, Calif.: Wadsworth Publishing Co., 1966. 408 pp.

A well-organized introductory reader including a section on "Education in a Technological Era" and a focus on problems such as leisure, automation, population, privacy, and government.

2. *New Developments in Science and Technology*

49. TAYLOR, Gordon Rattray. *The Biological Time Bomb.* N.Y.: World Publishing Co., NAL Books, 1968. 240 pp.

A pessimistic overview of the biological future by an authoritative popularizer of science. Covers sex, transplantation, death, mind control, genetics, and the creation of life, concluding that "The root of our problem, pragmatically, is the absence of any means of measuring satisfaction . . . Current indications are that the world is bent on going to hell in a handcart and that is probably what it will do." (p. 230) For a prestigious and optimistic overview, see Philip Handler (ed.), *Biology and the Future of Man* (Oxford, 1970. 936 pp. $12.50), the distillation of 175 distinguished American scientists working on 20 panels for the National Academy of Sciences. Although these two volumes have not been compared, the less "respectable" synthesis by Taylor may be far more relevant insofar as pointing out potential impacts on man.

50. HARRINGTON, Alan. *The Immortalist: An Approach to the Engineering of Man's Divinity.* N.Y.: Random House, 1969; Avon Discus edition, 1970. 287 pp. $1.25.

A well-written and provocative volume with the overstated central theme that fear of aging and death is "the central passion that drives us."

"The case for the immortalist point of view will rest on the evidence that since the beginning of recorded time man has engaged in a disguised drive to make himself immortal and divine, and that this overriding motive that accounts for much of his significant action, is now driving him toward his evolutionary crisis. The time has come for men to turn into gods or perish." (p. 29) The final chapter describes the society of immortal men, and an appendix deals with the inevitably raised question of population control, seen as a diminishing threat. It is concluded that "Humanity's push toward the utopia beyond time will not be slowed down by the warnings of demographers. Too much pressure has been built up behind it. Research is not going to be called off. The day will arrive when somebody wearing glasses and a sterilized apron will run through a laboratory yelling wildly and waving a test tube. Provided that the species refrains from destroying itself, there will be no way for this not to happen." (p. 262)

51. BENDER, A. Douglas, et. al. "Delphic Study Examines Developments in Medicine," *Futures*, 1:4, June 1969, pp. 289-303.

The results of a Delphi study conducted for Smith, Kline and French laboratories as an aid to the planning of a pharmaceutical company, and covering the areas of biomedical research, diagnosis, medical therapy, health care, and medical education. From these results, a scenario of "Medicine 1980" is presented. (pp. 294-300)

52. BJERRUM, Chresten A. "Forecast of Computer Developments and Applications 1968-2000," *Futures,* 1:4, June 1969, pp. 331-338.

Results of a Delphi study, with the general consensus that "rapid development of advanced computers and computer applications is expected to continue to the year 2000 and result in much more influence on society than today." (p. 335) Some of the forecasts: a 50% reduction of the labor force in present industry by the late 1980's, all major industries controlled by computers in the year 2000, patients in major hospitals controlled by computers around 1975, computer prices (despite advanced technology) to decrease by a factor of 100 (!) by the end of the 1980's, etc.

53. CALDER, Nigel (ed.). *Unless Peace Comes. A Scientific Forecast of New Weapons.* N.Y.: The Viking Press, 1968, 243 pp.

16 experts discuss what the quest for new destructive power is likely to produce in forthcoming decades. An important inventory of possible horrors that should not be ignored.

54. KERN, Edward. "A Good Revolution Goes on Sale," *Life,* October 16, 1970, pp. 47-52.

An overview of casette TV, with a chart of what to expect and when, as concerns six competing brand names. Also see feature articles in *The New York Times,* Sunday, July 5, 1970, Sec. 3, p. 1, and *Saturday Review,* August 8, 1970 (which lists 14 companies in the field). Many other articles and books will surely be published in the near future. This new technology may prove to have a far greater impact on education than broadcast television, once the bewildered consumer makes a choice between Cartrivision, Instavision, EVR, SelectaVision and other systems. Ultimately, we might even see a national or global casette university offering thousands of courses of instruction.

55. TEBBEL, John. "Libraries in Miniature: A New Era Begins," *Saturday Review,* January 9, 1971, pp. 41-42.

A brief overview discussing the Microbook Library of Encyclopaedia Britannica, the PCMI Library Information System of the National Cash Register Co. (utilizing UMF, or Ultramicrofiche), *The New York Times'* Information Bank, a new index from

University Microfilms, and possible applications of cassette video players to books. "We are approaching a new era that will certainly revolutionize libraries, probably reading habits, and possibly even publishing itself . . . What the transistor is to radio and television, high reduction photography is to the printed page." (Also see an editorial entitled "UMF and the Future," *Saturday Review,* April 19, 1969, p. 26.)

56. MEISE, Norman R. *Conceptual Design of an Automated National Library System.* Metuchen, N.J.: Scarecrow Press, 1969. 234 pp.
Demonstrates the feasibility of an automated system that utilizes existing technology. Also discusses bibliographic search, acquisitions, circulation data, cataloging, and tying together local libraries (public, academic, and special), regional centers, and a National Library Central (perhaps the Library of Congress, which is already moving toward automation). Although this volume is largely technical, it is nevertheless important for suggesting what would more or less appear to be the inevitable shape of future information systems.

3. *Population, Food, Ecology*

57. DJERASSI, Carl. "Birth Control after 1984," *Science,* 169: September 4, 1970, pp. 941-951.
Discusses contraceptive methods of the future and their feasibility. It is concluded that an "Orwellian" approach, such as disseminating an agent through drinking water, "is totally unfeasible by 1984." Fundamentally new birth control methods in the female (such as once-a-month pills) and a male contraceptive pill "probably will not be developed until the 1980's at the earliest, and then only if major steps . . . are instituted in the early 1970's." If new incentives for continued active participation of the pharmaceutical industry are not developed during the next decade, "birth control in 1984 will not differ significantly from that of today." (p. 951)

58. PADDOCK, William and Paul PADDOCK. *Famine—1975! America's Decision: Who Will Survive?* Boston: Little, Brown and Co., 1967. 276 pp.
The two brothers—one a retired diplomat, the other an agronomist and plant pathologist—have written a lucid, straightforward, yet well-documented book that consistently underlines the theme that famine is inevitable in the underdeveloped

nations. All of the familiar hopes about breakthroughs in synthetic foods, hydroponics, desalinization, ocean farming, agricultural research, fertilizers, irrigation, idle land, and land reform are smashed. "The timetable of food shortages will vary from nation to nation, but by 1975 sufficient serious food crises will have broken out in certain of the afflicted countries so that problem will be in full view. The Time of Famines will have begun." (p. 205) The U.S. is seen as the sole help of the hungry nations, but having to make painful decisions as to which hungry nations to aid, in the "Age of Food" when food becomes the main source of international power. For an optimistic view, see Lester R. Brown, *Seeds of Change: The Green Revolution and Development in the 1970's.* N.Y.: Praeger, 1970. 250 pp.

59. NICHOLSON, Max. *The Environmental Revolution: A Guide for the New Masters of the World.* N.Y.: McGraw-Hill, 1970. 366 pp. $10.00.

Also see Paul R. and Anne H. Ehrlich, *Population, Resources and Environment* (Freeman, 1970. $8.95) and Lynton Keith Caldwell, *Environment: A Challenge for Modern Society* (N.Y.: Natural History Press, 1970. $7.95). These three books are considered by Paul Shepard *(New York Times Book Review,* August 30, 1970, p. 3) to be the best among a dozen new books on the environment. It is not known by this compiler as to what degree these books deal with the future; however, Paul Ehrlich has written several pessimistic eco-scenarios. For example, see Paul Ehrlich, *The Population Bomb* (N.Y.: Ballantine Books, 1968; 3 scenarios, pp. 69-80). Also see a single scenario by Ehrlich, "Eco-Catastrophe," in Garrett de Bell, *The Environmental Handbook* (N.Y.: Ballantine Books, 1970, pp. 161-176).

4. *Cities*

60. DOXIADIS, Constantinos A. "The Coming Era of Ecumenopolis," *Saturday Review,* March 18, 1967, pp. 11-14.

Due to population growth, foresees "a universal city, Ecumenopolis, which will cover the earth with a continuous network of minor and major urban concentrations of different forms . . . the pressure of population on resources will be such that important measures will have to be taken so that a balance can be retained between the five elements of the anthropocosmos in a universal scale." (p. 13) The anthropocosmos—the real world of man—contains nature, man himself, society,

shells (or structures), and networks. For a listing of the extensive publications by Doxiadis and Associates, write The Athens
Center of Ekistics, P.O. Box 471, Athens, Greece.

61. DOWNS, Anthony. *Urban Problems and Prospects.* Chicago:
Markham Publishing Co., October 1970. 293 pp. $7.95; $3.95
paper.

11 essays, including Alternative Forms of Future Urban Growth
in the U.S., Alternative Futures for the American Ghetto,
Racism in America and How to Combat It, A Realistic Look at
the Final Payoffs from Urban Data Systems, and Competition
from Community Schools.

62. HODGE, Patricia Leavey and Philip M. HAUSER. *The Challenge
of America's Metropolitan Outlook, 1960 to 1985.* Prepared for
the National Commission on Urban Problems. N.Y.: Praeger,
1968. 90 pp.

A projection of growth in Standard Metropolitan Statistical
Areas, largely in suburban rings, and a growing concentration of
nonwhites in SMSA's, especially in central cities. "The problems
facing the central city schools—especially in respect to integration—are highlighted by an anticipated almost doubling (92
percent) of nonwhite youngsters under 15, while corresponding
white youth would diminish by 8 percent." (p. 55) "The projections clearly indicate that the present 'urban crisis' is likely
to be greatly exacerbated in the coming years and that serious
difficulties will face the nation in respect to intergroup relations, education, employment, housing, and provisions for the
aged." (p. 57)

63. BANFIELD, Edward C. *The Unheavenly City: The Nature and
Future of Our Urban Crisis.* Boston: Little, Brown and Co.,
1970. 308 pp. $6.95.

A social scientist's hard-nosed and gloomy analysis of urban
problems in the light of scholarly findings. "So long as the city
contains a sizable lower class, nothing basic can be done about
its most serious problems." (p. 210) "It is impossible to avoid
the conclusion that the serious problems of the cities will
continue to exist in something like their present form for
another twenty years at least." (p. 255) Present programs are
seen as prolonging these problems and perhaps making them
worse. In part this is due to false definitions of the situation,
perpetuating a "reign of error," e.g., defining so many situations
as "critical." In Chapter 7, "Schooling vs. Education," Banfield
advocates lowering the school-leaving age to 14 to get non-

learners out of school and therefore stop their anti-education, and the possibility of school districts contracting with industry for job training. Possibilities for changing schooling are not considered. In Chapter 10, various alternatives to free children from the grip of lower-class culture are explored, such as state removal from parents, boarding schools, and day nurseries—but little hope is offered here or in other areas, other than the possibility of replacing the conventional wisdom of do-gooding over the next decade or two as a consequence of social science brought to bear on policy questions.

64. U.S. Department of Housing and Urban Development. *Tomorrow's Transportation: New Systems for the Urban Future.* Washington: Office of Metropolitan Development, Urban Transportation Administration, May 1968. 100 pp.

The report, a summary of recommendations for a comprehensive program in all aspects of urban transportation, is the first major effort of its kind. After surveying trends in urbanization and urban transportation, it lists various inter-related strategies for action, including recommended future systems such as dial-a-bus, personal rapid transit, dual mode vehicle systems, automated dual mode bus, pallet or ferry systems, and fast inter-urban transit links.

5. *Manpower, Equality and the Economy*

65. GARDNER, John W. *Excellence: Can We Be Equal and Excellent Too?* N.Y.: Harper & Row, 1961; Harper Colophon edition, 1962. 171 pp. $1.45.

A well-known (indeed, perhaps classic) essay on three competing principles (hereditary privilege, equalitarianism, and competitive performance), the search for talent necessitated by our complex society, and the need to select a variety of talents.

66. MILLER, S. M. and Pamela ROBY. *The Future of Inequality.* N.Y.: Basic Books, 1970. 272 pp. $7.95.

Inequality is seen as increasing during the 1970's due to the elimination of unskilled work and the increasing importance of education for all. Only deliberate public policy of compensatory programs could lead to greater equality, and this appears unlikely. Yet there will be greater sensitivity to inequities, resulting in still more dissent. But the possibility of change is held forth: "What we are suggesting is a radical restructuring capable of appealing to a large number of voters who feel the need for change and do not see the possibility of a politically viable program." (p. 252)

67. U.S. Senate. Select Committee on Equal Educational Opportunity. *Equal Educational Opportunity.*

Part 1A: *Equality of Educational Opportunity, An Introduction.* Washington: USGPO, 1970. 413 pp. $1.50.

Part 1B: *Equality of Educational Opportunity, Appendix.* Washington: USGPO, 1970. pp. 415-741. $1.25.

Hearings held April 20-29, May 5 and 12, 1970 "to study the effectiveness of existing laws and policies in assuring equality of educational opportunity and to examine the extent to which policies are applied uniformly in all regions of the United States." (GPO brochure)

68. YOUNG, Michael. *The Rise of the Meritocracy, 1870-2033: An Essay on Education and Equality.* London: Thames and Hudson, 1958; Baltimore: Penguin Books, Pelican edition, 1961. 190 pp.

A brilliant and witty essay by a sociologist who write as a sociologist in the year 2033, defending the existing order and providing historical background for government leaders. (A short-term forecast is also provided, which proves disastrously inaccurate.) Brain-power planning became more effective as the measurement of merit (intelligence + effort) became more effective, so that "The world beholds for the first time the spectacle of a brilliant class, the five percent of a nation who know what five percent means." (p. 103) The most intelligent children obtained the best education, and to insure justice for late developers, quinquennial revaluations were held at Regional Centres for Adult Education. With the intelligent taking their rightful positions of leadership, the Pioneer Corps was established to provide the least responsible jobs for the least able people, and the Home Help Corps provided domestic servants again, after a lapse during the egalitarian age. Consequently, the gap between the classes became wider, with social inferiors being inferiors in other ways as well. Despite the Equalization of Income Act of 2005, tensions grew between the Technician's Party (which issued the "Chelsea Manifesto" in 2009, arguing for a classless and tolerant society where every human being could develop his own special capacities for leading a rich life), and the extreme conservatives who, seeing the principles of heredity and merit coming together, wished to turn full cycle and restore the hereditary principle.

Despite necessary simplifications (assuming an industrial society and "the dictatorship of biology" over women) there is considerable insight to be had from this essay, and the format serves as an exemplary model of a "future history."

69. LECHT, Leonard A. *Manpower Needs for National Goals in the 1970's.* N.Y.: Praeger, 1969. 183 pp. $7.50.

A report of ongoing research by the National Planning Association's Center for Priority Analysis, predicated on the assumption that the U.S. will move ahead to implement national goals in 16 critical areas: agriculture, area redevelopment, consumer expenditures, education, health, housing, international aid, manpower retraining, national defense, natural resources, private plant and equipment, research and development, social welfare, space, transportation, and urban development. It is concluded that "If we continue to follow present patterns of employment, discrimination, training, and education, our attempts to implement national goals and solve these problems will be hamstrung by substantial labor shortages. Even advanced technology and increased automation will not alter this picture for . . . each new development creates additional manpower demands requiring new skills. Hence, only advance planning in both private and public sectors can alleviate manpower bottlenecks that would cripple new programs at the outset." (book cover)

70. FOLGER, John K., Helen S. ASTIN, and Alan E. BAYER. *Human Resources and Higher Education.* Staff Report of the Commission of Human Resources and Advanced Education. N.Y.: Russell Sage Foundation, 1970. $17.50.

"As the pace of change in our society increases, the need will be even greater for manpower planning to avoid imbalances among the professions and the frustration of individual career plans. This work develops our understanding of the set of interrelated forces that determines the education and utilization of our major national asset—able men and women." (advt.)

71. BERG, Ivar. *Education and Jobs: The Great Training Robbery.* Foreword by Eli Ginzberg. N.Y.: Praeger (published for the Center of Urban Education), 1970. 200 pp. $7.50.

A well-researched sociological study of the relationship of education to employment, pointing out that many workers are over-educated, employee productivity does not vary with formal education, job dissatisfaction increases as educational level rises, and that "educational credentials have become the new property in America." Of particular interest is evidence indicating that elementary and secondary teachers are less likely to stay in teaching as they move up the credentials ladder. Unfortunately, Berg only analyzes the single dimension of education and jobs, without suggesting other purposes (such as citizenship and individual development) that schools might satisfy. (Although there is no trend data or forecasts, and only a hint of policy suggestions, this book nevertheless has broad implications for policy and is therefore included here.)

72. GALBRAITH, John Kenneth. *The New Industrial State.* Boston: Houghton-Mifflin, 1967. 427 pp.

A comprehensive view of modern economic life and the changes that are shaping its future, especially focusing on the Techno-structure (the complex of specialists and technicians now exercising decisive power), the Revised Sequence (where, instead of the consumer as sovereign, large business firms now control markets and arrange consumer behavior to serve their needs), the Educational and Scientific Estate which is replacing the waning power of the unions as a political force, and "the convergent tendencies of industrial societies, however different their popular and ideological billing." Galbraith concludes that "if economic goals are the only goals of the society it is natural that the industrial system should dominate the state and the state should serve its ends. If other goals are strongly asserted, the industrial system will fall into its place as a detached and autonomous arm of the state, but responsive to the larger purposes of society." (p. 399)

73. MISHAN, E. J. *Technology and Growth: The Price We Pay.* N.Y.: Praeger, 1969. 193 pp.

A popular version of *The Costs of Economic Growth* (N.Y.: Praeger, 1967. 190 pp. $6.50), written to convince the public "of the need of radical change in our habitual ways of looking at economic events." For a parallel questioning of "Progress," see Staffan B. Linder, *The Harried Leisure Class.* N.Y.: Columbia University Press, 1970. 182 pp. $7.00.

74. The Staff of the Wall Street Journal. *Here Comes Tomorrow! Living and Working in the Year 2000.* Princeton, N.J.: Dow Jones Books, 1967. 196 pp.

Originally a series of 13 *WSJ* articles. Essentially optimistic and even approaching a "gee whiz" simplicity. Nevertheless, a large number of trends and plans are drawn together to report where and how it's happening as concerns population, food, computers, communications, energy, air travel, space, cities, automobiles, homes, education, medicine, and war. "Some Office of Education officials estimate that (education) outlays will generate as much as 25% of the $2.3 trillion GNP expected in 2000." (p. 155) A Ford Foundation official suggests that "there's a very good possibility that company operations will get to be so educationally competent that they will become degree-granting." (p. 164) This "pop futures" volume provides a quick overview of possible material developments, in a spirit of unabated optimism that one decreasingly finds.

6. *Social Structure and Youth*

75. CARROLL, James D. "Noetic Authority," *Public Administration Review,* 29:5, September-October 1969, pp. 492-500.
"This paper suggests that the state is withering away in a psychological sense because of an increase in awareness in contemporary society and a growing questioning of authority. It also suggests the state is withering in a technological sense because of a failure to use organized knowledge to satisfy expectations and values. It then suggests that a new form of the state, the 'innovative state' characterized by a new form of authority, may in time emerge." (Abstract) "Noetic" refers to "the increase in awareness—consciousness—of man's social and physical environment that is occurring throughout much of the world." (p. 492) Noetic politics is the politics of knowledge and awareness in an increasingly complex society that is shifting to a mental base of operations and a collegial form of authority. The implications for educating institutions are not discussed, but are obviously profound.

76. BENNIS, Warren G. *Changing Organizations.* N.Y.: Mc-Graw-Hill, 1966.
Contrasts traditional ideas of bureaucratic organization with contemporary perceptions and organization change. Through forecasts of organizations of the future over the next 25 to 50 years, the end of bureaucracy is anticipated. The new social systems will be more complex, innovative, unprogrammed, with an emphasis on diverse goals and freedom of expression.

77. REICH, Charles A. *The Greening of America: How the Youth Revolution is Trying to Make America Livable.* N.Y.: Random House, 1970. 399 pp. $7.95. (Condensation in *The New Yorker,* September 26, 1970, pp. 42-111)

The best-seller that attacks the corporate state and the basic premises by which we live: 1) disorder, corruption, hypocrisy, war; 2) poverty, distorted priorities, and legislation by power; 3) uncontrolled technology and the destruction of the environment; 4) decline of democracy and liberty, powerlessness; 5) the artificiality of work and culture; 6) absence of community; and 7) loss of self.

To indicate the true significance of the new generation, three broad categories of consciousness are discussed: Consciousness I as the traditional outlook of the American farmer, small businessman, or worker trying to get ahead; Consciousness II representing the values of an organizational society—basically "liberal" but with the potential of becoming repressive; and Consciousness III as the new mode of independence and personal responsibility, seeking restoration of the non-material elements of man's existence.

"There is a revolution under way. It is not like revolutions of the past. It has originated with the individual and with culture, and if it succeeds it will change the political structure only as its final act. It will not require violence to succeed, and it cannot be successfully resisted by violence. It is now spreading with amazing rapidity, and already our laws, institutions, and social structure are changing in consequence. Its ultimate creation could be a higher reason, a more human community, and a new and liberated individual. This is the revolution of the new generation." (*New Yorker,* p. 42)

Reich has been widely attacked (by "Con II" people, of course) as a romantic, while "Con III" people undoubtedly find the book as a Bible for our times. In any event, "Con III" has rapidly become part of our national idiom.

78. MEAD, Margaret. *Culture and Commitment: A Study of the Generation Gap.* N.Y.: Doubleday and Natural History Press, 1970. 113 pp. $5.00.

A wide-ranging essay summarizing much of Mead's thinking over the past decades and adding new insights on our unique present that is "without any parallel in the past." The argument easily follows the chapter headings: The Past: Postfigurative Cultures and Well-Known Forbears (where lack of questioning and consciousness are the key conditions); The Present: Cofigurative Cultures and Familiar Peers (which is institutionalized through age grading); and The Future: Prefigurative Cultures and Unknown Children (where the child represents what is to come). All men are seen as equally immigrants into the new era, and "Today, nowhere in the world are there elders who know what the children know, no matter how remote and simple the societies are in which the children live. In the past there were always some elders who knew more than any children in terms of their experience of having grown up within a culture system. Today there are none." (pp. 77-78)

79. KENISTON, Kenneth. "You have to Grow Up in Scarsdale to Know How Bad Things Really Are," *The New York Times Magazine,* April 27, 1969.

Behind this innocent title lies a profound explanation of the broad trends resulting in student revolt. Rejecting the "Oedipal Rebellion" interpretation of Feuer and the "Historical Irrelevance" theory of Brzezinski and Bell, Keniston sees the fusion of two revolutions. On the one hand, there is a continuation of the old revolution of the industrial society, involving "the progressive extension to more and more people of economic, political, and social rights, privileges and opportunities originally available only to the aristocracy." Affluent youth take these values for granted seeing them as rights and not as goals. While demanding these rights, a new revolution—consonant with a post-industrial society—is developing. Beyond affluence is a concern with the quality of life and a stress on the values of individuality, participation, openness, and continuing human development.

80. GOODMAN, Paul. *New Reformation: Notes of a Neolithic Conservative.* N.Y.: Random House, 1970. 208 pp. $5.95.

"My subject is the breakdown of belief, and the emergence of new belief, in sciences and professions, education, and civil legitimacy . . . By 'Reformation' I mean simply an upheaval of belief that is of religious depth . . . The crisis of legitimacy is deeper than political revolution; it is what I have here been calling religious: the young have ceased to 'believe' in something, and the disbelief occurs at progressively earlier years." (pp. x-xi, 127)

Although "rather sour on the American young," Goodman has even stronger words (as usual) on the school system, which is seen as "manned by the biggest horde of monks since the time of Henry VIII." (p. 21) The widening wisdom of the times that children must learn to learn "usually means picking up the structure of behavior of the teachers and becoming expert in the academic process. In actual practice, young discoverers are bound to discover what will get them past the College Board examinations." (p. 78)

"By and large, though not for all topics and all persons, the incidental process of education suits the nature of learning better than formal teaching." (p. 69) Accordingly, Goodman's suggested "Reformation" of education includes incidental education as the chief means of learning and teaching, eliminating most high schools, college training following entry into the professions, and delaying socialization to protect children's free growth. "Our aim should be to multiply the paths of growing up, instead of narrowing the one existing school path." (p. 87) For ages 6-11, a system of radically decentralized tiny schools is proposed, each with 28 children and 4 teachers (a licensed teacher, a college senior, a literate housewife and mother, and an intelligent high school graduate or dropout). Due to savings of topdown administration, special services, and construction, it is estimated that the mini-schools would cost 25% of present urban school costs. (p. 99) (Perhaps this is overstated, but such a scheme may yet be tried by the financially desperate cities.)

C. Educational Trends and Descriptive Futures

1. *General*

81. COOMBS, Philip H. *The World Educational Crisis: A Systems Analysis.* N.Y.: Oxford, 1968. 241 pp. Bib., pp. 217-226.

A competent overview of international educational trends, indicating that problems of rising demand and system obsolescence are afflicting all nations in every part of the world. Although the discussion is organized around inputs and outputs, it is nevertheless highly readable, covering not only the formal system but nonformal or "periphery" education. An excellent annotated bibliography of 74 items is provided.

82. U.S. Congress, House Committee on Science and Astronautics. *The Management of Information and Knowledge.* Washington: USGPO, 1970. 130 pp. 60 cents.

Seven provocative papers prepared for the Eleventh Meeting of the Panel on Science and Technology, by Herman Kahn, Stafford Beer, Daniel J. Boorstin, Thomas F. Green, Paul Armer, Osmo A. Wiio, and George Kozmetsky. Especially see

"Education as an Information System" by Kozmetsky and "Education and Schooling in Post-Industrial America: Some Directions for Policy" by Green.

83. BYRNES, James C., with the assistance of Michael FOLK. *The Quantity of Formal Instruction in the United States.* Prepared for the U.S. Office of Education by the Educational Policy Research Center. Syracuse: EPRC, August 1969. 67 pp.

Examining the age-graded educational system, the development and maturation of a nearly universal system of secondary school instruction is considered as "the most significant event of the 20th Century in the development of educational institutions in the United States." Yet, the proportion of high school graduates completing a four-year post-secondary degree stands today roughly what it was about the turn of the century. The report concludes by describing two specific alternative states for the quantity of instruction (as measured by time), which highlights two possible extremes for future policy: a continuous rise in the amount of instruction received vs. stabilization.

84. SANDOW, Stuart A. *Emerging Education Policy Issues in Law: FRAUD. Number One of a Series.* Syracuse: Educational Policy Research Center, Syracuse University Research Corporation, November 1970. 47 pp.

An experimental Delphi exercise conducted with a small group of attorneys, based on a news event of a hypothetical case of fraud that had been successfully pursued through the courts. 80% of the respondents saw the possibility of a fraud issue arising and succeeding in five years. Sandow is pursuing his study of possible precedent cases that may have profound impacts on education.

85. U.S. Office of Education. *Education in the Seventies.* Office of Program Planning and Evaluation, Planning Paper 68-1, May 1968. 44 pp.

Projections of enrollments, staff, and expenditures to 1975 for elementary, secondary, and higher education.

86. *The New York Times,* "Annual Education Review," Monday, January 11, 1971, pp. 47-78.

39 brief overview articles under seven headings: reforming education, some ventures in reform, styles and values, urban education, private and parochial schools, higher education, and management and finance. The 1970 edition (January 12, 1970 - coming at the turn of the decade) is more oriented toward

descriptive futures, whereas the 1971 edition appears more oriented toward action, or a prescriptive future. Both are excellent overviews of contemporary thinking.

87. PETERSON, A.D.C. *The Future of Education*. London: The Cresset Press, 1968; N.Y.: Humanities, May 1969. 234 pp.

In predicting future development, the author states at the outset that "education has one advantage over other social activities. It has lagged so far behind the changes in society as a whole that we already know that it at least needs considerable adaptation, before it is relevant even to the society in which we are now living." (p. 1) Although concerned with education in England, there may be considerable relevance to the U.S. as concerns the description and prescription of developments in content, methods, administration, the teaching profession, tertiary education, and financing.

88. MORPHET, Edgar L. and others (eds.). *Designing Education for the Future: An Eight State Project*. 7 volumes, 1966-1969.

A massive project involving the 8 mountain states and headquartered in Denver. Although the 7 volumes, final report, and 5 sound filmstrips that resulted tend to be rather conventional, leaving one with the impression of blind men somewhat better informed about their elephant of inquiry, there are nevertheless some valuable contributions here, and the ambitious structuring of the entire project is to be especially commended. Most of the following are published by Citation Press, with Morphet and Charles O. Ryan as co-editors of the first three, and Morphet and David L. Jesser as co-editors of the remainder. Each volume is $2.00 paperbound.

Vol. 1. *Prospective Changes in Society by 1980*. N.Y.: Citation, 1967. 268 pp. (16 articles by non educators.)

Vol. 2. *Implications for Education of Prospective Changes in Society*. N.Y.: Citation, 1967. 323 pp. (20 articles, largely by professional educators, in response to Vol. 1.)

Vol. 3. *Planning and Effecting Needed Changes in Education*. N.Y.: Citation, 1967. 317 pp. (26 articles, largely by professional educators, on planning for and effecting change in schools, school systems, metropolitan areas, and at the state level.)

Vol. 4. *Cooperative Planning for Education in 1980: Objectives, Procedures, and Priorities*. N.Y.: Citation, 1968. 105 pp. (Four worthwhile articles concerned with prospective social change and the implications for educational planning.)

Vol. 5. *Emerging Designs for Education.* Denver: Designing Education for the Future, May 1968. 240 pp. (Four articles on implications of societal changes for the educational program, alternative local school district models, and alternative models for state financing.) Citation, 1968.

Vol. 6. *Planning for Effective Utilization of Technology in Education.* Denver: Designing Education for the Future, August 1968. 372 pp. (32 articles, many of them from representatives of potential supplying organizations.) Citation, 1969.

Vol. 7. *Preparing Educators to Meet Emerging Needs.* Denver: Designing Education for the Future, 1969.

2. *Elementary and Secondary*

89. MORPHET, Edgar L. and David L. JESSER (eds.). *Emerging State Responsibilities in Education.* Denver, Colo.: Improving State Leadership in Education (1362 Lincoln Street), 1970. 168 pp.

An initial publication of a new project financed under Title V of ESEA. "In this publication, the implications of recent and prospective changes in society for the emerging roles, functions and relations of state education agencies primarily concerned with the improvement of provisions and procedures needed for planning and effecting improvements in elementary and secondary education are considered in some detail. Some of the major alternatives in organization and procedures are also discussed." (p. vi)

90. CULBERTSON, Jack (ed.). "Education and Public Policy Symposium," *Public Administration Review,* XXX:4, July-August 1970, pp. 331-375.

Seven important articles as follows: "Educational Governance and Policy-Making in Large Cities" (Luvern L. Cunningham), "Low-Income Families and the Schools for their Children" (Theodore R. Sizer), "Federal Influences on Educational Policy" (Roald F. Campbell), "New Relationships Between Education and Industry" (Francis Keppel), "The State and Educational Policy" (Lawrence D. Haskew), "The Changing Nature of the School Superintendency" (Sidney P. Marland, Jr.), and "The Financing of Elementary and Secondary Education" (H. Thomas James).

91. EURICH, Alvin C. and the Staff of the Academy for Educational Development (eds.). *High School 1980: The Shape of the Future in American Secondary Education.* N.Y.: Pitman Publishing Corporation, 1970. 304 pp. $8.50.

Articles on the reformed curriculum in English, Social Studies, Science, Foreign Languages, and Vocational Education, in addition to views of the future of school buildings, guidance and testing, the school without walls, relevance, etc.

92. GOODLAD, John I. *The Future of Learning and Teaching.* An Occasional Paper of The Center for the Study of Instruction. Washington: National Education Association, 1968. 24 pp.

Address at 1967 inaugural ceremonies of Sam Lambert as NEA Executive Secretary. Discusses impact of computer on schools and informal education, the need for "human-based schools" and a humanistic curriculum. By the year 2000, "School, as we now know it, will have been replaced by a diffused learning environment involving homes, parks, public buildings, museums, and an array of guidance and programming centers." (p. 22) Teachers are warned that if they do not legitimize the computer, the profession will be bypassed.

93. McLUHAN, Marshall and George B. LEONARD. "The Future of Education: The Class of 1989," *Look,* 31:4, February 21, 1967, pp. 23-25.

A short and provocative forecast of education by two well-known writers. Mass education is seen as a child of the mechanical age, and with the advent of new technologies, "the very first casualty of the present-day school system may very well be the business of teacher-led instruction as we now know it." The new education "will be more concerned with training the senses and perceptions than with stuffing brains. . . The new student who makes his own educational space, his own curriculum and even develops many of his own learning methods will be unique, irreplacable."

94. BRUNER, Jerome S. "Culture, Politics, and Pedagogy," *Saturday Review,* May 18, 1969, pp. 69-72+.

Discusses learning in the future in light of the knowledge explosion and new retrieval techniques, and argues that "there are three forms of activity that no device is ever going to be able to do as well as our brain with its 5×10^9 cortical connections, and I would suggest that these three represent what will be special about education for the future.

"The first is that we shall probably want to train individuals not for the performance of routine activities that can be done with great skill and precision by devices, but rather to train their individual talents for research and development . . . in the sense of problem-finding rather than problem-solving . . . A second special requirement for education in the future is that it provide training in the performance of 'unpredictable services' . . . acts that are contingent on a response made by somebody or something to your prior act . . . Third, what human beings can produce and no device can is art—in every form . . ." (pp. 71-72)

95. KRAFT, Ivor. "The Coming Crisis in Secondary Education," *The Bulletin of the National Association of Secondary School Principals,* 49-298, February 1965, pp. 5-42.
The entire issue is focused on this trenchant article, which contends that the coming crisis will be fully upon us by 1975. Three components of the crisis involve the incompetence and timidity of educators, administrators, school boards, and policy makers, leaving secondary education leaderless and aimless; the polarization of schools into services for largely college oriented youth and services for lower class youth; and the content and subject matter of education or the discrepancy in relating the learner to what is to be learned. The remainder of the issue is devoted to 14 respondents.

96. ROBINSON, Thorington P. *The Implication of Selected Educational Trends for Future School Systems.* Santa Monica: System Development Corporation, January 1968. SP-3046. 94 pp.
An extrapolation of two major trends: 1. The trend toward the assumption by the schools of tasks and responsibilities previously undertaken by the family, other public agencies, and industry; and 2. The trend toward providing individualized education to all school students. Based on these trends, two skillfully constructed and plausible scenarios are presented.

97. GREEN, Thomas F. "Schools and Communities: A Look Forward," *Harvard Educational Review,* Spring 1969.
A philosopher's discussion of school-community relationships in the 1980-1990 period, focused on both change and continuity.

98. TOFFLER, Alvin (ed.). *The Schoolhouse in the City.* N.Y.: Praeger, 1968. 255 pp.
Sponsored by Stanford and Educational Facilities Laboratories. 21 authors offer answers on urban school construction problems, present case studies of developments in three cities (educational parks in Baltimore and Pittsburgh; Linear City in

Brooklyn), and project the possible future of the schoolhouse in the city.

99. THOMAS, Thomas C. *On Improving Urban School Facilities and Education.* Menlo Park: Stanford Research Institute, Educational Policy Research Center, Policy Research Report EPRC-6747-1, May 1969. 126 pp.

An examination of education parks, mini-schools (storefronts), and neighborhood schools in terms of the reactions by the following stakeholders: white liberals, pro-integration blacks, pro-local control blacks, and teachers. It is concluded that "For different reasons, neither of the two facility innovations—education parks and mini-schools—offer much promise to urban education. One probably should not be implemented, and the other probably will not be implemented. Neighborhood schools will most likely remain the choice of most school districts." (p. 125) Nevertheless, "There will be considerable educational change over the next decade, though it may be cloaked in violence." (p. 126)

100. Educational Facilities Laboratories. *Educational Change and Architectural Consequences.* A Report on the Facilities for Individualized Instruction. N.Y.: EFL, 1968. 88 pp. Free.

In view of the new "spirit of innovation, experimentation, venturesomeness" four school designs are suggested (pre-primary, primary, middle, and secondary) "as a stimulus to open up the options in school design," in that "Too many of our schools still stand as handicaps to new programs and new thinking in education." (p. 85)

3. *Higher Education*

101. KERR, Clark. *The Uses of the University.* Cambridge: Harvard University Press, The Godkin Lectures, 1963. 140 pp.

Although primarily known for introducing the concept of the "multiversity," there is also a provocative chapter entitled "The Future of the City of Intellect." Planners might well contemplate the statement (p. 102) that "Change comes more through spawning the new than reforming the old."

102. EURICH, Alvin C. and the Staff of the Academy for Educational Development. *Campus 1980: The Shape of the Future in American Higher Education.* N.Y.: Delacorte, 1968. 327 pp.

A competent anthology of largely descriptive forecasts by the top writers on higher education, who adhere quite well to the objective of looking at "Campus 1980." Topics include the magnitude of higher education, higher education and the national interest, cities and universities, universities and the world, professionalism, teaching, community colleges, continuing education, college students, curriculum, instructional organization, instructional technology, graduate education, campus architecture, and the university and change.

103. MAYHEW, Lewis B. (ed.). *Higher Education in the Revolutionary Decades.* Berkeley: McCutchan, 1967. 466 pp.

A reader presenting an excellent selection of 34 articles, some of which are cited elsewhere in this bibliography. Although many of the articles deal with trends in the revolutionary decades since World War II, the inclusion of several future-oriented articles implies that forthcoming decades will also be revolutionary. Especially see the scenario by Alvin C. Eurich, "A Twenty-First Century Look at Higher Education," (pp. 443-453) in which universities are seen as stressing wisdom rather than fact-mongering, using television lectures by the world's leading scholars, judging students by standardized criteria of achievement rather than time spent in college, employing microfilmed libraries and portable television sets in dormitory rooms, and allowing individual determination of course mixes. (Eurich offers a similar but updated scenario in *Reforming American Education,* Item 151.)

104. EASTON, David. "The New Revolution in Political Science," *The American Political Science Review,* 63:4, December 1969, pp. 1051-1061. (Presidential Address delivered to the 65th Annual Meeting of the American Political Science Association, September 1969, New York City.)

Describes a new future-oriented "post-behavioral revolution" with its battle cries of relevance and action, taking place not only in political science but simultaneously in the other social sciences. It is seen as "the most recent contribution to our collective heritage" and "an opportunity for necessary change."

Several of the tenets that are suggested for the post-behavioral credo are: substance must precede technique, behavioral science conceals an ideology of empirical conservatism, to know is to bear the responsibility for acting and to act is to engage in reshaping society, etc. "The search for an answer as to how we as political scientists have proved so disappointingly ineffectual in anticipating the world of the 1960's has contributed significantly to the birth of the post-behavioral revolution." (p. 1053) "Both our philosophers and our scientists have failed to reconstruct our value frameworks in any relevant sense and to test them by creatively contemplating new kinds of political systems that might better meet the needs of a post-industrial, cybernetic society." (p. 1058)

105. CAFFREY, John (ed.). *The Future Academic Community: Continuity and Change*. Washington: American Council on Education, 1969. 327 pp. $7.00.

Proceedings of the 1968 ACE Annual Meeting, including articles by Bertrand de Jouvenel, Alvin C. Eurich, Constantinos Doxiadis, John Gardner, etc.

106. JOHNSON, Byron Lamar. *Islands of Innovation Expanding: Changes in the Community College*. Beverly Hills, Calif.: Glencoe Press, 1969. 352 pp.

An authoritative report on a 1967-68 non-statistical survey of innovation in instruction at more than 200 junior colleges. From the context of change in society, education, and junior colleges in general, Johnson discusses specific innovations such as co-op work-study, programmed instruction, the systems approach to instruction, gaming, students as teachers, independent study, etc. Aids and obstacles to innovation are then discussed, with concluding comments on the need for evaluation. Several trends are extrapolated into the short-range future.

107. EURICH, Alvin C., Lucien B. KINNEY, and Sidney G. TICKTON. *The Expansion of Graduate and Professional Education During the Period 1966 to 1980*. Studies in the Future of Higher Education, Report No. 2. N.Y.: The Academy for Educational Development, April 1969. 96 pp.

Based on a sample of 149 universities, all of which were visited in 1967 by a team under the direction of Lewis B. Mayhew. The universities studied expected a growth of 130% in graduate and professional school enrollments from 1967 to 1977. But their plans were frequently not written down in any detail, "nobody knows how much the new and expanded graduate programs will cost in the future," (p. 6) and it was implicitly expected that there would be extensive aid from the federal government. No cutbacks in programs are being planned anywhere: "the theory seems to be that society is going to need more of everything for decades ahead." (p. 6) This document may be somewhat outdated due to recent cutbacks in federal funding of science.

108. JENCKS, Christopher and David RIESMAN. *The Academic Revolution*. Garden City: Doubleday, 1968. 580 pp. $10.00.

An authoritative overview focusing on the growth of professionalism and the consequent emergence of the "university college" as "the model for the future." Recent dissent and subsequent change, however, may make this thorough volume somewhat obsolete in the next few years. Although largely empirical, the final chapter is devoted to "Reforming the Graduate Schools," a concern that is largely overlooked in the many volumes devoted to undergraduate education.

109. RUNKEL, Philip, Roger HARRISON, and Margaret RUNKEL (eds.). *The Changing College Classroom.* San Francisco: Jossey-Bass, October 1969. 368 pp. $9.50.

"Original reports of innovations in college teaching written for this book by . . . college teachers who describe their work in experimental colleges in state universities, liberal arts colleges, urban colleges, private religious colleges, junior colleges, and a Negro college . . . The classes discussed range in size from a dozen to well over a thousand students. The subjects range from mathematics, speech, and writing to psychology, organizational management, and creativity . . . A commonality of goals and an underlying theory unite the underlying practices and experiments: increasing the relevance of education to meet the values and needs of students and increasing the students' freedom, self-direction, and learning-how-to-learn." (advt.)

110. ROURKE, Francis E. and Glenn E. BROOKS. *The Managerial Revolution in Higher Education.* Baltimore: Johns Hopkins, 1966. 184 pp.

A thorough analysis, based on questionnaires and interviews, that estimates the degree to which more rationalized college and university administration has taken place, as regards use of EDP equipment, offices of institutional research, and allocation of resources. Several of the conclusions are that the potential of computers is still largely unrealized, institutional self-study will become increasingly common and varied, and that there is an "unmistakable" trend toward more rational procedures in the management of money and space. The emerging style of university administration is toward greater candor, a cabinet style of governing, and new forms of decision-making. One of the great unresolved questions is whether the new managerial techniques lead to a centralization of power.

111. WALLERSTEIN, Immanuel. *University in Turmoil: The Politics of Change.* N.Y.: Atheneum, 1969. 147 pp. $4.95.

A deep, astute, and elegant essay by a political sociologist. "Three questions about the university in society have come to the fore--none of them new but all posed with renewed urgency and simultaneously. One question is the degree to which it is appropriate for the university . . . to collaborate with the government. The second question is the degree to which it is appropriate for the university to attach some priority to the needs and concerns of the oppressed groups within the society. The third question is how the university may itself best be governed . . ." (p. 9)

"However it acts in relation to the government, the university is engaged in politics." (p. 11) Changing university linkages to government is seen as having relatively little impact on external policy, but changing university policies in view of their growing role as a mechanism for distributing social status and as urban property owners is seen as having a profound impact on society. Finally, overt clashes with the ethnic left and the ideological left is seen as part of a long-range trend to libertarian and participation values. "We are at the early stage of this conflict, the stage of initial testing of strength." (p. 133) This, in turn, will evolve to a stage of constitution-drafting, "perhaps for thirty years or so." (p. 129)

"Thus reform of curricula is not a primary issue. It will come about almost automatically as a consequence of other changes we have been discussing, and it will not come in any significant measure without them." (p. 146)

112. LADD, Dwight R. *Change in Educational Policy: Self-Studies in Selected Colleges and Universities.* A General Report Prepared for The Carnegie Commission on Higher Education. N.Y.: McGraw-Hill, 1970. 231 pp. $5.95.

Brief but well-drawn case studies of the collegial process of attempted reform at Berkeley, New Hampshire, Toronto, Swarthmore, Wesleyan, Michigan State, Duke, Brown, Stanford, Columbia, and UCLA. "While the scope and degree of the proposed changes vary, all have in common the use of the traditional, collegial process of study, analysis, discussion, and debate leading to a decision based on general acceptability . . . Unhappily, the results of these studies seem to lend support--at least in a negative way--to the efficacy of pressure politics as a way of bringing about change." (p. 197)

"The situations reviewed here suggest that these studies have rarely succeeded in bringing about any fundamental change in educational policies on the campuses involved except where a significant portion of the faculty had accepted the desirability of some change before the study began or where pressures for change from outside the faculties were much in evidence." (p. 200)

"It is quite obvious that we can have personnel policies and purchasing policies and library policies in any university, however large. All large bureaucracies have these. What is less obvious after examination of these studies is whether or not large institutions can have *educational* policies—whether the American tradition of giant institutions has not, in the case of higher education, reached the point of diminishing returns." (concluding comment, p. 209)

4. Adult Education

113. MOSES, Stanley. *The Learning Force: An Approach to the Politics of Education.* Prepared for the U.S. Office of Education by the Educational Policy Research Center. Syracuse: EPRC, March 1970. 40 pp.

The Learning Force includes all students in Core institutions (elementary, secondary, and higher education) as well as those in the Periphery (corporation and military training programs, proprietary schools, anti-poverty programs, correspondence schools, formal courses conducted over educational television, and other adult education programs conducted by Core institutions, museums, libraries, unions, etc.). Moses supplies trend data (1940-1975) indicating that enrollments in the Periphery (assessed on a head count rather than an FTE basis) are growing at a rapid rate and will be about 25% greater than Core enrollments by 1975. It is concluded that "Activities in the Periphery provide the basis for developing a new framework for the considerations of educational policy. A consideration of the total Learning Force provides the basis for making an accurate assessment of the true dimensions of education in American society, not only regarding enrollments . . . but also total educational expenditures and employment. A consideration of the total learning force also provides the basis for making more rational decisions regarding policy for the Core as well as providing the basis for new initiatives in the Periphery." (p. 37)

114. TOUGH, Allen. *The Adult's Learning Projects: A Fresh Approach to Theory and Practice in Adult Learning.* Toronto:

Ontario Institute for Studies in Education, July 1971. Approx.
210 pp. and $7.00 (U.S. and Canadian).

The latest and most sophisticated of a series of studies conducted by Tough and his associates on self-initiated learning
behavior. A "learning project" is a series of "learning episodes"
totalling more than 7 hours, an episode being defined as an
effort "in which more than one half of a person's motivation is
to gain and retain certain knowledge and skill that is fairly clear
and definite."

Among 66 adults, the in-depth interviews discovered that 65
had conducted at least one learning project in the past year,
with an average of 8 distinct projects totalling 700 hours a year
of learning effort. Less than 1% of these projects were motivated by academic credit, and about 70% of the projects were
planned by the learner himself. Ten 16-year olds and ten
10-year olds were also interviewed, with a parallel discovery of
significant non-school learning activity.

Despite the small data base, Tough raises a number of fundamental questions for further research and for educational policy
directed toward learners of all ages. Four clusters of suggestions
are offered for making schools and colleges more useful in the
light of observed learning behavior: producing graduates who
are willing and able to set appropriate learning goals, providing
students with a greater choice of how to learn, freeing the
student to choose a larger proportion of subject matter that he
wants to learn, and decreasing the emphasis on credit as a
motivation for learning. For adults, recommendations are made
for better help and resources with both planning and actual
learning, and for new ways of helping people become more
competent as learners.

115. ZIEGLER, Warren L. (ed.). *Essays on the Future of Continuing
Education—World-wide*. Syracuse: Syracuse University Publications in Continuing Education, S.U. Press, July 1970. 141 pp.
$3.00.

Eight articles discussing trends in adult education and methods
of thinking about and planning for the future.

116. LIVERIGHT, A. A. *A Study of Adult Education in the United
States*. Boston University Center for the Study of Liberal
Education for Adults, 1968. 138 pp.

Although not primarily aimed at trends or futures, both are
considered somewhat in this authoritative overview. Of especial
note is the statement that "Even if nothing further is done to

stimulate participation, adults involved in continuing education will triple in number within the next twenty years." (p. 13) Views an upgrading image (from "remedial" to "lifelong" learning) and new program directions involving more courses specifically for adults, more non-credit courses, credit for experience, new degree programs, etc.

117. ANDERSON, Darrell and John A. NIEMI. *Adult Education and the Disadvantaged Adult.* Syracuse: S.U. Publications in Continuing Education and ERIC Clearinghouse on Adult Education, Occasional Papers No. 22, November 1970. 96 pp. Bib., pp. 71-96. $1.50.

A review of the adult education literature to determine the role of education in altering the personal and social characteristics of disadvantaged adults, concluding that "Any plan for a remedy for disadvantage must be concerned with cultural change which involves an alteration in the over-all way of life. Piecemeal approaches directed toward the alleviation of individual distress will not solve the problem because they will not alter the basic cultural environment . . . Thus, it may be more economical in the long run to establish new programs unrelated to present educational institutions than to attempt to reconstruct existing systems."

The bibliography of 317 items is alphabetical and unannotated.

118. BIENVENU, Bernard J. *New Priorities in Training: A Guide for Industry.* N.Y.: American Management Association, 1969. 207 pp. $10.50.

Argues that the bewildering rate of change demands that training become a continuous process, whereas at the present time, 9 out of 10 employee training programs are sporadic affairs. Advocates a "total training" process.

5. *Educational Personnel*

119. U.S. Office of Education. *The Education Professions: 1968. A Report on the People Who Serve Our Schools and Colleges.* Washington: USGPO, OE-58032, June 1969. 377 pp. $2.75.

The first annual assessment of the state of the education professions, as required by the Education Professions Development Act of 1967. A thorough analysis of trends and future requirements through 1975 at all levels, including preschool, elementary, and secondary programs; vocational, post-secondary vocational, and adult education programs; and undergraduate and graduate education, with analysis of personnel in both public and private institutions, and teacher training at each level. Despite "the lack of adequate and comprehensive data on educational personnel . . . the report will hopefully prove to be a positive step toward building a sophisticated bank of information which can be useful to all levels of education." (p. iii)

120. STONE, James C. *Breakthrough in Teacher Education.* San Francisco: Jossey-Bass, 1968. 206 pp. $7.50.

Discusses the Breakthrough Programs (largely sponsored by the Ford Foundation): "a scattering of models from which new patterns in teacher education might spread. Most of the nation's colleges continue to prepare the majority of future teachers in conventional programs." (p. 155) Especially see chart of trends in teacher preparation (pp. 175-76) and new models for innovation proposed in the last chapter.

121. ROSOVE, Perry E. *An Analysis of Possible Future Roles of Educators as Derived from a Contextual Map.* Santa Monica: System Development Corporation, SP-3088, March 8, 1968. 82 pp.

A subsequent report to SP-3026 that presents the "complete" results of an experiment in the use of contextual mapping. "The mapping process results in the identification of 98 different possible future roles for educators and also, as a by-product, it identifies 101 potential future issues in education." (p. 3) It is concluded that "the projections of current trends in 18 areas as displayed on the contextual map suggest that (the crisis in education) is merely beginning and will become increasingly complex, fractious, and more costly to resolve in the two decades ahead." (p. 30) To prevent an evolutionary form of drift, four new concepts are proposed: the learning environment as a real time facility (blurring the distinction between work and education); the continuous, vertical, learning organization serving all educational levels; the learning environment as a multipurpose facility; and (the major conclusion of the study as derived from the above three concepts) the generic role of the "learning facilitator" (rather than the present generic role of "teacher") as a counselor, engineer, instructor in the use of learning resources, and researcher.

6. *Educational Technology*

122. OETTINGER, Anthony, with the collaboration of Sema MARKS. *Run, Computer, Run: The Mythology of Educational Inno-*

vation. Harvard Studies in Technology and Society. Cambridge: Harvard University Press, 1969. 302 pp. $5.95.

An authoritative, caustic, myth-crumbling essay concluding that "The formal education system is bound to society in a way that is almost ideally designed to thwart change. Little *substantive* technological change is therefore to be expected in the next decade." (p. 215) The "present innovation fad . . . favors highly visible quickie approaches creating the illusion of progress." (p. 220)

123. ROSSI Peter H. and Bruce J. BIDDLE (eds.). *The New Media and Education: Their Impact on Society.* Chicago: Aldine, 1966; Garden City: Doubleday Anchor, 1967. 460 pp.

Eleven articles by sociologists on recent and projected technological developments, and the impact of the news media on school systems, higher education, adult education, and the total society.

124. Educational Facilities Laboratories. *The Impact of Technology on the Library Building.* N.Y.: EFL, 1967. 20 pp. Free.

A brief and competent summary of expert opinion concerning the impact of computers on college library buildings.

D. Educational Policy Proposals: Reforms or Thorough Alternatives?

1. Commission Reports

a. General

125. National Goals Research Staff. *Toward Balanced Growth: Quantity with Quality.* Washington: USGPO, July 1970. 222 pp. $1.50.

Outlines options open to policy-makers and advantages and disadvantages of various actions in areas of population growth and distribution, environment, education, consumerism, technology assessment, basic natural science, and economic choices. The introduction by Daniel Moynihan discusses the movement from program to policy-oriented government. The overall theme of balanced growth seeks a more interdependent development, as opposed to policies in the past that "have dealt in a largely independent fashion with specific objectives in their own context." Although judged by some to be overly equivocal, this important document suggests a new direction in public decision-making. The tone contrasts quite markedly, for example, with the certitude of purpose in *Goals for Americans: Programs for Action in the Sixties* (Prentice-Hall, 1960).

126. National Commission on the Causes and Prevention of Violence. *To Establish Justice, To Insure Domestic Tranquility.* Final Report. Washington: USGPO, December 1969. 338 pp. $1.50. Especially see Chapter 9 on campus disorder, which recommends a code of conduct for student-faculty-administration relations, contingency plans for dealing with campus disorders, more rapid and effective decision-making, better communications both on the campus and with alumni and the general public, caution against reactive legislation, and a focus on "striving toward the goals of human life that all of us share and that young people admire and respect." (p. 281) Chapter 10, on "Challenging Our Youth" recommends a lowering of the voting age, draft reform, expanded programs of public service and opportunities for inner-city youth, more research on marijuana use, lowered penalties for use and possession of marijuana, and better communication to bridge the generation gap.

127. National Commission on Technology, Automation, and Economic Progress. *Technology and the American Economy.* Vol. 1. Washington: USGPO, February 1966. 115 pp. The overall conclusion of the Commission is that "our society has not met the challenge of technical progress with complete success. There is much to be done." (p. 6) Of the many recommendations for facilitating adjustment to change, those concerning education are among the most important: universal high school graduation, free public education through grade 14, an open ended system of education stressing lifelong learning, etc. Chapter 9, "Improving Public Decision Making," has an excellent discussion of the role of "social accounting," systems analysis, and "inventing the future."

128. Commission on Tests. *Report of the Commission on Tests. I. Righting the Balance.* (118 pp. $2.00) *II. Briefs.* (194 pp. $3.00) N.Y.: College Entrance Examination Board, 1970. $4.50 for both volumes in boxed set. Recommends that the College Board modify and improve its tests and associated services in seeking to serve its distributive, credentialing, and educative functions. It is suggested that the Board act for both its traditional institutional clientele and for its student clientele, and that the "other half" of non-college-going high school students be served through a job entry testing program and regional centers for guidance in continuing educa-

tion. Thus, the theme of "Righting the Balance" in the first volume. The second volume consists of 14 papers by Commission members, serving as background to the many recommendations made.

129. NATIONAL ACADEMY OF SCIENCES, Committee on Science and Public Policy, and SOCIAL SCIENCE RESEARCH COUNCIL, Committee on Problems and Policy. *The Behavioral and Social Sciences: Outlook and Needs.* A Report by the Behavioral and Social Sciences Survey Committee. Englewood Cliffs: Prentice-Hall, 1969. 230 pp. $7.95.

A systematic self-portrait by 6-10 member panels for each of ten social science disciplines, largely based on a questionnaire survey of research units at 135 universities. Separate reports are being published for each of the disciplines: anthropology, economics, history as social science, political science, sociology, psychology, geography, linguistics, psychiatry, and statistics.

This summary volume provides a good layman's overview of the social sciences: what they do, how they do it, and what they can be expected to contribute toward the formulation of public policy. Major recommendations are as follows: a system of social indicators culminating in an *Annual Social Report to the Nation* that identifies and measures fundamental changes in the quality of life for all people; in support of the above, a special technical commission to investigate and recommend procedures for a national system of statistical data reporting designed for social scientific purposes; the creation of new interdisciplinary programs of teaching and research symbolized by the organizational concept of a Graduate School of Applied Social Research; and an annual increase of 12-18% in federal support of basic and applied research.

130. QUATTLEBAUM, Charles A. *Federal Educational Policies, Programs and Proposals. A Survey and Handbook. Part I: Background; Issues; Relevant Considerations.* Washington: USGPO, House Document No. 398 (Printed for the Use of the Committee on Education and Labor), December 1968. 167 pp. 75 cents.

A valuable overview of a variety of areas as follows:

—Federal Policies in education, 1777-1960

—Congressional enactments concerning education and training, 1961-1966

—History, organization, and functions of USOE and NSF

—Recommendations of 17 governmental and 10 nongovernmental ad hoc advisory commissions, 1929-1967
—Policies advocated by 23 government bodies and 55 private
organizations.

b. Elementary and Secondary

131. National Advisory Commission on Civil Disorders. *Report of
the National Advisory Commission on Civil Disorders.* Special
introduction by Tom Wicker. N.Y.: E.P. Dutton and Bantam
Books, March 1968. 609 pp.
Based on Chapter 16 ("The Future of the Cities"), Chapter 17
("Recommendations for National Action") contains an excellent survey of inner-city education, with many proposals for
reform. (pp. 424-457)

132. President's National Advisory Commission on Rural Poverty.
The People Left Behind. Washington: USGPO, September 1967.
160 pp.
Chapter 5 lists 33 recommendations for changing educating
systems so that rural citizens may be better equipped to participate in the modern world.

133. U.S. House of Representatives, Committee on Education and
Labor, General Subcommittee on Education. *Needs of Elementary and Secondary Education for the Seventies: A Compendium of Policy Papers.* Washington: USGPO, Committee
Print, March 1970. 982 pp.
"The first section of the compendium consists of essays which
have been prepared at the invitation of the Subcommittee by a
distinguished group of more than a hundred university faculty
members and administrators, industrialists and businessmen,
journalists, social philosophers, professional educators, educational researchers, scientists, and other prominent citizens,
reflecting perhaps every shade of opinion about education.
They have been asked both to predict what will be the compelling issues of the seventies and beyond and to suggest poten-
tially fruitful alternatives. The choice of specific topics, however, has been left to the individual writers.

"The second section of the anthology is comprised of the
formal statements which were submitted by witnesses when
they testified at the Subcommittee hearings.

"This collection of papers represents perhaps the most extensive
survey of the educational needs of the seventies that has been

attempted to date." (Foreword by Congressman Roman C. Pucinski, p. v.)

Such a self-assessment can only be heartily seconded. This document is a gold mine, a non-indexed encyclopedia of alternatives.

134. Central Advisory Council for Education (England). *Children and Their Primary Schools. Vol. 1: Report; Vol. 2: Research and Surveys.* London: Her Majesty's Stationary Office, 1967. 556 pp. and 633 pp. respectively. (May be ordered from Sales Section, British Information Services, 845 Third Avenue, New York, New York 10022. Vol. 1, $4.95; Vol. 2, $5.85.)

Known as "The Plowden Report," this thorough and comprehensive study looks at "primary education in all of its aspects and the transition to secondary education." The following are but a few of the many conclusions and recommendations: a higher priority in the educational budget should be given to primary schools (for dollars spent on older children will be wasted if not spent on them during their primary years); "Finding Out" has proven to be better for children than "Being Told"; family background is important; half-time education for 3 and 4 year olds should be provided to ease the transition from home to school; and learners must develop self-confidence in early years.

135. *Living and Learning. The Report of the Provincial Committee on Aims and Objectives of Education in the Schools of Ontario.* Toronto: Ontario Department of Education (44 Eglinton Avenue West), 1968. 221 pp.

A lovely document, summarizing a wide array of literature and special reports, written cogently and forcefully, and amplified by photographs and drawings. The Committee arrived at two fundamental principles: a) the right of every individual to have equal access to the learning experience best suited to his needs, and b) the responsibility of every school authority to provide a child-centered learning continuum that invites learning by individual discovery and inquiry. (p. 179) Based on these principles, 258 recommendations are made in four broad categories reflecting the sequence of the Report: The Learning Program, Special Learning Situations, The World of Teaching, and Organizing for Learning. The appropriate body for consideration and action is listed with each recommendation.

136. U.S. Congress. House of Representatives, Committee on Education and Labor. *To Improve Learning: A Report to the*

President and the Congress of the United States by the Commission on Instructional Technology. Washington: USGPO, March 1970. 124 pp. 50 cents.

Concludes that technology could bring about far more productive use of the teacher's and the student's time, but "that one-shot injections of a single technological medium are ineffective. At best they offer only optional 'enrichment.' Technology, we believe, can carry out its full potential for education only insofar as educators embrace instructional technology as a system and integrate a range of human and nonhuman resources into the total educational process." (p. 7)

The report recommends establishing the National Institutes of Education within the Department of Health, Education and Welfare, and a National Institute of Instructional Technology within the NIE. The NIIT would establish a resource center, conduct demonstration projects, train and retrain teachers and specialists, and bring education and industry together.

The Commission, chaired by Sterling M. McMurrin and staffed by members of the Academy for Educational Development, will publish its full report in two volumes through the R.R. Bowker Co. Appendix G of this summary report lists about 140 papers prepared at the request of the Commission and about 80 papers sent to the Commission for information. Presumably, these will be drawn together in the full report.

137. Advisory Council on Vocational Education. *Vocational Education: The Bridge Between Man and His Work.* General Report of the Advisory Council. Washington: U.S. Office of Education, November 1968. 220 pp. $2.25.

Part I reviews growth and development, financing, administration, research, teacher education, vocational guidance, supporting services, and contemporary local programs. Part II deals with achievements and limitations, social and manpower environments of vocational education, and innovations and new directions (including an excellent summation of 15 trends on p. 191). It is concluded that "there is a growing recognition that far too many youths are leaving school inadequately prepared to enter the labor market and that the schools must assume the responsibility for the vocational preparation for a much larger portion of the school population than they are now accommodating." (p. 193) Part III offers 23 legislative recommendations (including the formation of a Department of Education and Manpower Development at the Cabinet level), and 3 administrative recommendations directed to the Commissioner of Education (including the establishing of a Learning Corps).

138. U.S. Congress. Senate Committee on Labor and Public Welfare, Special Subcommittee on Indian Education. *Indian Education: A National Tragedy—A National Challenge.* Washington: USGPO, November 1969. 220 pp. $1.00.

The work of the Subcommittee, chaired by Senator Edward Kennedy, fills 4,077 pages in seven volumes of hearings and 450 pages in five volumes of committee prints. This report is a condensation, concluding with 60 recommendations for action. "We are shocked at what we discovered . . . We have concluded that our national policies for educating American Indians are a failure of major proportions. They have not offered Indian children—either in years past or today—an educational opportunity anywhere near equal to that offered the great bulk of American children." (p. xi)

c. Higher Education

139. *The Report of the President's Commission on Campus Unrest. Including Special Reports: The Killings at Jackson State; The Kent State Tragedy.* N.Y.: Arno, 1970. 529 pp. $5.95. (Report also appearing in *The Chronicle of Higher Education,* V:2, October 5, 1970, pp. 2-24.)

The Scranton Commission report on "a crisis of violence and understanding," finding that most student protesters are neither violent nor extremist. Many recommendations for law enforcement, the President, government, the university, and students.

140. American Academy of Arts and Sciences, Assembly on University Goals and Governance. *A First Report of the Assembly on University Goals and Governance.* Boston: AAAS (280 Newton Street), 1971. Reprinted in *The Chronicle of Higher Education,* V:15, January 18, 1971.

A blue ribbon panel headed by Martin Meyerson, listing 85 theses to stimulate academic reforms in all areas of higher education, and nine themes pervading the report: learning as the central mission, institutional self-knowledge as a basis for educational reform, extending choice in admissions and attendance, experimentation and flexibility in undergraduate and graduate education, diversification and differentiation, preserving the private and public systems, enhancing the professoriate by broadening the basis of recruitment, governance by delegation and accountability, and inventing new procedures and institutional forms to make co-operation and self-help more of a reality.

141. Carnegie Commission on Higher Education
—General Information pamphlet available from The Commission, 1947 Center St., Berkeley, Calif. 94704
—All publications may be ordered from McGraw-Hill Book Co., Hightstown, N.J. 08520

A monumental endeavor, headed by Clark Kerr, concerned with the functions, structure, and governance of higher education, innovation and change, demand and expenditures, available resources, and effective use of resources. 67 special studies have been commissioned, and special reports "of urgent public interest" have appeared since December 1968. The final report of the commission is due in June 1972.

SPECIAL REPORTS
—*Quality and Equality: New Levels of Federal Responsibility for Higher Education.* (December 1968, 54 pp.) Supplement with Revised Recommendations. (June 1970. $1.00)
—*A Chance to Learn: An Action Agenda for Equal Opportunity in Higher Education.* (March 1970. 29 pp. $1.00)
—*The Open-Door Colleges: Policies for the Community Colleges.* (June 1970. $1.00)
—*Higher Education and the Nation's Health: Policies for Medical and Dental Schools.* (October 1970. 128 pp. $2.95)
—*Less Time, More Options: Education Beyond the High School.* (December 1970)
—*From Isolation to Mainstream: Problems of the Colleges Founded for Negroes.* (February 1971, 81 pp.)
—*Dissent and Disruption: Proposals for Consideration by the Campus.* (April 1971)
—*The Capitol and the Campus: State Responsibility for Postsecondary Education.* (April 1971. 144 pp. $2.95)
SELECTED SPECIAL STUDIES
—Earl F. Cheit, *The New Depression in Higher Education.* December 1970. 250 pp. (price n.a.) Examines 41 private and public colleges and universities, finding 70% of them either "in financial difficulty" or "headed for trouble."
—Irwin T. Sanders and Jennifer C. Ward, *Bridges to Understanding: International Programs of American Colleges and*

Universities. December 1970. $7.95. Finds international studies still largely underdeveloped and present levels of activity in serious jeopardy.

—Lewis B. Mayhew, *Graduate and Professional Education, 1980: A Survey of Institutional Plans.* August 1970. $3.95.

—Heinz Eulau and Harold Quinley, *State Officials and Higher Education: A Survey of the Opinions and Expectations of Policy-Makers in Nine States.* March 1970. $5.95.

(About a dozen others have been published as of February 1971. Also, see Ladd, Item 112.)

142. President's Task Force on Higher Education, *Priorities in Higher Education.* Washington: USGPO, 1970. 30 cents. (Recommendations published in *The Chronicle of Higher Education,* October 19, 1970, pp. 3-4.)

Chaired by James M. Hester, the Task Force makes recommendations on financial aid for disadvantaged students, Negro colleges, support for health-care professional education, increased tax incentives for support to higher education, the expansion of opportunities for post-high-school education, the support of high-quality graduate and professional education, clarification of institutional purposes, improvement in the quality of the curriculum and methods of teaching and learning, clarification of institutional governance, and establishing a National Academy of Higher Education modeled after the National Academy of Sciences.

143. The President's Committee on Education Beyond the High School. *Second Report to the President.* Washington: USGPO, July 1957. 114 pp.

Originally intended as an interim report similar to the first one (November 1956), funds were cut off and this report serves as a final statement. There are a number of recommendations concerning inputs: the need for teachers, assistance to students, expansion and diversity of educational opportunities, and financing higher education; but there is no concern for the quality of educational services as there is at present. However, there are two remarkable insights that are still relevant for contemporary policy-making: the recognition of peripheral education in corporations, the military, etc., such that "we have become a 'society of students' " (p. 1), and the emphasis on the neglected federal role in collecting information. "We have been struck above all else by the astounding lack of accurate, consistent, and up-to-date facts, and by how little this Nation knows about its enormously vital and expensive educational enterprise in contrast to how much it knows, in great detail, about agriculture, industry, labor, banking and other areas." (p. 15) Indeed!

144. Commission on Post-Secondary Education in Ontario. *Post-Secondary Education in Ontario: A Statement of Issues.* Toronto: Ontario Department of Education (44 Eglinton Avenue West), 1970. 20 pp. Free.

An interim statement by the Wright Commission, briefly outlining issues such as expected number of students, institutional characteristics, costs, the economic argument for education, the manpower argument for education, certification, education and social justice, the example of the U.S., measurements, technology, structural problems, students' share of cost, etc. An excellent overview of essential questions.

145. National Science Foundation. *Toward A Public Policy for Graduate Education in the Sciences.* Report of the National Science Board. Washington: USGPO, NSB 69-1, 1969. 63 pp. 40 cents.

Primarily addressed to graduate education and research in the natural sciences, the social sciences, and engineering, many of the conclusions of the report are nevertheless applicable to the arts and humanities. Graduate education is seen as having developed without an explicit national policy, and in that enrollments are expected to double and costs quadruple by 1980, substantial federal funding is seen as necessary. Recommendations are made to educational institutions, state and regional planners, and the federal government. "These recommendations are made in the firm conviction that no instrumentality of society can contribute more importantly to the future strength and well-being of the Nation and its citizens than does graduate education." (p. xii) Perhaps.

146. National Science Foundation. *Graduate Education: Paramenters for Public Policy.* Report prepared for the National Science Board. Washington: USGPO, NSB 69-2, 1969. 168 pp. $1.25.

"Presents the statistical evidence, forward projections, analyses, and interpretations which underlie the conclusions and recommendations offered in the First Report . . . However, this is much more than an Appendix . . . It is both a unique analysis of the present status of graduate education and the source of a large body of information and useful correlations which should be invaluable to rational planning for graduate education and indeed for all of higher education." (p. iii) The three chapters cover dimensions of graduate education (no. institutions, distribution of enrollment), correlates of quality (high quality found largely in large institutions and large departments), and financial perspectives. Many public policy issues are raised, such as creating new institutions vs. expanding existing ones, geographic priorities, offsetting a possible decline in quality during the next decade, etc.

147. STEINHART, John S. and Stacie CHERNIACK. *The Universities and Environmental Quality—Commitment to Problem Focused Education.* A Report to the President's Envrionmental Quality Council. Washington: Executive Office of the President, Office of Science and Technology, September 1969. 71 pp. 70 cents.

A report on several multidisciplinary environmental programs. Despite some promising starts, there is still a severe shortage of ecology professionals, and the report suggests actions that the federal government can take, such as assisting in the formulation at colleges and universities of Schools of the Human Environment.

2. *Other Prescriptions*

a. General

148. PLATT, John. "What We Must Do," *Science,* 166: November 28, 1969, pp. 1115-1121.

A concise and powerful overview of the multiple crises that we are confronting, with the view that "it has now become urgent for us to mobilize all our intelligence to solve these problems if we are to keep from killing ourselves in the next few years." Two overview charts are provided (for the U.S. and the World), indicating the priority of problem areas and the estimated time to crisis, broken down in three future periods (1-5 years, 5-20 years, and 20-50 years). For the U.S. the problem areas, in order of priority, are total annihilation, great destruction or change (physical, biological or political), widespread almost unbearable tension (slums, race conflict), large-scale distress (transportation, urban blight, crime), tension producing responsive change (water supply, privacy, drugs, marine resources), other problems important but adequately researched (military R&D, new educational methods), exaggerated dangers and hopes (mind control, heart transplants), and non-crisis problems being overstudied (man in space and most basic science). It is concluded that "The task is clear. The task is huge. The time is horribly short. In the past, we have had science for intellectual pleasure, and science for the control of nature. We have had science for war. But today, the whole human experiment may hang on the question of how fast we now press the development of science for survival."

Although this is one man's list of priorities, it is critically important that more thinking be generated along these lines. Although education is not directly mentioned in this article, the implications should be obvious.

149. GARDNER, John. *Self-Renewal: The Individual and the Innovative Society.* N.Y.: Harper & Row, 1963. 141 pp.

A lucid and powerful essay advocating "The Ever-Renewing System" and "Educating for Renewal."

150. USDAN, Michael D., David W. MINAR, and Emanuel HURWITZ, Jr. *Education and State Politics: The Developing Relationship Between Elementary-Secondary and Higher Education.* N.Y.: Columbia University, Teachers College Press, 1969. 190 pp.

An excellent although preliminary attempt to analyze statewide coordination as of summer 1967, based on the experience of 12 states (California, Florida, Georgia, Illinois, Indiana, Massachusetts, Michigan, New Jersey, New York, Ohio, Pennsylvania, and Texas).

The two general findings are that in most states the interlevel relationship verges on open political conflict; yet, "state policy-makers seldom recognize the relationship as something worthy of attention. They have been content, in the general style of American politics, to take problems piece-by-piece, confronting them only when necessary and then in as small portions as possible. The point, however, is that as the pressures rise and conflict grows, the probability of problems being handled successfully on this basis declines. The financial crisis of American education requires massive, broad scale consideration." (p. 188)

"On the whole, we have been pushed toward the conclusion that interlevel coordination in education is a desirable, if not essential, step. Such coordination need not be and indeed would not be likely to be tight and neat. But without some effort to bring the forces of education together into some form of integrated structure, the ability of the states to undertake rational planning in education is bound to suffer." (p. 187)

151. EURICH, Alvin C. *Reforming American Education: The Innovative Approach to Improving Our Schools and Colleges.* N.Y.: Harper & Row, 1969. 269 pp. $6.50.
"Education must be vastly improved to meet the challenges of the present and the future; the innovative approach is the most promising strategy for bringing about such improvement." Taking a wide-angle view, the author discusses rigid dogmas, the necessity for bold public policies, provocative new developments, new patterns of reform at all levels, and education as a futurist enterprise. An updated scenario (see Item 103), "A Twenty-First Century View of American Higher Education," (pp. 175-199), touches on university cities, sea-grant colleges on floating ocean cities, the revival of philosophy and the humanities to deal with spiritual malaise, learning terminals with graphic tables and multi-purpose TV type displays, computerized learning, internationalization, individualization, etc.

152. ROGERS, Carl R. *Freedom to Learn: A View of What Education Might Become.* Columbus, Ohio: Charles E. Merrill Publishing Co., 1969. 358 pp.
An eminent psychologist feels that "all teachers and educators prefer to facilitate experiential and meaningful learning, rather than the nonsense syllable type. Yet in the vast majority of our schools, at all educational levels, we are locked into a traditional and conventional approach which makes significant learning improbable if not impossible . . . It is not because of any inner depravity that educators follow such a self-defeating system. It is quite literally because they do not know any feasible alternative." (p. 5) Alternatives are suggested toward building "a fully functioning person" and a plan for self-directed change in an educating system is proposed. Although the comments are directed at all levels, a special chapter is devoted to "A Revolutionary Program for Graduate Education," in that the graduate level "is frequently the furthest behind the main stream of our culture and is the least educational in any true sense." (p. 189)

153. TAYLOR, Harold. *The World as Teacher.* N.Y.: Doubleday, 1969. 322 pp. $6.95.
The result of a two-year study of the education of American teachers in world affairs. Proposes a wide array of reforms, to make education more relevant to the emerging world society.

154. GATTEGNO, Caleb. *Towards a Visual Culture: Educating Through Television.* N.Y.: Outerbridge & Dienstfrey, 1969. 117 pp. $4.95.

A serious essay of McLuhanesque proportions on the potentials of television in education: "a call to use television for what it can give, which is really tremendous and by most still unsuspected." (p.4) ". . . only recently, through television, has (man) been able to shift from the clumsiness of speech . . . to the power of the dynamic, infinite visual expression . . . we can foresee the coming of an era where . . . we shall be able to share vast conscious experiences at once . . . The future is requiring that we learn to consider ever larger wholes in whatever social position we find ourselves . . . a visual culture is the answer to such a trend . . . sight is far swifter means of experiencing and communicating than speech." (p. 5)

155. GANS, Herbert J. "The Mass Media as an Educational Institution," Center for Urban Education, *The Urban Review,* 2:1, February 1967.

A challenging discussion of policy implications based on the premise that "both the school and the mass media are, in the broadest sense, political institutions competing for cultural power in the society." Because of "the media's demonstrated ability at engaging a child's interest and holding his attention more adequately than the school," it is suggested that "perhaps school learning should not be a compulsory process" and the school should become more audience oriented. "The School's conception of the child, which developed in an era in which there was no democracy or equality for children . . . needs to be replaced." The conception of the teacher as a professional with a monopoly of knowledge "is no longer applicable in an era when the mass media have informed both children and parents."

156. ILLICH, Ivan. *De-Schooling Society.* N.Y.: Harper & Row, World Perspective Series, April 1971.

Two preview articles in the *New York Review of Books* ("Schooling: The Ritual of Progress," December 3, 1970, pp. 20-26; "Education Without School: How It Can Be Done," January 7, 1971, pp. 25-31) suggest that this may be the most important and controversial book of 1971. In the first article, Illich summarizes much of the thinking that appears in his collection of essays *Celebration of Awareness: A Call for Institutional Revolution.* (Doubleday, 1970. 189 pp. $5.95.) He views the entire schooling system as the modern equivalent of the church, and attacks the multitude of myths that inhibit learning and equal opportunity. In the second article he outlines a thorough alternative involving reference services to educators at large who would be chosen by polling or consulting former clients. By doing so, "we can depend on self-motivated learning instead of employing teachers to bribe or compel the student . . . we can provide the learner with new links to the world instead of continuing to funnel all educational programs through the teacher." (p. 25) A thorough de-schooling of society is considered to be at the root of any movement for human liberation. Recent essays by Illich also appear in *CIDOC Cuaderno* (see below). Especially see No. 1007, 1970. ($4.00 for single copy)

157. REIMER, Everett. *An Essay on Alternatives in Education.* Cuernavaca, Mexico: Centro Intercultural de Documentacion (Apdo. 479), CIDOC Cuaderno No. 1005, 1970. 93 pp. To be published in *Interchange* (see Item 192), 2:1, along with six responding articles.

Reimer is a colleague of Illich who thinks along similar lines. It is not clear (and probably not important) as to who has originated what idea, for, as explained in the introduction to this essay, Reimer and Illich have been conversing for almost 15 years since meeting in Puerto Rico. Paolo Friere, Paul Goodman, and others have also contributed to this body of thought.

In this comprehensive essay, Reimer views school as "the universal church of the technological society" and sees the formation of a universal international curriculum. Yet, "The conclusion is inescapable: no country in the world can afford the education its people demand in the form of schools." Even in the U.S., where the richest one-tenth of the population gets ten times as much public funds for education as the poorest one-tenth, it is estimated that an additional $80 billion would be required to fully meet educational demands. Given the growing importance of schooling benefits, it is inevitable that the rich outdistance the poor both within and between nations, unless they grow in charity faster than they grow in privilege. "Since there is no precedent for such behavior, it seems wiser to turn to the other alternative, namely, not to separate education from activities which provide for more basic needs." It is also considered essential that learning resources be allocated outside the school system (as the only means of attaining equity), and that control of these resources should be in the hands of persons seeking to learn.

Schools will not be abandoned, but are seen as only one way of organizing the resources required for learning (time, space, objects, and people). A system of lifetime educational accounts is advocated (not unlike the voucher system), in addition to four laws that would effectively disestablish the school system as an educational monopoly: a law separating school and state (similar to the first amendment of the U.S. Constitution), a law forbidding favoritism based on schooling ("Where and how one has been schooled is as irrelevant to one's capacity to do a job as race or religion"), a law requiring equal sharing of public educational resources, and an effective extension of anti-monopoly laws to the field of education. This fundamentally new dimension may significantly change the nature of our ongoing national debate over education for many years to come.

158. FREIRE, Paolo. *The Pedagogy of the Oppressed.* N.Y.: Herder & Herder, November 1970. $5.95.

A Brazilian educator argues that "every human being, no matter how 'ignorant' or submerged in the 'culture of silence,' is capable of looking critically at the world in a dialogical encounter with others, of perceiving his personal and social reality, and of dealing critically with it."

159. FARBER, Jerry. *The Student as Nigger: Essays and Stories.* N.Y.: Contact Books, August 1969; Pocket Books, September 1970. 142 pp. 95 cents.

The pungent title essay of this policy manual for institutional clients is already an underground classic, having appeared (by Farber's estimate) in about 500 publications. But far more is offered here. "The Student and Society: An Annotated Manifesto" begins with the assertion that "School is where you let the dying society put its trip on you . . . it's not what you're taught that does the harm but how you're taught. Our schools teach you by pushing you around, by stealing your will and your sense of power . . . Students can change things if they want to because they have the power to say 'no'." (p. 17)

In "The Four-Fold Path to Student Liberation," Farber advocates The Way of Direct Action (non-violent), The Way of the Provo (not always practical but always aesthetic), The Way of the Square (student government) and The Way of the Self

("When people stop playing 'student,' they will be able to learn without surrendering themselves in exchange.") Also see "A Young Person's Guide to the Grading System" and a brilliant satire of academic behaviorists: "Teaching Johnny to Walk: An Ambulation Instruction Program for the Normal Preschool Child."

Whether or not one is sympathetic, educators should recognize that volumes such as this are increasingly influential in shaping educational policy.

b. Elementary and Secondary

160. BERMAN, Louise M. *New Priorities in the Curriculum.* Columbus, Ohio: Charles E. Merrill Publishing Co., 1968. 241 pp. Bib., pp. 197-238.

A well-researched proposal "to open up the possibility of the development of process-oriented persons within our schools." Each chapter discusses a process and the need for it: perceiving, communicating, loving, decision-making, knowing, organizing, creating, and valuing. Bibliography of about 600 items.

161. KOHL, Herbert R. *The Open Classroom: A Practical Guide to a New Way of Teaching.* N.Y.: New York Review/Vintage, 1969. 116 pp. $1.65.

"This book is a handbook for teachers who want to work in an open environment . . . It is important not to equate an open classroom with a 'permissive' environment," (p. 15) Kohl explains alternatives to textbooks and the domination of the teacher, learning from the experience of the students, establishing rules and routines only as necessary for a particular class, discipline, and how a teacher can survive in an oppressive bureaucracy while maintaining an open and exciting classroom treating students as people. It is contended that these principles of non-authoritarian education are applicable to all fields of learning.

162. UMANS, Shelley. *The Management of Education: A Systematic Design for Educational Revolution.* Garden City: Doubleday, 1970. 226 pp. $5.95.

The Director of the Center for Innovation of the New York City Board of Education discusses PPBS, change models, educational programs of industry and government, and various trends in electronic media. Advocates a new educational system, "incorporating only those elements of education that have proven to be important." (p. 23) The "Blueprint for the

Future" envisions the total community as the school, with the
school building of today just one small station, along with
educational environment centers (neighborhood facilities offering a full range of services for all people at all times), satellite
development centers, block schools, skills centers, and the " 'No
School' School."

163. Sudbury Valley School. *The Crisis in American Education: An
Analysis and A Proposal.* Framingham, Mass.: The Sudbury
Valley School Press (Winch Street), 1970. 109 pp. $1.50.

"This book presents the action and thought which brought
forth The Sudbury Valley School, and will bring forth other
schools like it throughout the country." A bold new solution is
proposed to overcome "Our Un-American Schools: . . . for
education in America today, the grand strategy must be to
make the schools the embodiment of the American Dream for
young and old alike—to make the schools bastions of Individual
Rights, Political Democracy, and Equal Opportunity for all
people and for all time." (p. 45) The Sudbury Valley School
opened in July 1968 as a day school for students aged four
years and up . . . "a prototype democratic school for all to see
and to study." The second step in the tactic of change is to
establish satellite public schools, culminating finally in public
schools with public support.

164. GROSS, Ronald and Beatrice (eds.). *Radical School Reform.*
N.Y.: Simon and Schuster, 1969. 350 pp. $7.95.

A wide-ranging anthology of 23 articles. "Radical means going
to the root, posing the fundamental problems, and responding
with theories and practices which are genuine alternatives to
present theory and practice . . . radical means unorthodox ways
of promoting learning that fall outside the scope of conventional or even innovative school practice. This book reflects the
entire range of radical thought and practice, from the grand
demand that compulsory public education be repealed and the
formal educational system dismantled to reports of intensely
practical teachers working constructively within the existing
situation but nevertheless using truly unorthodox teaching
techniques." (p. 14)

Especially see: Kenneth B. Clark, "Alternative Public School
Systems," (reprinted from *Harvard Educational Review,* Winter
1968) which discusses regional state schools, federal regional
schools, college and university-related open schools, industrial

demonstration schools, labor union sponsored schools, and army schools.

165. GOODLAD, John I., M. Frances KLEIN, and Associates. *Behind the Classroom Door.* Worthington, Ohio: Charles A. Jones Publishing Co., 1970. 116 pp. $2.75 paper.

Based on organizational, curricular, and instructional thrusts which have been widely recommended and which one "might reasonably expect to be substantially implemented," the authors studied 150 classrooms in 67 schools and found that all of the changes recommended over the past 15 years "were blunted on school and classroom door." They also found a universal sameness, "a considerable discrepancy between teachers' perceptions of their own innovative behavior and the perceptions of observers," supplementary and enrichment activities differing little from regular activities, non-identified goals in the classroom and the school as a whole, and school personnel appearing to be very much alone in their endeavors.

Perhaps the most telling observation about our educational system is that there is not, below the level of intense criticism and endless recommendations for improvement, any effective structure by means of which countervailing ideas and models may be pumped in and developed to the point of becoming real alternatives. Stated conversely, the system is geared to self-preservation, not to self-renewal." (p. 99)

166. SILBERMAN, Charles E. *Crisis in the Classroom: The Remaking of American Education,* N.Y.: Random House, Fall 1970. 525 pp. $10.00.

Based on a three and one-half year study commissioned by the Carnegie Corporation, this broad indictment of all levels of education is based on a thorough review of the literature, extensive interviews and correspondence with educators and critics, and first hand investigation in more than 100 schools by the author and in about 150 more schools by his three-member staff.

Silberman finds the schools to be "intolerable," severely afflicted by "mindlessness," operating on the assumption of distrust, offering a banal and trivial curriculum, and pre-occupied with order and control (which in turn creates discipline problems, rather than eliminating them). More than 200 examples of school practice are provided in support of these charges, which are no less severe than those made by the so-called "romantic" critics of the past decade.

Based on an analysis of the superiority of English primary schools, "informal education" (also known as free schools, open learning systems, etc.) is strongly advocated.

167. GLASSER, William, M.D. *Schools Without Failure.* N.Y.: Harper & Row, 1969. 235 pp. $4.95.

A psychiatrist sees the schools as largely failure-oriented which is "the most impractical result of education." By failing to satisfy the basic needs of love and attaining self-worth, the author estimates, from his experience in the central city of Los Angeles, "that 75 percent of the children do not achieve a satisfactory elementary education." Parents do not complain because "they cannot compare their children's failure with a successful school experience of their own . . ." (p. 113)

Based on the principles of his previous book, *Reality Therapy,* Glasser makes many proposals that he has employed successfully: class meetings, reasonable rules, student conversations with adults, inviting graduates back to talk with students, abolishing grading, giving recognition to students with bad records when they start to do well, and using failing students to tutor younger failing students. Although oriented primarily toward elementary education because it is considered most important, the ideas in the book are applicable to all levels. Especially see Chapter 5 on Relevance, the attack on Fact and Memory Education in Chapter 6, and Chapter 13 on Morality (or the need to learn and experience the value of truthfulness, which is often discouraged by schools). A simply-written, sensitive, and gentle book encouraging profound and humane reform.

168. FANTINI, Mario, Marilyn GITTELL, and Richard MAGAT. *Community Control and the Urban School.* Introduction by Kenneth B. Clark. N.Y.: Praeger, July 1970. 288 pp. $7.95; $2.95 paper.

"A comprehensive study of the participation issue in urban public schools. Tracing the development of public education and the bureaucratization of school systems since the 1900's, the authors examine where and for whom the attempt to provide universal education failed. They offer a persuasive case for community control as a means of achieving the participation they consider to be an intrinsic part of the education process." (advt.)

169. FANTINI, Mario D. and Milton A. YOUNG. *Designing Education for Tomorrow's Cities.* N.Y.: Holt, Rinehart and Winston, 1970. 160 pp.

Present educational systems are found to be outmoded and inadequately structured (has anyone yet to find them adequate?), and, as a suggestion for strategies of major reform, the authors use the development of the Fort Lincoln New Town school system in Washington, D.C. as a case study.

170. HAVIGHURST, Robert J., Frank L. SMITH, Jr., and David E. WILDER. *A Profile of the Large City High School.* Washington: National Association of Secondary School Principals, 1970.
A study of 700 high schools in 45 cities with more than 300,000 population, recommending new approaches such as a single experimental high school at a central location, temporary shifting of faculty to provide more racial integration and distribution of experience, allowing students to divide attendance among two or more schools, employing an open attendance rule allowing inner-city students to enroll in comprehensive or middle-class schools, and constructing one or more large high schools in a kind of educational park enabling greater diversity of students.

171. FISH, Kenneth L. *Conflict and Dissent in the High School: An On the Scene Analysis* N.Y.: Bruce Publishing Co., 1970. $6.95.
"A comprehensive, nationwide study of student unrest by a high school principal for the National Association of Secondary Schools under a grant from the Ford Foundation. A first hand report on why eruptions occur with recommended action for the future." (advt.)

172. Syracuse University Research Corporation, Policy Institute. *Disruption in Urban Public Secondary Schools.* Syracuse: SURC Policy Institute (723 University Ave.), August 1970. 61 pp. + Appendices. (Prepared for USOE).
A broad survey of the literature combined with 27 on-site visits and 683 usable questionnaires. Of the urban high schools surveyed, 85% experienced some type of disruption during the last three years, and disruptions were found to be *more* frequent in racially integrated schools. The traditional punitive methods of dealing with disruptions (expulsion, arrest, in-school detention, etc.) are seen as often producing counter-productive results. Many remedies are proposed, including overcoming bigness, recruiting and promoting black personnel, special schools for disruptive students, utilizing young adult security personnel, etc.

173. WESTIN, Allen F. et. al. *Civic Education in a Crisis Age: An Alternative to Repression and Revolution.* N.Y.: Columbia

University, Center for Research and Education in American Liberties, September 1970. 27 pp.

Finds that a large majority of nearly 7000 junior and senior high school students surveyed feel they are regularly subjected to undemocratic decisions, and proposes ten objectives for civic education.

174. Montgomery County (Md.) Student Alliance. "A Study Report of the Montgomery County Public School System. Wanted: A Humane Education. An Urgent Call for Reconciliation Between Rhetoric and Reality," in Diane Divoky (ed.) *How Old Will You Be in 1984? Expressions of Student Outrage From the High School Free Press.* N.Y.: Discus Avon, 1969. $1.25 paper.

The 250 selections from the underground press in the Divoky volume are of some interest, but the "Study Report" (pp. 329-350) is extremely well done and compares favorably (in its maturity and insight) with many if not all of the other "adult" reports cited here. The county public schools are attacked for basing the system on fear, dishonesty, distruction of eagerness to learn, causing alienation, demanding blind obedience to authority, stifling self-expression, narrow scope of ideas, prejudice, and instilling self-hate. "The extent to which school officials appear unaware or unconcerned about how students feel and the effects of the schools is frightening and disturbing." (p. 334) 24 recommendations are made, including an ombudsman, an end to secret files, student input in teacher evaluations, eliminating letter grades, a free press, shorter and more flexible learning modules, relevant courses, informing students of their rights, a student voice on the school board, etc.

175. BLISHEN, Edward (ed.). *The School That I'd Like.* Middlesex, England: Penguin Books, 1969. 171 pp.

A charming collection of astute comments by English children, ages 11-18, based on a competition conducted by *The Observer* in December 1967. Blishen concludes that: "Standing out above everything else is the children's desire to teach themselves, rather than to be the passive targets of teaching: a great restlessness about classrooms, timetables, the immemorial and so often inert routine of schools. The children seem to sense what their elders are slow to sense, that you enter the world of the late twentieth century ill-armed if all you have done is to submit, to some degree or other, to a pre-determined, pinched, examination-harried course of instruction, from which in its nature most of the excitement and surprise of learning is excluded . . .

"The evidence of all this writing is that our children are immensely anxious to be reasonable, to take account of practical difficulties. Some of these entries were dullish or dulled, but there was very little in them that was foolish. I can't imagine any educationist anxious to learn from what the children say who would not emerge from this book with his head full of perfectly firm and very sensible ideas." (pp. 13-14) Quite so, and one would hope to see many American counterparts of this volume, to supplement critiques provided in underground newspapers.

176. POSTMAN, Neil. "Once Upon a Time—A Fable of Student Power," *The New York Times Magazine,* June 14, 1970. pp. 10-11.

Although brief, this delightful scenario describes a very clear alternative to schooling that was put into effect during an officially declared state of emergency in New York City. The Emergency Education Committee developed a curriculum for all children in the 7th-12th grades, known as Operation Survival, obliging them to clean up neighborhoods, beautify the city, direct traffic (freeing the police to fight crime), deliver mail, publish neighborhood newspapers, assist in hospitals, register voters, substitute for certain adults whose jobs the students could perform without injury or loss of efficiency (thus freeing the adults to attend school or assist students in saving the city) and, with the aide of college students, conducting an auxiliary public transportation system (thereby reducing auto traffic). Consequently, young people assumed a proprietary interest in their environment and came to be respected by the old, leading to a revival of courtesy and a decrease in crime. "Amazingly, most of the students found that while they did not 'receive' an education, they were able to create a quite adequate one." Difficulties developed, however, from teachers who felt their training to be wasted, and the inability to tell dumb children from smart children due to the cessation of testing. "But the Mayor . . . promised that as soon as the emergency was over everything would be restored to normal. Meanwhile, everybody lived happily ever after—in a state of emergency, but quite able to cope with it."

177. Center for the Study of Public Policy. *Education Vouchers: A Preliminary Report on Financing Education by Payments to Parents.* Cambridge, Mass.: The Center (56 Boylston Street), March 1970. 219 pp.

A report of the first phase of research contracted by USOE which explores the following areas: determining the value of vouchers and the restrictions (if any) on private supplementation, insuring adequate information for intelligent choices by parents, procedures for allocating scarce places, education vouchers compared with state "purchase of services" from private schools, and the relationship of vouchers to racial segregation and the First Amendment prohibition against establishment of religion. The second phase of this important research will demonstrate the feasibility of an experimental project.

178. COONS, John E., William H. CLUNE III, and Stephen D. SUGARMAN. *Private Wealth and Public Education*. Cambridge: Belknap Press of Harvard University, 1970. 520 pp. $12.50.

Three lawyers thoroughly analyze discrimination by wealth in state systems of school finance and American value systems in general, proposing a plan of "power equalizing" based on manipulation of state and local taxes. The primary hope for change is through court actions. For the latest proposals, see John Coons and Stephen B. Sugarman, *The Family Choice in Education Act: A Heuristic Model for State Education.* Berkeley: Institute for Governmental Studies, Spring 1971. Approx. $1.50. (Also to appear in *California Law Review,* May 1971). For parallel proposals in higher education, see following item.

c. Higher Education

179. "Learn Now, Pay Later," *The New Republic,* February 20, 1971. pp. 12-13.

A brief report on the Pay as You Earn (PAYE) plan proposed by Yale University, which might alleviate the financial problems of higher education by removing much of the cost burden from taxpayers and placing it on the beneficiaries. Any student would be able to borrow money, and repayment would be over a period of about 35 years at an amount dependent on the level of income; thus, students in high-paying fields of work would repay more than they borrowed, while those making less would repay less. If the Yale pilot idea is successful, the scheme may be tried nationally, with a resource bank similar to FHA, and loan repayments incorporated in federal income tax and payroll withholding.

The genesis of the Yale plan is not known; however the idea has appeared in at least three recent instances:

—William J. PLATT and Janet ABRAMS, *A Self-Financing Fund for Student Charges in Higher Education,* Educational Policy Research Center at Stanford, Research Note EPRC-6747-7, October 1968. 22 pp.

—James TOBIN and Leonard ROSS, "A National Youth Endowment: Paying for the High Costs of Education," *The New Republic,* May 3, 1969. pp. 18-21.

—Michael CLURMAN, "How Shall We Finance Higher Education?," *The Public Interest,* No. 19, Spring 1970. pp. 98-110.

The PAYE plan is intended to promote equality of opportunity, similar to voucher proposals for elementary and secondary education.

180. ZWEIG, Michael. *The Idea of a World University.* Edited with a foreward by Harold Taylor. Carbondale: Southern Illinois University Press, 1967. 204 pp.

A thorough exploration of a recurring idea for an institution "which would match on an intellectual scale what the United Nations was designed to accomplish in a political dimension . . . a rough estimate would be that since the end of World War I, more than one thousand such proposals have been made." (Taylor in Foreward, pp. v-vi). Zweig explores the needs, alternatives (international exchanges, area study programs, etc.), the history of the proposal, and what should be done.

181. WOLFF, Robert Paul. *The Ideal of the University.* Boston: Beacon Press, 1969. 161 pp. $5.95.

A well-written essay responding to the events at Columbia and attempting to develop a program of practical reform of present-day institutions, based on the view that "the competition for scarce places at top colleges corrupts the secondary school education, and even corrodes primary education as well." After a discussion of 4 models (the university as A Sanctuary of Scholarship, A Training Camp for the Professions, A Social Service Station, and An Assembly Line for Establishment Man), the final chapter proposes that "performance in high school must be made irrelevant to college admission and college performance must be made irrelevant to graduate and professional admission." (p. 142) Degrees would be abolished, including the Ph.D. and its questionable "contribution-to-knowledge" requirement, in turn freeing students for truly meaningful work. Professional training would be an alternative to undergraduate education, rather than a linear sequel to it, and undergraduate admissions would be by lot among those attaining some minimum performance.

182. LAWRENCE, Ben, George WEATHERSBY, and Virginia W. PATTERSON (eds.). *Outputs of Higher Education: Their Identification, Measurement, and Evaluation.* Papers from a seminar held at Washington, D.C., May 3-5, 1970, conducted by the Western Interstate Commission for Higher Education in cooperation with the American Council on Education and the Center for Research and Development in Higher Education at Berkeley. Boulder, Colorado: WICHE, July 1970. 130 pp. $3.50.

10 important essays examining purposes, priorities, responsibilities and capabilities of higher education, under the rationale that "Educational decision-makers are seeking honest, viable responses to the issues of public accountability, flagging financial support, and an earlier overreaction to short-term need. They are seeking forthright approaches to the polarization of opinion about the role of the university in a free society ordered by law." (p. 7) Bibliography of about 200 items in three categories: output variables and models for their analysis; goals and/or psycho-social effects of education on its constituencies; and educational costs.

183. AXELROD, Joseph, et. al. *Search for Relevance: The Campus in Crisis.* San Francisco: Jossey-Bass, 1969. 244 pp. Bib., pp. 212-237.

Tying together Nevitt Sanford's theory of student development, old ideals, and present student protest, four "total design" models are proposed: a cluster college on the campus of an urban college or university, a B.A. program in Future Studies, a community college, and an Experimental Freshman Year Program. Bibliography of about 400 items.

184. The Committee on the Student in Higher Education. *The Student in Higher Education.* New Haven, Conn.: The Hazen Foundation, January 1968. 66 pp.

"This report was written to bring attention to the possibility of developmental higher education . . . These recommendations call for a major qualitative change in planning for the future of higher education. The Committee has no quarrel with the computer experts, the technical planners, and the budgetary wizards who are telling us how many students, teachers, and classrooms we will need by 1980 . . . but it is not enough, for they are not concerned with the character of education. It takes another kind of planner to consider and envision the quality of human relationships in the college environment." (p. 57) Many recommendations such as the whole freshman year as an orientation to learning, a reduction of competition, a proliferation of experimentation, a reforming of physical structures, etc. Clearly written with a humane concern.

185. GAFF, Jerry G. and Associates. *The Cluster College: Innovations and Consequences.* San Francisco: Jossey-Bass, 1970. $8.50.

"Provides the first systematic study of the cluster college, a collegiate model which permits schools to preserve the best features of both the small college and the large university. The authors describe and analyze the purposes and practices of these schools, illuminating such details as the utility of the cluster concept, the various methods of accommodating cluster colleges in different universities, the innovations in curriculum, grading, instruction, governance, and residence requirements." (advt.)

186. PATTERSON, Franklin and Charles R. LONGSWORTH. *The Making of a College: Plans for a New Departure in Higher Education.* Hampshire College, Working Paper No. 1. Cambridge: MIT Press, 1966. 364 pp. $4.95 paper.

Planning papers for a new liberal arts college in South Amherst, Massachusetts, which "defines an organized vision of liberal education for a new era . . . to help its students learn to live their adult lives fully and well in a society of intense change, immense opportunity, and great hazards."

E. For Students of the Future

1. *Journals*

187. *Futures. The Journal of Forecasting and Planning.* Guildford, Surrey, England: Iliffe Science and Technology Publications, Ltd. (32 High Street). $22.50 annually. (U.S. subscribers may order through Iliffe-NTP, Inc., 300 E. 42nd Street, New York, New York 10017).

Published quarterly since September 1968, quite valuable but overpriced. "Contains articles and original papers on the probable and possible long-term trends in science, technology, economics, politics, and social conditions, and on the means by which desirable goals may be selected and achieved." (Journal masthead) A serious publication with an international focus.

188. *The Futurist. A Journal of Forecasts, Trends and Ideas About the Future.* Washington: World Future Society (P.O. Box 19285, Twentieth Street Station, Washington, D.C. 20036). $7.50 annually.

Published bi-monthly since February 1967 and improving with each issue since its original inception as "A Newsletter for Tomorrow's World." Includes a variety of short articles, book reviews, speech extracts, as well as a member's book service offering a 10% discount on a list of about 60 books, most of them worthwhile. For an additional $10.00 per year, the WFS Supplemental Program offers current news on who is doing or writing what, and abstracts of recently published books. The first General Assembly of the World Future Society will be held May 11-14, 1971.

189. *Technological Forecasting: An International Journal.*
Published quarterly since Spring 1969 by American Elsevier Publications (52 Vanderbilt Avenue, New York, New York 10017). Vol. 1, $24.00; Vol. 2 and subsequent volumes, $26.00 annually. The journal is largely concerned with methodology rather than substantive forecasts.

190. *Policy Sciences: An International Journal for the Policy Sciences.*
Edited by Edward S. Quade, in association with Harold D. Lasswell and Yehezkel Dror, and published quarterly since Spring 1970 by American Elsevier Publications (52 Vanderbilt Avenue, New York, New York 10017). *"Policy Sciences* will provide a forum for the developing interest in the application of structured rationality, systematic analysis, and interdisciplinary knowledge to problems of public policy. It will include applied studies analyzing specific problem areas, theoretic studies on the methods, content, and problems of the policy sciences, and papers dealing with the policy sciences as a subject for research and teaching and as a new profession." (advt.)

191. *Notes on the Future of Education.* (Donnelly J. Barclay, ed.)
Published quarterly since Fall 1969 by the Educational Policy Research Center at Syracuse, 1206 Harrison Street, Syracuse, N.Y. 13210. Subscriptions are free. The research from which these brief articles are drawn is conducted under a contract with the U.S. Office of Education. Especially see 1:2 (articles on the quantity of instruction and "The Learning Force"), 1:3 (special

issue on methodology, with articles on macro-system fore-casting, the applications and limitations of the Delphi method to education, and econometric models), II:1 (three policy articles prepared for the National Reading Center, which plans to coordinate a massive attack on functional illiteracy in the U.S.), and II:2 (special issue on three improbable probabilities: that we will be older, dumber, and poorer).

192. *Interchange: A Journal of Educational Studies.* (Andrew Effrat, ed.)
Published quarterly since Spring 1970 by the Ontario Insti-tute for Studies in Education, 252 Bloor Street West, Toronto 5, Ontario, Canada. $5.00 per year. Especially see Vol. 1, No. 4, "Education for the Future," and Vol. 2, No. 1, "Alternatives in Education."

193. *Education and Urban Society.*
Published by Sage Publications, 275 So. Beverly Drive, Beverly Hills, Calif. ($8.00 annually), since November 1968. Subtitled: "An Independent Quarterly Journal of Social Research with Implications for Public Policy.

2. *Major Bibliographies*

194. CALDWELL, Lynton K., assisted by William B. DEVILLE and Hedvah L. SHUCHMAN (comps). *Science, Technology, and Public Policy: A Selected and Annotated Bibliography* (2 vols.). Prepared for the National Science Foundation by the Program in Public Policy for Science and Technology, Department of Government. Bloomington: Indiana University, revised edition, 1969. 492 pp. and 544 pp. respectively.
This massive and valuable reference work contains an estimated 5000 items, with annotations of varying length for each, and classified in 12 major sections and 46 sub-sections. "To provide a definitive treatment limited to publications in English for the years 1945-1967 would increase the size of the bibliography by at least half. The size might easily be doubled if relevant edito-rials and articles in news magazines and in popular journals were included." (Vol. II, p. i.)

195. WEBSTER, Maureen (Comp.), with the assistance of H.G. MEYERS, Don ADAMS, and Jerry MINER. *Educational Plan-ning and Policy: An International Bibliography.* Syracuse: Educational Policy Research Center, June 1969. Working Draft, 654 pp.

Seeking to be comprehensive, international, and action-oriented, 4,927 items are included, largely written in the present decade. An elaborate categorization is provided, with indexes by author, country and region. The six major categories are titled Education and National Development, Comprehensive and Partial Planning, Financing Educational Plans, Influences on Plan Targets, Productivity and Efficiency, and Bibliographies. An updated edition of about 8000 entries will be published in Fall 1971. The major shift in focus is toward non-school education and alternative futures for learning.

196. ROJAS, Billy (Comp.). *Future Studies Bibliography*. Amherst, Mass.: University of Massachusetts, Program for the Study of the Future in Education, School of Education, January 1970. 107 pp., mimeo.

A listing of about 1500 items in 16 categories and 52 sub-categories. An updated version (August 1970) cites about 2000 items.

197. MARIEN, Michael (Comp.). *Alternative Futures for Learning: An Annotated Bibliography of Educational Trends, Forecasts, and Proposals*. Syracuse: Educational Policy Research Center, May 1971. Approx. 250 pp. $5.00.

An array of about 900 items, nearly all books and monographs, and about two-thirds annotated in varying degrees. The format is roughly the same as in this selected bibliography, except that "trends and futures" are not separated from "proposals." There is less emphasis on trends and forecasts that are unrelated to education, but a greater array of proposals, especially those that are outdated to some degree.

An additional bibliography, *Alternative Futures for Mankind: An Annotated Bibliography of Societal Trends, Forecasts, and Proposals,* will hopefully be published in Fall 1971. It will be of interest especially to students of the future (professional and otherwise). It will cover about 1000 items, including an overlap of about 200 items from the above bibliography. A new edition of *Essential Reading for Education,* selecting the most worthy items from both of these bibliographies, will probably appear in fall 1971.

3. *Futures Teaching and Research*

198. ROJAS, Billy (Comp.). *Future Studies Syllabus*. Amherst, Mass.: University of Massachusetts, Program for the Study of

the Future in Education, School of Education, revised edition, July 1970. 36 pp.

Outlines of 16 global and specialized futuristics courses presently being conducted at the college level. A 1971 edition will present outlines of about 70 courses.

199. ELDREDGE, H. Wentworth, "Education for Futurism in the United States: An On-Going Survey and Critical Analysis," *Technological Forecasting and Social Change* 2 (1970), pp. 133-148. Also see a briefer version, "Education in Futurism in North America," *The Futurist,* IV:5, December 1970, pp. 193-196.

An excellent survey of futures research and teaching. As of July 1970, approximately 90 institutions of higher learning (of which 7 were in Canada) were offering futurism or technological forecasting courses, with perhaps 100 academics involved in all of North America.

However, the focus and quality of the courses varies immensely. Generally, the intellectual roots were shallow, with very little awareness "of mankind's age-old Promethean strivings." Furthermore, "there was almost a complete lack of any implicit, much less explicit, social change theory." Various predictive techniques and teaching methods used are also covered, and the article is concluded with 17 summary propositions on the teaching of futurism.

200. McHALE, John. *Typological Survey of Futures Research in the U.S.* Binghamton: State University of New York, Center for Integrative Studies, June 1970. 103 pp., mimeo.

A survey of the current state of futures research programs in the United States, conducted for the National Institute of Mental Health during the June 1969-June 1970 period, "in order to elicit a representative profile of such ongoing work, i.e. who is doing what, in which social sector, how it is being done and to which specific end(s)." (p. 1) Based on 135 usable returns (out of 356 letters sent out), McHale concludes that there are not more than 1000 full-time and less than 500 part-time workers in the field. (p. 19) Various charts and appendices list organizations, individuals, characteristics of the work, various definitions of futures research, communication needs, a discussion of the World Future Society, and informal change agencies that are actively creating alternative social arrangements. Although it is pointed out that this is not a directory or a social register of futurists, the study is nevertheless the best approximation for the time being.

Based on the returns (which undoubtedly characterize the mainstream), McHale concludes that the disciplines represented are heavily biased in the area of the physical sciences and engineering, which may tend "to push the overall developmental direction of the field towards 'professional respectability' and institutional propriety based on methodologies and models drawn from these areas . . . this direction if sustained may limit severely the 'lookout' and 'early-warning' capability of futures research." (p. 42) The age range concentration and sex ratio of the researchers also comes under criticism, and it is pointed out that "much of the work in this area is, indeed, tied closely to the traditional and largely unexamined premises for human action which are imbedded in our local ideological systems and value assumption. It is largely 'culture bound' in a period when one of the key aspects of ongoing change is the degree to which the more stereotyped socio-cultural premises . . . are undergoing considerable modification." (p. 43)

"One might conclude here that the potential contribution of futures research in the manifold service of the society is very great--but that present state of development, and the range of supported inquiry is not wholly conducive to the fullest use of that potential." (p. 45)

F. Addenda

ASIMOV, Isaac, "The Fourth Revolution", *Saturday Review,* Oct. 24, 1970, pp. 17-20. (Part of a special issue entitled "Toward the Global Village", Asimov envisions worldwide electronic literacy.)

BAGDIKIAN, Ben H. *The Information Machines: Their Impact on Men and the Media* N.Y.: Harper & Row, Feb. 1971. 359 pp. 8.95 (A broad overview based on RAND research and a Delphi exercise.)

COLLIER, Barnard Law, "Brain Power: The Case for Bio-Feedback Training", *Saturday Review,* April 10, 1971, pp. 10-13, 58. (Reviews possibilities of a radically new area of human learning.)

CARTTER, Allan M, "Scientific Manpower for 1970-1985", *Science,* 172: April 9, 1971, pp. 132-140. (Views graduate school as 30-50% too large for needs of 1970's and 1980's.)

Commission on Population Growth and America's Future. *Population Growth and America's Future.* Interim Report of the Commission. Washington: USGPO, 1971. 56 pp. 40 cents.

DOYLE, Frank J. and Daniel Z. GOODWILL. *An Exploration of the Future in Educational Technology.* Montreal: Bell Canada (c/o F.J. Doyle, Business Planning, Room 1105, 620 Belmont St.), Jan. 1971. 70 pp. Free. (Delphi study concluding with a scenario of Education 1990. Optimistic, but provocative.)

"International Education for Spaceship Earth". *New Dimensions.* Booklets on the Social Studies and World Affairs, No. 4. N.Y.: Foreign Policy Association (345 E. 46th St.), 1970. 84 pp. Free.

MACLURE, Stuart, "England's Open University: Revolution at Milton Keynes", *Change: The Magazine of Higher Education,* 3:2, March/April 1971, pp. 62-68. (A prospective breakthrough in educational technology and opening higher learning to all ages.)

MAYHEW, Lewis B. *Colleges Today and Tomorrow.* San Francisco: Jossey-Bass, 1969. 255 pp. 7.75. (A Thorough overview of problems and proposals.)

MERTINS, Herman, and Bertram M. GROSS (eds.), "Changing Styles of Planning in Post-Industrial America", *Public Administration Review* (Special Issue), XXXI:2, May/June 1971.

MILLER, Arthur R. *The Assault on Privacy: Computers, Data Banks, and Dossiers.* Ann Arbor: University of Michigan Press, 1971. 333 pp. 7.95. (Especially see "The Little Red Schoolhouse Goes Electronic", pp. 105-122)

NEWMAN, Frank (Task Force Chairman). *Report on Higher Education.* Washington: U.S. Dept. of Health, Education, and Welfare, March 1971. 140 pp. (Major proposals reprinted in The Chronicle of Higher Education, March 15, 1971, pp. 4-8.)

WAYS, Max, "Don't We Know Enough To Make Better Public Policies?", *Fortune,* April 1971, pp. 64+. (Confronts the paradox of growing knowledge and growing ignorance. Of fundamental importance.)

III. INDEXES

A. Index by Major Author

Jungk	27	Reich	77
Kahn	22, 34	Reimer	157
Keniston	79	Riesman	108
Kern	54	Robinson	96
Kerr	101, 141	Roby	66
Kilpatrick	6	Rochberg	11
Kohl	161	Rogers	152
Kostelanetz	34	Rojas	196, 198
Kraft	95	Rosove	121
Ladd	112	Rossi	123
Lawrence	182	Rourke	110
Lecht	69	Runkel	109
Leonard	93	Ryan	88
Liveright	116	Sandow	84
Lundberg	23	Sheldon	32
Magat	168	Silberman	166
Marien	197	Slater	38
Marty	3	Snow	20
Mayhew	19, 103	Steinhart	147
McHale	24, 200	Stone	120
McLuhan	34, 93	Stulman	29
Mead	78	Taylor, G.	49
Meise	56	Taylor, H.	153
Mesthene	46	Tebbel	55
Michael	1	Theobald	35
Miller	66	Thomas	99
Mishan	73	Toffler	37, 98
Moore	32	Tough	114
Morphet	88, 89	Umans	162
Moses	113	Usdan	150
Muller	47	Wager	26
Nicholson	59	Wallerstein	111
Oettinger	122	Weaver	10
Orwell	42	Webster	195
Paddock	58	Westin	173
Patterson	186	Wiener	22, 34
Peccei	25	Wolff	181
Peterson	87	Young	68
Platt	148	Ziegler	16, 115
Postman	176	Zweig	180
Quattlebaum	130		

National Association of Secondary School Principals

National Commission on the Causes and Prevention of Violence — 126

National Commission on Technology, Automation, and Economic Progress — 127

National Education Association — 92

National Goals Research Staff — 125

National Planning Association — 69

National Science Foundation, National Science Board — 145, 146

New York Times — 86

Observer (England) — 175

Ontario Institute for Studies in Education — 114, 192

Organisation for Economic Co-Operation and Development — 8

Policy Institute of the Syracuse University Research Corporation — 172

President's Commission on Campus Unrest (Scranton Commission) — 139

President's Committee on Education Beyond the High School — 143

President's Environmental Quality Council — 147

President's Task Force on Higher Education — 142

Program in Public Policy for Science and Technology (Indiana) — 194

Program for the Study of the Future in Education (Mass.) — 196, 198

Provincial Committee on Aims and Objectives of Education in the Schools of Ontario (Canada) — 135

Social Science Research Council — 129

Sudbury Valley School — 163

Systems Development Corporation — 96, 121

U.S. Congress. House Committee on Education and Labor — 130, 133, 136

U.S. Congress. House Committee on Science and Astronautics — 13, 14, 82

U.S. Congress. Senate Committee on Labor and Public Welfare — 138

U.S. Dept. of Health, Education, and Welfare — 30

U.S. Dept. of Housing and Urban Development — 64

U.S. Office of Education — 85, 119

Wall Street Journal — 74

Western Interstate Commission for Higher Education — 182

World Future Society — 188

World Institute — 29

C. Index of Bibliographies

Topic	Author and Listing No.	No. Items
Forecasting	Jantsch - 8	420, annotated
Educational Planning	Coombs - 81	74, annotated
	Webster - 195	4927, not annotated (8000 in new edition)
Higher Education:		
Outputs and Costs	Lawrence et. al. - 182	200, not annotated
Reform	Axelrod - 83	400, not annotated
Educational Recommendations and Proposals	Quattlebaum - 130	105 governmental and nongovernmental commissions and interest groups
Adult Education for the Disadvantaged	Anderson and Niemi - 117	317, not annotated
New Curriculum Prescriptions	Berman - 160	600, not annotated
Futures Courses	Rojas - 198	16 syllabi (70 in new edition)
Technology and Public Policy	Caldwell - 194	5000, annotated
	Mesthene - 46	70, annotated
Future (General)	Ferkiss - 36	900, not annotated
	Toffler - 37	359, not annotated
	Rojas - 196	2000, not annotated
	Marien - 197	1400, part annotated in two documents of 800 each
Utopias	Armytage - 4	500 in notes
	Weiss - 4	500 chronological, not annotated

Index

DATE DUE

GAYLORD   PRINTED IN U.S.A.